Joseph Newton Hallock

The Christian Life

For devotional reading and family worship

Joseph Newton Hallock

The Christian Life
For devotional reading and family worship

ISBN/EAN: 9783337037734

Printed in Europe, USA, Canada, Australia, Japan

Cover: Foto ©Lupo / pixelio.de

More available books at **www.hansebooks.com**

THE
CHRISTIAN LIFE:

FOR

Devotional Reading

AND

Family Worship.

WITH NUMEROUS ILLUSTRATIONS.

BY

REV. JOSEPH NEWTON HALLOCK,

EDITOR OF "THE CHRISTIAN AT WORK."

THIRD EDITION.

"Forgetting those things which are behind, and reaching forward to those things which are before, I press toward the mark for the prize of the high calling of God in Christ Jesus."—PHIL., iii., 13, 14.

NEW YORK:
THE CHRISTIAN AT WORK.
1892.

COPYRIGHT, 1892, BY
THE CHRISTIAN AT WORK.

PREFACE.

NO one is more surprised at the publication of this volume than myself. When I wrote these articles it was not with the intention of printing them in book form. They were simply written for and printed in the now well-known department, "The Christian Life," which was many years ago introduced in *The Christian at Work* by the writer, who until the present time has edited it exclusively. Although written for a religious paper, and not for preservation in this more permanent form, I have been induced to print this book at the request of many who have found these editorials on the Christian life helpful, and have learned each week to look for and prize them. This volume, therefore, consists simply of a few selections of original articles and editorials from this department of the paper, and is especially intended for a place in the family library. Nothing, however, is here printed that has appeared within the last two or three years, and many of the articles were written long before that time, some of which I have partially rewritten for this especial presentation. This part of the book needs no introduction to its new readers, many of whom will doubtless be already somewhat familiar with portions of it. I can only hope that these short and rather hastily written sketches may not lose whatever of helpfulness they seem to have possessed by being thrown into this more permanent form, where they can be read more leisurely and critically, and at such times as the various members of the family may feel so inclined. The true Christian life is progressive, and both the old and the young need all the encouragement and help in this direction that can possibly be given them. The mission of this little book is simply to give such help, and, with this object particularly in mind, it has been issued in such illustrated form as to be attractive to the young, although its matter is intended more especially to instruct, comfort, and help the older members of the family.

The various forms of prayers for family worship, at the close of the volume, are not added to make the book popular. Indeed, there is in many minds a deep-seated prejudice in regard to any printed forms of prayer; and the same objection appears, only less in degree, to printed forms of grace at meals, and even to the children's prayers. Prayer is a mockery unless it comes from the heart, and hence some feel that sincere feelings and impulses can be expressed by no set form of words, but simply by the spontaneous and unrestrained language that comes bursting from a full heart. We sympathize with such; indeed, there is no prayer mentioned in the Bible as being more acceptable to God than the simple, broken-hearted, and almost despairing cry of the publican, "God be merciful to me a sinner." Such a prayer from a broken and contrite spirit will always be heard. But while we feel the necessity of always praying "from the heart," we should be careful and not allow ourselves to be unreasonably prejudiced against set expressions, sentences, or devout and fixed forms of prayer. A spirit of devotion does not necessarily imply the ability to always give clear expression in words. Many a good Christian is rather hindered than helped by inability to adequately express his feelings of love, gratitude, and devotion in the hearing of others. The early disciples realized this, even while in the Master's inspiring presence; and with a directness and simplicity which, in our ignorance and poverty of utterance, we will do well to emulate, they asked to be taught *how* to pray. Our Saviour recognized their need, and respected their request by complying with it. He gave them a "form" of prayer; and who will say they were afterward less sincere and devout in their worship because they sometimes felt impelled to use the very words of the Master?

I am indebted to so many of my friends for valuable suggestions and material assistance in regard to this feature, that I can here only acknowledge my great obligations and return thanks to all collectively. It may be interesting to the reader, as it was to me, to learn the significant fact that from nearly thirty of our best-known and most devout clergymen—to each of whom I had sent a private note requesting, for this purpose, a short, simple, and original form of family prayer—came back the modest response: "I have tried, but made a miserable failure. I pray thee have me excused." These were the very men I did not wish to excuse, and as all most heartily endorsed this feature of my book, I sent to each a second and more urgent note, in response to which, from nearly every one, I received such chosen or original form of prayer as he deemed most suitable for family worship.* In most instances the prayer is original in its language, and was written especially for this volume, one of the longest and best of these being the excellent Sunday morning prayer from our well-known friend and contributor, Rev. Dr. Cuyler, near the close of the book and underneath his portrait. It will be seen, therefore, that the various forms of family prayers in the last few pages of this book have either been very carefully chosen, or written especially for this purpose, by the best and most sincere Christian men of our time. The feature was suggested by the fact that in social conversation with the writer, many persons have plead timidity, ignorance, and kindred excuses as an apology for neglecting family prayers. Very many, when the subject has been referred to, have confessed that they would be glad to observe this time-honored custom of their fathers, but feel a reluctance, which they cannot overcome, to engage in prayer in the presence of others. This is not a sufficient excuse for the neglect of a plain duty, but as it prevails to a great extent it is well to try to remove it. With these excellent forms of prayer at hand, no one can reasonably plead such an excuse. If necessary, a prayer may be read; all joining in the Lord's Prayer at the close. But it is still better to study the prayers and familiarize one's self with the different forms of expression, as here set forth from the hearts and lips of these earnest Christians. Words

---

* I trust I commit no breach of confidence in stating that such well-known names as Behrends, Hall, Phillips Brooks, R. S. Storrs, Fisher, Taylor, Doolittle, Ingersoll, Parkhurst, Whitaker, C. L. Thompson, Junor, Deems, Chester, Ludlow, Van Dyke, and many others equally well known for their piety and good works, are among those to whom I wrote, nearly every one of whom is here represented by an original form of prayer, or such a selected form as he deemed most suitable for the family.

and sentences are simply vehicles of thought, ideas, and feelings, and the best and most worthy Christian must learn how to use them before he can convey his sentiments to others, or even fitly express his emotions of reverential love, gratitude, and praise. It is true

> "Prayer is the simplest form of speech
> That infant lips can cry."

But we should not be content to forever remain infants in the Christian life. We must strive to attain to those heights of spiritual vision where we shall find in our own experience come welling up from our hearts and lips

> "Prayer—the sublimest strains that reach
> The Majesty on High."

It is a duty, therefore, as well as a great and blessed privilege, to familiarize the mind with the Lord's Prayer, and with the prayers of good men. These different forms of expression should by no means supersede or interfere with the daily practice of extempore prayer; rather use them as the lame use a staff—to lean upon at such times as you feel the need, and cannot do better without their assistance. If used in this way, they will prove, we trust, with the rest of the book, a constant source of strength and help.

J. N. HALLOCK.

NEW YORK CITY, December 14, 1891.

ADDENDA FOR THIRD EDITION.

TO THE TABLE OF CONTENTS:
  Page 18.—Christ the Shepherd.
  "   39.—Underneath the Everlasting Arms.
  "   123.—Burden-Bearing.
  "   133.—A Prepared Life.
  "   165.—Seeking Relief in Prayer.
  "   302.—Thirty-and-eight Years.

TO THE ILLUSTRATIONS:
  Page 301.—St. Peter's and Castle of St. Angelo.
  "   318.—Christ Among the Doctors.
  "   332.—Jesus Stilling the Tempest.

CONTENTS

	PAGES
PREFACE	3 to 6
CONTENTS	" 7 " 8
FULL-PAGE ILLUSTRATIONS	" 9 " 10
FRONTISPIECE.	

	PAGE		PAGE
What is Christian Life?	11	"Full of Mercy"—Forgiveness	98
Our Besetting Sin	15	The Real Source of Power	100
Heavenly Mindedness	17	"And Good Fruits"	101
Christ the Vine	21	Bread upon the Waters	103
The Signs of the Times	23	What is Prayer?	107
Letting the Light Shine	25	The Anchor of the Soul	110
Glorification through Death	27	In the Shepherd's Care	113
The Mountains and their Suggestions	31	The Wheat and the Tares	117
The Lord our "Rock"	36	God's Special Care	119
"Ye must be born again"	41	The Christian's Possessions	121
Speak the Truth "in Love"	44	A Spiritual Atmosphere	125
Little Sermons	47	A Good Name	129
Home without Spiritual Life	49	God's Discipline	131
Faithful unto Death	51	Crossing the Rubicon of Trial	133
"If"	52	A City of Refuge	137
The Value of Time	53	"Watch"	139
Christian Sympathy	55	God's Instruments	141
The Grace of Ignorance	57	Is Life Worth Living?	145
The Christian's Race	61	Character	148
Mary Magdalene's Reward	63	Will it Pay?	151
Walking with God	67	"Peace, be Still!"	154
The Blessings and Power of Prayer	69	Christian Cheerfulness	155
		"He Saith"	157
True Religion not Damaged by Adversity	71	A Stranger and a Pilgrim	159
		God "Our Father"	161
Girding on the Armor	75	Faith of Woman	163
Don't be too Busy	77	Despondency	167
Little Things	79	Be not Weary in Well Doing	170
The Love of God	83		
Not Incomplete	85	Affliction and Tribulation	171
"First Pure"	87	Laboring in the Vineyard	173
"Then Peaceable"	91	Sufficient unto the Day	174
"Gentle and Easy to be Entreated"	94	A Beloved Disciple	177
		Put your Heart in It	179

CONTENTS.

	PAGE
Called and Chosen: And Faithful	181
One Restful Day	183
The Joy of the Morning	185
Our Tender Shepherd	187
Lessons of the Day	190
Every-day Christian Life	192
Perfect Trust	194
Our Old Enemies	195
Moral Beauty	199
What Are We Doing?	200
"No God"	202
Cause and Effect	204
God's Omniscience	206
The Father's Way	208
God's Crucible	210
Full and Free Forgiveness	211
Little Sins	213
Crowns	214
What is Rest?	215
My Presence Shall Go with Thee	216
Planning and Doing	217
Not Our Own	219
Restraining Grace	221
Under Sealed Orders	223
Waiting on the Lord	224
Neither Cold nor Hot	225
God's Laws Inflexible	227
Grace Will Tell	229
Take Near Views	231
The Branch and the Vine	233
Self-Denial	238
Ambition for Greatness	239
Just Once	241
Common Sense in Religion	243
Jesus of Nazareth passeth by	244
The Real Source of Power	246
Ask and Ye shall Receive	247
Individual Responsibility	249
Doing Heartily	251
Perverting the Truth	253
A Rainbow in the Clouds	255
Words Fitly Spoken	258
Recognition in Heaven	261
Power in Right Music	263
Light and Love	267
Alone with God	268
Euroclydon	269
The Prince of Peace	272
Giving up Old Hopes	274
Advantages of Confessing Christ	275
Our Responsibility	279
How Are We Building?	281
The Master Impulse	282
Light is Sown for the Righteous	283
The Devices of the Tempter	285
Their Eyes were Holden	288
The Daily Task	291
Sunlight in Autumnal Days	293
The Will of God	297
Conquer as You Go	299
But One Petition	303
He Will Bring it to Pass	307
Treasures in Earthen Vessels	309
Work That Endures	311
Personal Obligation	315
Childhood of Jesus	317
His Ways Are not Our Ways	319
The Human Tide	323
The Living Bread	325
An Olive-tree	329
A Few Days	331
Does Jesus Care?	333
The Church at Laodicea	337
Sadness and Solace	341
Waiting for Feeling	343
Missionary Work	347
In Everything Give Thanks	350
Giving Thanks	351
New Year Thoughts	355
The Hopes of Easter-tide	357
Sweetness of Spirit	360
If They Could Come Back	361
Old-fashioned Christians	364
On Christmas Day	367
Fidelity	370
The Preciousness of Christ	373
Your Sunday Reading	376
What Will Ye Give Me?	378
The World	380
Beginning at Jerusalem	383
Children's Prayers	390
Family Prayers	391–413
Common Forms of Grace during Meals	414–415
The Lord's Prayer	416

FULL-PAGE ILLUSTRATIONS.

	PAGE
Frontispiece.	
The Mount of Olives	30
Mount Ararat	33
The Mountains and their Suggestions (View on the Jordan)	35
Mount Olivet from St. Stephen's Gate	37
Gethsemane	43
I Will Instruct Thee (Text)	45
O Lord, How Manifold (Text)	59
Mary Magdalene's Reward	63
Ark of the Covenant	65
Florence Nightingale	73
Christ Blessing Little Children	81
The Wild Palm	89
He That Walketh Uprightly (Text)	100
The Annual Overflow of the Nile	105
Anchor of the Soul	111
In the Shepherd's Care	115
Thou Shalt Guide Me (Text)	135
A City of Refuge	137
The Altar of Sacrifice	143
Tribute Money	150
The Sea of Galilee	176
He That is Without Sin	197
The Way of Peace	209
Thou Crownest the Year (Text)	235
Jesus of Nazareth Passeth By	245
Characteristic Oriental Scene	265
The Prince of Peace	273
Sunlight in Autumnal Days	295
He That Overcometh (Text)	301
Wash Me, and I Shall be Whiter than Snow	306

FULL-PAGE ILLUSTRATIONS.

	PAGE
Thy Kingdom Come (Text)	313
The Ascension of Our Lord	321
The Table of Shew Bread	327
Elijah Fed by Ravens	328
Steps in the Rocks Leading to Mt. Sinai	335
Laodicea	339
The Pool of Siloam	343
Ancient Gethsemane	345
Thanksgiving	353
Bird's-eye View of Jerusalem	385
Watch and Pray (Text)	387
Rev. Theodore L. Cuyler, D.D.	411

WHAT IS CHRISTIAN LIFE?

COMMON error is to suppose that we are doing the Lord's work only when we are engaged in devotional exercises or laboring for the conversion of sinners, or for the edification of Christians. That which a man does heartily, as unto the Lord, is the Lord's work. The farmer, when he is carefully and wisely cultivating the soil, is doing the Lord's work. Plowing is as truly a religious act as praying. The merchant when he makes an honest exchange is doing the Lord's work. Dealing justly is as truly a religious act as warning sinners to flee from the wrath to come. A man is doing God's work when he is doing that which pleases

God. A man is doing the Lord's work when he is faithful to his employer—does a fair day's work; when he takes proper care of his health; when he governs his temper; when he is careful to speak the exact truth; when he is courteous to strangers and lends a helping hand to the needy; when he has a word of encouragement for the desponding; when he sets an example of industry and honesty; when he returns good for evil; when he leads such an upright, benevolent, God-honoring life, that men take knowledge of him that he has been with Jesus. Religion does not consist solely in reading the Bible, praying, attending church and laboring for the conversion of men. These are important duties, but they do not include the whole of duty. God's will has reference to every act of our lives.

Let us see wherein this differs from the secular life. The two may be, and frequently are united in the same individual. We are all obliged to attend to the everyday business of life, and it is right that we should do so, but this Christian life is something different from, while at the same time it enters into an ordinary life. Some of the most prominent characteristics of a truly Scriptural and spiritual Christian life are the following:

1. Christian life is life in Christ. He is our very life. "Not I, but Christ liveth in me," and to the close we are dependent on him for everything, and do all things through Christ who strengtheneth us.

2. Christian life is life in the Spirit. Christ seals it, sustains it, and is the substance of it. We "live in the Spirit" and "walk in the Spirit." All our graces are "the fruit of the Spirit." We are illuminated by the Spirit, "strengthened" by the Spirit, and "filled" with the Spirit, and we are warned against grieving and quenching this Blessed Friend.

3. Christian life is resurrection life. The believer is regarded as a man who has died with Christ as to his old sins and sinful nature, and is no longer his former self. His life is not a modification or improvement of the old life, but a new nature imparted directly from the heart of Christ and as free from all former sin as Christ is now free, as fully accepted in the beloved as the beloved Son himself; as truly the child of God as Jesus is; and with

aspirations as high and heavenly as his high and heavenly origin; "buried with Christ," "risen with Christ," "quickened together with Christ," made to "sit together with Christ in heavenly places," called to "know the power of his resurrection, and the fellowship of his sufferings."

4. Christian life is a life of separation from the world and sin. "It has crucified the flesh with its affections and lusts." It can say, "The world is crucified unto me, and I unto the world." It must "seek the things that are above," and "mortify the members that are on the earth." It must "put off the old man with his deeds;" its "conversation" must be as "in heaven," remembering ever that they who mind earthly things are "enemies of the cross of Christ."

5. Christian life is a life of conflict; "conflict with the flesh," which "lusteth against the Spirit;" conflict with principalities and powers—the rulers of the darkness of this world—wicked spirits in heavenly places. And the nearer we get to the gates of triumph, the thicker grow the opposing hosts, and the more trying the ordeal of temptation. But the panoply is sufficient and the victory is sure.

6. Christian life is a strife, an ardent desire for practical holiness. Nothing is more emphasized in the Epistles of Paul than the common virtues of life, the ordinary relationships, the petty moralities, the domestic and social obligations, which a true spiritual life ought to bring out and show in the best light. Such a life ought not even to need being so pointedly reminded of these things. But the blessed Teacher knows that these very things are the truest test of real spirituality, and the most influential testimonies of our religion before the world. As the greatest minds are always the most perfect masters of details, as the truest chronometer is as exact in measuring seconds as hours, so the holiest saint will ever prove the most faithful father, husband, wife, child, servant or neighbor.

7. Finally, the true Christian life is a life not only of working and suffering, but of waiting and hoping for the coming of Christ and the glory of his resurrection, looking for the blessed hope and the glorious appearing of the great God, our Saviour Jesus Christ, "pressing

toward the mark for the prize of the high calling of God in Christ."

> Let not thy days be passed in hope or fear
> Of joys and cares that future time may bring :
> To-morrow is not thine for any thing.
> The need for love and duty lieth near.
> Nor brood o'er thoughts and follies of thy past :
> It is too late for thought or action there.
> From "all existence" learn thy lesson vast,
> And put to shame thy life of petty care.
> To-day is all that thou canst call thine own :
> *Now* is the hour for noble thoughts and deeds.
> Let Truth, Love, Beauty, speak to thee alone,
> Or give thyself to help the common needs.
> Thus shall thy life grow ever more sublime,
> And thou shalt learn of deeper things than time.

OUR BESETTING SIN.

WHEN day after day we find ourselves drawn—often against our better instincts—in the same direction and trapped by the same sin, we must come at last to the unpleasant conclusion that we have a certain partnership in evil, that there is something in the realm of wickedness which has a right to be called *our* sin. It does not affect the conclusion whether we are angered at the partnership, or blush at it, or accept it without feeling; the fact of partnership is there. The easily besetting sin is steadily and powerfully influencing us, however we may disguise the fact.

There are two ways of looking at this easily besetting sin. Many of us it blinds to our true position. Our tendencies are not generally evil; so we reason that we do not do this thing, we do not do that; we are not as bad as some other men, and these things we emphasize, while we are apt to pass over slightingly the one sin we do commit. "Men must be allowed their little weaknesses," we say, and we feel that one evil among so much good ought not to be very severely regarded.

This is assuredly a most comfortable way of regarding besetting sins, and I think that as a general thing men are thus linked to evil mainly by a single sin. Few ever break the whole law; our natures fortunately are not large enough to make us guilty of all; the restraints of circumstances are usually such as to leave a loophole in the life of every person for only a few, and often it happens to be a simple, willful, persistent besetting sin that we are entertaining and excusing. If we are unable to feel as we ought on this subject, Christ's words ought to destroy our complacency and incite us to action: "Whosoever shall keep the whole law and yet offend in one point, he is guilty of all."

Surely the great Comforter, who delighted in nothing so much as giving men peace, would not have said that if it had not been necessary and if it had not been a tremendous truth.

When we come to our besetting sin, instead of asking for indulgence we have really come to the crisis of spiritual life. It is no trifle, however small it may be; but, on the contrary, it just represents the point where we are bound to evil, and to break with sin entirely is to break with it at this point. The first consciousness of the new birth is usually a determination to break with this sin; then we may believe we are living unto God. We can see the important place this sin occupies by looking at the weakness it introduces into the whole life. If we are free from a multitude of other sins, so much the better, but also so much the more important is it to break with that one. Though every organ of the body but one be healthy, fatal disease in that one is fatal to all. Why should it not be in the soul, even as in material things? No chain is stronger than its weakest link, and this holds good in character. Our great enemy, walking up and down in the earth, finds the weak spot, and then farewell to strength; our easily besetting sin conquers us.

Everything is concentrated here; it is the key to the whole position. As long as there is one place of communication between the soul and sin, so long the old life is let in, and we shall find ourselves as weak as our weakest point. In all other respects we may be models; in great matters we may be firm; and yet a little folly may destroy all and bring our entire character down to its own weak level.

The Christian's character is like a chain of large and massive links which lies on the deck of an ocean steamer in rusty coils, to be used to keep the great ship away from danger. Can you imagine the captain examining such a chain, and on finding one link with a flaw in it, saying, "On the whole this is a good chain; one weak spot, but all the rest as strong as need be; it will do?" The judgment of that captain is wisdom itself in comparison with the utter folly of those of us who risk our eternal well-being on one wilful, known besetting sin.

HEAVENLY MINDEDNESS.

IT is the part of wisdom to let worldly cares and enjoyments hang loosely about us, so that when "the inevitable hour" comes we may let them fall like a mantle, and take our departure unregretfully. Ripened fruit falls easily. So when the heart of the Christian is truly weaned from the world, death may come at any time and find him ready. It is possible to be in the world and yet not of it, to perform its proper tasks and allotted duties fully and bravely, while yet our supreme desires and affections are set on things above. If we allow worldly cares and perplexities to weave themselves about our hearts so firmly that they cannot rise above the level of our common life, then are we companioning ourselves with the beasts of the field, who live in the present only, and whose whole range of being is comprised within the circle of sensual gratification. Heavenly-mindedness comes from a contemplation of the things that are pure, and right, and holy; from a study of God's Word, and an application of its precepts to our daily life. It is not possible to have this frame of mind except it be with a consciousness that we are accepted of God, and have received forgiveness of sins. While the windows of the soul are darkened by sin and unbelief, we cannot expect that the sunshine will pour in to cheer and lighten its innermost recesses, and draw its thoughts heavenward. The mind that is set on spiritual delights, that loves to commune with God, and finds its chiefest joys in doing his service, will not be ruffled by every disappointment in life, or broken by its calamities, for these things it rightly regards as transitory, and of no account in comparison with things that come after, that are sure and eternal. Clothed in such serenity and peace, the soul may move through the midst of trials and griefs, such as come to all of us, like a great strong ship whose course is not stayed by the buffeting of the winds and waves, because it has a certain port to gain, and a pilot who knows how to guide it there.

"Lo, I am with you alway," were the farewell words of our blessed Saviour to his mourning disciples, but the promise made to them was meant for every one of earth's sorrowing children. "I," the Infinite One, the "friend that sticketh closer than a brother," the loving, tender shepherd, "I am with you." And for how long a time? "Alway." Have bereavements come upon you? Have earthly friends become estranged and forsaken you? Have misfortunes overtaken you, and swept away every temporal comfort? Do grief and care walk hand in hand beside you? Are the wayside blossoms beaten down by the storms of adversity? Is the song gone out of your heart and the light out of your life? Oh! famishing, drooping soul, look up! Hear the tones of infinite pity and love, "I will not leave you comfortless." "Lo, I am with you alway." What though the daily task be hard, and the life path be rough? What though affliction, sorrow, pain, sit ever unwelcome guests around your hearthstone? What though death touch with icy fingers the lips you love, and set his seal upon the marble brow, and hush forever the voice whose tones made sweetest music? Reach out and touch the Divine hand extended toward you; open your eye of faith to behold your Saviour walking with you in loving companionship, heeding all your sighs and counting all your tears. Lean upon his arm which is ever outstretched to enfold and uphold you, and that moment you will be able to say,

> " I'm walking close to Jesus' side,
> So close that I can hear
> The softest whispers of his love
> In fellowship so dear,
> And feel his great almighty hand
> Protects me in this hostile land."

CHRIST THE SHEPHERD.

EXT to that of Father, one of the dearest and tenderest of all the figurative characters of Christ is that of the Shepherd, the Good Shepherd. The Master was wont frequently to apply that title to himself, and to speak of his followers as his flock. In nearly all the Eastern countries we know there was no occupation held in more respect and honor than that of the shepherd. A man could not be a good shepherd unless he was kind, patient, tender, and watchful. He had to be all this to care properly for the tender and defenceless lambs, and to protect his flock from the

ravages of wild beasts. The good shepherd knew each member of his flock by name, and was known of them. They came gladly at his call; they followed willingly whithersoever he led the way. Not one, from the smallest and weakest to the oldest and strongest, was overlooked or neglected. By daylight and starlight, through sunshine and storm, the shepherd stood by his flock with ever-watchful eyes. How completely the figure of the shepherd sets forth the relations which the Saviour bears to those who put their trust in him. Only the tenderness, love, and patience of Christ are infinite, wide, and boundless as eternity. The pastures where he feeds his flocks are always fresh and bountiful; those who follow him need never thirst or hunger, or have aught to fear. How sweet the thought of being one of the flock of Christ, to be cared for, to be watched over, to be guided day by day by the wonderful and compassionate Son of God. Who would not gladly follow the beckonings of such a shepherd as he?

Christ is also called the Door. He is the door that opens eternal life, the only one. There is no other way to heaven but through the merits of the blood of Christ. Men have been seeking for other doors ever since the world began; they have knocked and knocked at what they thought were doors, but no answer has come back, and they have not entered in. Christ is the Open Door, and all who seek an entrance through him will find the way prepared for their feet, and happy welcome all along to cheer them on, greetings and God-speeds to lighten the journey. Christ the Door is ready to-day to receive to himself all those who will come and enter into communion with him. Shall any one who reads these words say he has not known the door?

CHRIST THE VINE.

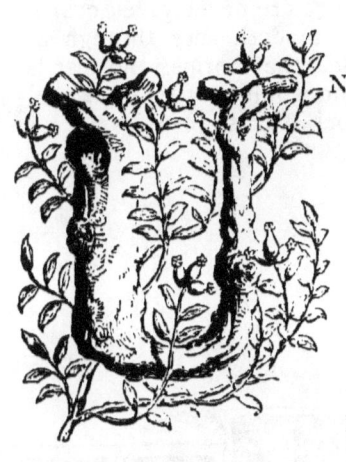

UNDER this title our Saviour is often presented to us, and of all the figurative titles applied to Christ in the Scriptures there is none more suggestive than that of the vine. "I am the vine," says the Master to his disciples, "ye are the branches." What figure could illustrate more strikingly than this the vital union which exists between the true believer and Christ, the Head of the Church! The true Christian has his very being in Christ, receives from Him every invigorating impulse, every enlarging desire and motive, every perfecting grace. The branches of the vine are strong and fruitful just in proportion as they are firmly and deeply engrafted on the main body. If, for any reason, they become partially disconnected, their hold upon the vine loosened, they at once grow poor and feeble, and if not soon reunited, wither and die. The Christian who neglects the means of grace, who falls into a loose and careless observance of God's laws, soon loosens his connection with the Vine, and is in danger of becoming a dead and withered branch in the vineyard.

As the natural vine holds up and supports its branches free from the earth and its entanglements, so does Christ the Vine bear aloft his followers above the world, above its cares and perplexities, above its trials and griefs. All the branches have to do is just to cling firmly, to trust wholly and grow. It is the Vine that gives the life, the strength, the power to bear fruit. The sincere, trustful Christian depends upon the Vine. Christ is his all in all.

In contrast to the above, Christ is also called a Rock. He is a firm and sure basis for all who will build upon him. He is the Rock, the everlasting, unchangeable Rock. Those who flee to him for refuge are never given over or betrayed to the enemy. He standeth sure through all the vicissitudes of this world, the storms, the perils, dangers, seen and unseen. Who would not seek the shelter of this Rock, the living Rock, Christ Jesus?

THE SIGNS OF THE TIMES.

CRISES in history always call forth men able and ready to meet them. One may look for them in vain beforehand, and be ready to despair of their existence, but somewhere, out of the way, they are in course of preparation, and when the time comes they appear. So whenever God has a special work to be done he raises up a special man to do it, and prepares him specially for it. All these giants in history have this one great characteristic in common, that they understood the times. We do not read very much about the tribe of Issachar in the Scriptures, and yet it is no faint praise that is lavished upon them in the words, they were "men that had understanding of the times to know what Israel ought to do." They were quiet, observant men, who kept their eyes upon the signs of the times, and were therefore well fitted to be wise and able counsellors. There is a very practical meaning in these words; they reveal to us very clearly what churches, that is, ministers, members, and people are meant to be. They should be like the children of Issachar, men who have understanding of the times to know what ought to be done.

It is hardly necessary to illustrate this in national life. No man can be a true or practical statesman who has not a clear and timely sagacity. No merchant can be successful who has not the talent of clear discernment, and can any one think for a moment that religion is a matter of less concern and interest than any earthly business? Many act so indeed, but I believe that if you could summon all the merchant princes of the earth, and ask them seriously what they consider the most important matter in the world, they would admit that the merchandise of religion is of more importance than the merchandise of silver. All men recognize it theoretically, but here is the great difficulty,—the wares of religion, so to speak, are immaterial, and cannot be seen or handled, and so they come to be considered unreal. Religion thus has no market value. Spiritual things cannot be estimated in money, and a man's services as a minister of the Gospel cannot be computed in dollars and cents. These are all spiritual things, and far removed from earthly rewards, but at the same time salvation has its value; even to the carnal judgment that value is greater than that of silver or gold.

"Godliness is profitable," and profit is what every merchant aims to secure; godliness pays. Why, then, cannot practical men be persuaded to give this subject practical attention? You who have "understanding of the times," why not apply the same talents to religion as to business. Take the weight and dimensions of "the pearl of great price." Calculate the value of its daily help and strength, put religion to the test, and let us see whether, even in regard to this world, it does not bring gain; so that although in a lower sense you may be forsaking all to follow Christ, yet in a higher sense is it not true that every one who hath forsaken houses or lands or brethren for Christ does receive for it an hundred-fold?

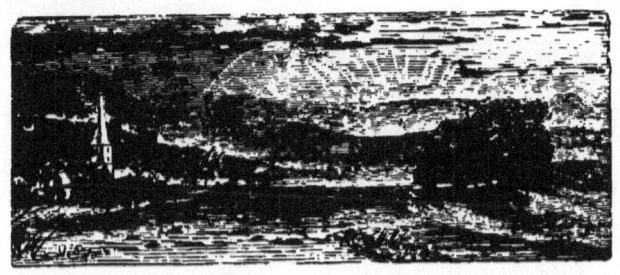

LETTING THE LIGHT SHINE.

WHEN a person is first converted to Christianity, it is generally a very easy matter to let others know something of the comfort and satisfaction which religion affords. Then, as time goes on, there seems to grow a certain reserve in alluding to the subject. This is not owing to coldness or indifference, perhaps, but to a kind of unwillingness to introduce a topic which might not be altogether agreeable to others. We should not act without judgment, but we must not forget that our Saviour told his disciples to let their light shine in such a way that others could see it. And when Jesus gave that injunction he knew all about the different dispositions, temperaments, and characters which must, through all ages, go to make up such as should be his disciples or followers. And there are so many ways in which the Christian's light may shine that no one is exempt from the Saviour's requirement in this respect. Mr. Moody says: "It is a great deal better to live a holy life than to talk about it. Lighthouses don't ring bells and fire cannon to call attention to their shining—they just shine." Nothing will commend religion to others like living a Christian life, and yet it may sometimes, at chosen intervals, be one's duty to talk about it too. How often it happens that a person, perhaps at the cost of considerable effort, makes some serious remark, that is eagerly, even hungrily responded to by a companion supposed to be utterly thoughtless and careless concerning such subjects.

A young lady when dying was in great distress of mind. On being asked why she had not thought of her soul and its interests while in health, she replied that no one had spoken to her about such things. The most pathetic and deplorable part of it was, that she had been living in a community of church-going Christian people. What kind of "lights" could they have been, that this poor child had failed so piteously to see them shining, and so knew nothing of glorifying her Father in Heaven! Like the several flowers in a garden, laden each with the dew of heaven, which, when shaken with the wind, they let fall at each other's roots, and thus are jointly nourished, Christians should become helpers, one to the other, in the Christian life. The dew of God's grace is given freely as the dew of heaven, and in falling it lights on hearts of many different moulds. The perfume of some lives is surely richer and fuller than that of others, and yet when shaken with the wind of God's love each lowly flower sends out its dew, a portion of its own sustenance, to help sustain or nourish others.

Many true, earnest Christians lament the fact that they seem to be able to do almost nothing to show forth the love they have for God, and their real desire to promote the cause they have so near at heart. But there is always the strong, potent power of prayer. A lady once spoke of certain friends whom it was her duty and privilege to benefit, without their being able to make return; "but," she added, "they are good people and we have their prayers, which I value a great deal." Quite as much as temporal benefits, and even vastly more, are the prayers of good people, whose only payment can be prayer for God's blessings, sure to be sent in answer. Woe to those so-called Christians who profess to serve God, but make no effort to send out a saving light into a world of sinners. Example in the right direction is much, and it often happens that a word of warning or encouragement falls as dew upon the flowers. Any earnest, prayerful effort to send out a saving light in the great garden of the Lord will surely gain the commendation of the great Lord of the harvest at last.

GLORIFICATION THROUGH DEATH.

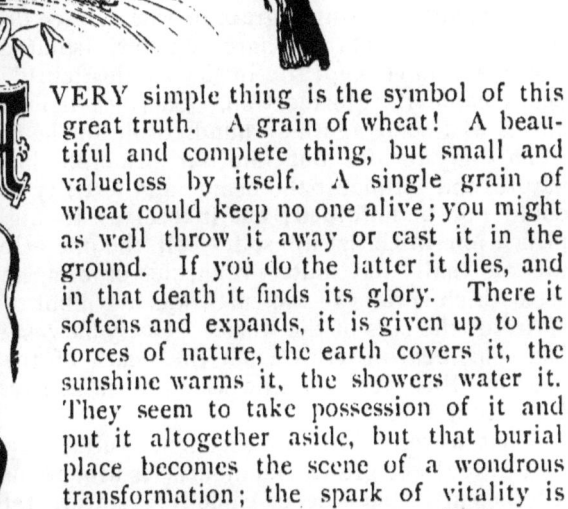

A VERY simple thing is the symbol of this great truth. A grain of wheat! A beautiful and complete thing, but small and valueless by itself. A single grain of wheat could keep no one alive; you might as well throw it away or cast it in the ground. If you do the latter it dies, and in that death it finds its glory. There it softens and expands, it is given up to the forces of nature, the earth covers it, the sunshine warms it, the showers water it. They seem to take possession of it and put it altogether aside, but that burial place becomes the scene of a wondrous transformation; the spark of vitality is kindled by the very elements which seem to work its destruction. It lengthens downward and upward, becomes a green, beautiful stalk, and at length is laden with a score of such grains as it was itself, and becomes the prolific parent of countless harvests in the future, until travelling in the West some day you will see vast towers and enormous buildings which look like the enginery of war. These are not buildings for defence, but the storehouses for the resurrections of your single grain of wheat.

From the interminable fields, stretching far as the eye can reach, undulating in the breeze like the waves of a tawny ocean, they bring in the grain, increased an hundredfold, and store it for the consumption of the world. When a famine occurs, even if it be in China, those great buildings are opened, and ship after ship departs laden with the golden grain to relieve misery and save life. What could the single grain of wheat have done toward that grand object? A hard, narrow, isolated thing, it could not have kept life in the smallest child. Only by death came its glorification. Sacrifice it in the sowing, and it will come again an hundredfold in the harvest.

This mysterious but familiar principle underlies all nature, and without it the beauty and fertility of the world could not be unfolded; but it receives its highest exemplification in Christ himself. All the operations of nature are really but mute prophecies of him, and the first seed which sprang in the earth was a symbol of the Lamb slain for the sins of the world. Every harvest which God has sent, bearing fruit from the death of the seed, has been an illustration of him who pre-eminently was glorified through death.

What a wonderful, transcendent fruitage sprang from that grave! It grows and flourishes around us, it covers all the earth, but whence came it? Nature tells that the harvest which now waves beneath the sun has been lying on the ground all through the winter, chilled with the frosts, drenched with the rains, buried in the grave of darkness, covered with a shroud of snow, but now it stands erect, crowned with beauty and bounty.

How true a symbol this is of the Saviour's stormy life, the dreary seed time when the Divine seed was placed in the ground amid the wreck of life and beauty. But out of that hiding-place of God's power, out of that grave sprang life and immortality. All the nations of the world shall eat of the fruit of that harvest. Thus our Saviour lost his life, and found it again in the lives of others to whom he had imparted life.

His personality became enlarged and increased by that very self-sacrifice which seemed at the time to have destroyed it.

Some time since there were discovered some grains of

wheat, bound tightly up in a mummy's wrappings. For centuries they had rested there unseen, until the dust of ages had gathered upon them. Hard, unfruitful kernels they had remained through all that time, of no use to the mummy and of no value to the world; but they were taken out and planted, and in one year had multiplied into a harvest. It was indeed a wonderful conservation of life which had preserved them for centuries, but can you imagine anything more fruitless? When they died their fruitfulness began.

Death, then, is not one of our enemies. It is deliverance from all the toils and troubles of life; it is reunion with loved ones, never to part again. The path lies through the valley of the shadow, and the chill night winds blow tumultuously, but this only leads to the brightness of the better world beyond. All our gain lies in death, the pain and peril lie in survival.

What shall we do with our lives? We may live only to enjoy ourselves and care only for selfish amusement, we may close our eyes to all the sin and misery that reigns in the world, and keep out of sight the whole region of conscience, and so we may win the passing, perishable things of sense. But let us not think that a universal law will cease its operations on our account. This is a process of death, not of life. If we do this, we shall be like the cold, hard corn of wheat, which abideth alone in an isolated death-in-life, incapable of any growth, because kept out of the ground, living for itself.

THE MOUNT OF OLIVES.

THE MOUNTAINS AND THEIR SUGGESTIONS.

THEIR crowning rocks tower above us, and we almost look to see the angels alight, and their shining garments flash out against the blue sky. A thin white cloud floats up now along the mountain's verdure to its undimmed crest, just such as we believed in happy childhood bore angels. Alas, that we have grown wiser! But why mourn the sweet credulity of earlier days? Knowledge has brought pain, but reveals truth overtopping the wonder and bliss of dreams. We would be loath to barter the larger, richer pleasures of added

31

years, surely, for the child's heedless joy. From the humming bird, who scarce sways the scarlet blossom it woos at our feet, to the massive, superb peak almost kissing the zenith, what a range of creation and thought! We bow in heart, adoring, to the Maker of all. He numbers alike the hairs of our head, and sows the universe with myriad worlds; those worlds, shining upon us from their far heights, a reproach to our murmurings and restlessness. Mountains and stars tell us of fresh hopes and eternal repose. Even unbelief Nature sways to reverence. We knew one between whose riper faith and child worship there yawned a chasm of infidelity. Often a stroll in God's fair forests awoke in him the latent religious instinct, while doubt clouded it in God's sanctuary. From the mountain peak, when John Randolph saw the sun rise, flushing the illimitable circumference of view with light and glory, he said solemnly to his body servant, the only one present, "Never doubt there is a God." Such wonder of landscape and tint, such dome of sky, mocked at a chance creation. Sooner far shut from thought proud St. Peter's architects, and say that aisle and dome and altar and ornaments were blown together by idle breezes. But Bible faith, worshipping the Creator, gathers many an association dear and sublime from sacred pages. How the most notable of these haunt about mountains! On Mount Ararat rested the ark and the remnant of our race above water that whelmed a world's woe and wickedness. Mount Moriah uplifted the altar that put to proof Abraham's surpassing faith, and brought, as ever, proportional blessing. Amid "thunderings, and the lightnings, and the noise of trumpets, and the mountain smoking," rang the law of a holy life from Mount Sinai. A Balaam and a Moses alternate grand dramas on Mount Pisgah. From two mountains, responsive blessings on the righteous, and cursings on the wicked nation, were uttered. God revealed to Elijah on Mount Carmel and Mount Horeb two chapters in the Bible which we may never read without bated breath. If we turn from the old to the new, from the dawning to the day of revelation, we remember how the devil, on "an exceeding high mountain," tempted Jesus in his humanity, with a temptation that might not befall other men.

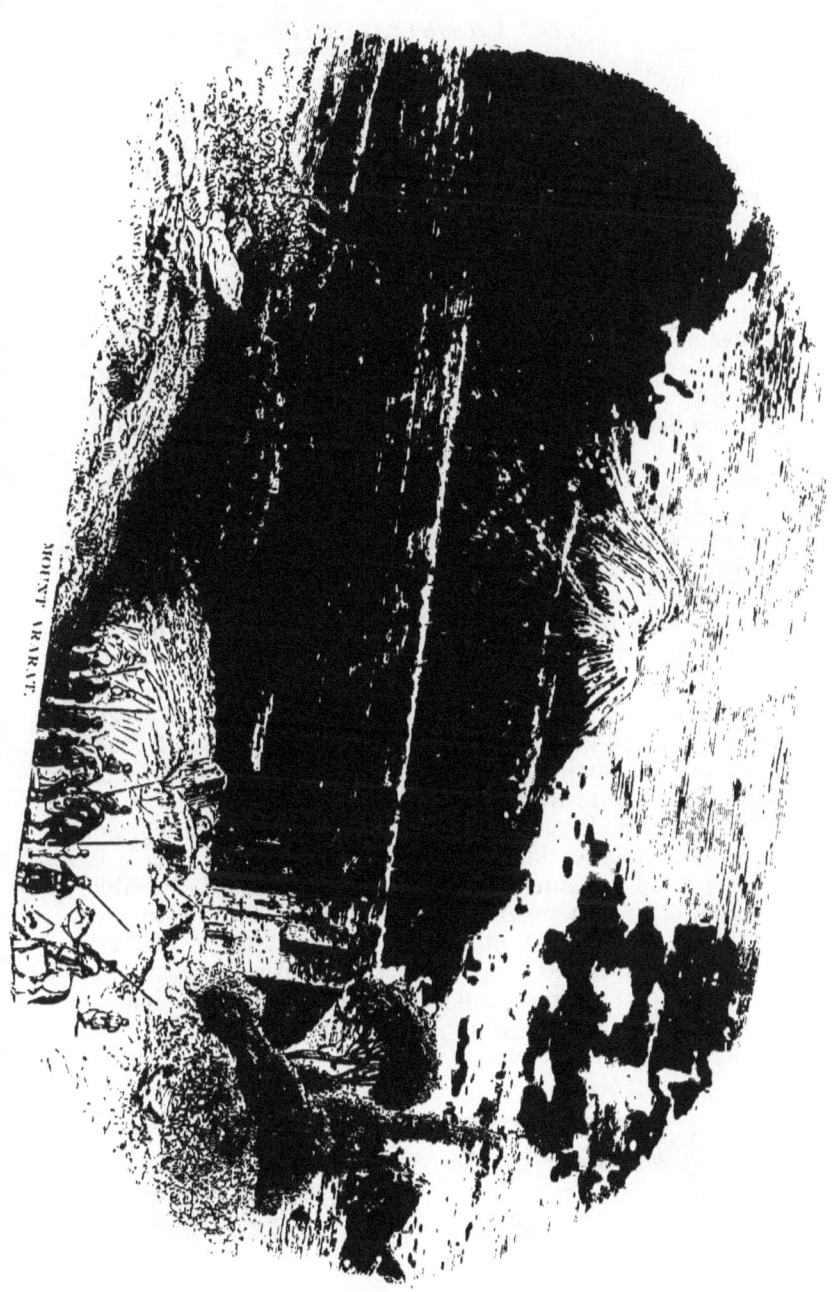

MOUNT ARARAT.

"All the kingdoms of the world and the glory of them" rolled at his feet in sumptuous pomp of procession. All that might gladden desire, or thrill imagination, or satiate ambition was there for his use; but with the condition—worship the bestower. "It is written," answers with quelling power. As the "Son of Man," Jesus opposed Scripture to alluring evil, but he speaks "with authority" in his Godhead, when he preaches the sermon on the mount. Who of us that would pray to be his disciple does not long to embody in a saintly life this the fullest of his teachings? Slowly we turn to the Mount of Transfiguration, though it shines with the supernatural; but at the foot of the cross—Mount Calvary—emotion overpowers. A beautiful ascension from Mount Olivet, and then the Lord our Saviour disappears from view. The pen of inspiration begins with the creation of the world, it closes with the revelation of heaven, and our spirit faints within us at the immensity, the supernal beauty of the vision. What an enlargement of sense to have seen in a single view from the mountain, "that great city, the holy Jerusalem, descending out of heaven from God!" Its stupendous walls, splendid with twelve diversely colored jewels, and set with twelve lustrous gates, three to a side, each several gate a pearl. Through their broadly flung portals we catch a glimpse of "the mansions" of pure gold, as it were transparent glass, "the river of water of life" overshadowed by its trees of fruit and healing, and we long to enter in. The walls shut out hope, but wide open stand the gates of pearl. They invite all to throng through, only an angel of might guards each, and we must beware to ask the Lord of the city for a passport. His promise is pledged to give freely to those who ask. For all who enter, strong and beautiful in their new immortality, there are joy, glory, power and holiness, the presence and the peace of God.

THE MOUNTAINS AND THEIR SUGGESTIONS.
(View on the Jordan.)

THE LORD OUR "ROCK."

THE Bible is specifically distinguished from all other early literature by its delight in natural imagery. It is a matter of easy observation in the poetical and prophetical portions of Scripture how largely they deal with natural scenery, and the natural features of the earth. Things spiritual are illustrated by things natural, and God's dealings with his ancient people early impressed this upon them. There was that mysterious Rock to which they owed their lives during all their desert wanderings—type of that smitten Rock from which the waters gushed forth and followed them in their march. In like manner their descendants were placed in what was then one of the most beautiful districts upon the earth, full of glorious mountains and valleys, so that they became by these means and by the touch of God's hand upon their hearts, sensible to the appeal of natural scenery in a way equalled by no other people. We find their literature, therefore, full of expressions not only testifying to a vivid sense of the power of nature over man, but showing the connection between natural and spiritual things. Rocks they learned to know and love and prize as the most enduring and stable of all things, and therefore the Lord was "their Rock."

In that land of mountains, where stood the goodly Lebanon and the snow-capped Hermon, they became familiar with the grandeur of God's works. The everlasting hills inspired them with ideas of permanence and eternity. In the diversity of the scenery, the rocks, which formed a large part of the landscape, lost all their ruggedness and roughness, became picturesque in their outlines, and clad in perpetual verdure, were beautiful to the eye. How

MT. OLIVET FROM ST. STEPHEN'S GATE.

often they found safe refuges in those same rocks, where the enemy could not find them and dared not attack them. The munitions of rocks were their defence, and a great part of the strength of the country.

Just what the rocks are to the earth, the Lord is to human life—its strength and stability. Human life never amounts to very much unless it has Divine elements in it; man is but the sport of circumstances without them. There is no certainty of safety for any man who has not the Lord in his life. He may have resisted sin for a long time, and been tried often without failing; he may be considered by his fellow-men noble and upright and true and good, but after all he has no rock in his life. Principle is strong, good habits are even stronger, but nothing less than deep-seated religious convictions and experiences, combined with a firm hold on the "Lord our Rock," and that help which comes from the "Everlasting Hills" of God's grace and power can make one secure. These are the foundations of life which are everlasting. They are not vague hopes or shadowy dreams like the architecture of the clouds, but are solid, substantial realities. They are not mere illusions; like those pictures reflected on the bosom of a lake, to be destroyed in an instant by the merest trifle, a pebble dropped by an idle hand, the wing of a passing breeze, a withered leaf falling from its tree, but they are truths which shall last when the heavens themselves shall be rolled up like a scroll.

Were the truths concerning God destitute of certainty, they might be brilliant indeed, but it would be the brilliance of the mirage, not of rock, gleaming in the sunlight. We need this element of certainty in our changing lives; in God alone we find it. He never changes. Amid the great mysteries of life which lie around us unexplored, in 'hopeless confusion, we can feel the everlasting arms underneath us. Amid the perpetual mutations of earth we may cling to the Eternal One, the Rock of Ages, against whom the waves of time and change will beat in vain. In the promise of the Gospel we have sure ground, beaten hard by the march of earth's wisest and best men, with whom we may with confidence exclaim, "The Lord is my Rock."

UNDERNEATH THE EVERLASTING ARMS.

THE eternal "God is thy refuge, and underneath thee are the everlasting arms." Surely no promise could have been more infinitely precious than this, when its words fell upon the ears of the Israelites. It was wonderfully adapted to the circumstances of a people who had been travelling houseless and homeless for a long time. The words had a homelike sound. The thought of stability and permanence must have been like music in the ears of this homesick people. Every blessing seemed to be contained in this promise, an abiding and unchanging dwelling-place where no evil could befall them, an everlasting arm to sustain and support them, strong enough to bear every burden, every care.

The words come down to us as a priceless legacy from the God who is the same yesterday, to-day, and forever, and we may each know for ourselves the comfort contained in them for every weary, heavy laden soul. The eternal God is our refuge, what need we care then if dark clouds of sorrow lower, and the bitter waters of affliction overflow us? God will never leave nor forsake us, and pavilioned in his eternal love we need fear no evil.

And God is not only a refuge, he is a dwelling-place. Too many of us are accustomed to go to God only in times of weakness, or to fly to him as a very present help only in time of trouble. When the clouds gather and the storm breaks, then we turn to God to protect us, but when the storm has passed, and all is bright and fair again, we forget him as if we were now self-sufficient. We make God our refuge only, instead of our dwelling-place; we go to him as a covert for a little season till the danger is overpast, we do not make him our home. If we made God our dwelling-place as well as our refuge, it would alter our lives completely, and increase our happiness an hundredfold.

Think for a moment what a blessed thing it is to dwell in God; then there is not one trouble that comes to us that we have to bear alone, not one joy that we have to share alone, not one purpose to make alone, not one temptation to conquer alone and unaided. The least event in our history quite as much as the greatest does not happen to us alone, but God shares our life with us, and every moment we are dwelling in him with the everlasting arms beneath and about us.

What a revolution it would make in our lives if we realized this! How many things would be left undone that now are done, how many new duties would be begun! What a new sanctity and sweetness would fill our joys, what deeper responsibility would invest our thoughts and actions, what victories we would gain over temptations that have heretofore defeated us! We would attach a new sacredness and greatness to our common life if we once felt that God was our constant dwelling-place, not simply our refuge in times of distress and trouble. Of course such times will come, but underneath us are the everlasting arms, strong enough to bear us up through any trouble. Should we ever be crushed by the burdens and cares of life as they gather about us, we can feel also the tightening of those everlasting arms which have borne so many precious souls through deepest waters safely to the other side.

"YE MUST BE BORN AGAIN."

CHRIST taught that if there is no change of heart now, there will be no true religion here or bliss hereafter. "Ye must be born of water and of the spirit." This is a moral necessity. It could not from the nature of things be otherwise. "How can two walk together except they be agreed?" How can you love a holy God while you love and cherish sin? How can you at the same time love the world and the world-crucifying Christ? How can you appreciate and take delight in exercises for which you have no relish? How can you be a loyal subject of King Jesus while in rebellion against him? How can you enjoy the companionship of regenerate souls with whom you have no affinity? Then think of the great hereafter—of heaven. How sweet is that word! It is the condensed expression of beauty, bliss, glory. All want to go thither at last. But do you know that heaven is a perfectly holy world, a purely religious place, a vast temple of incessant worship? Do you know that all its inhabitants from earth are regenerated people, its joys are the joys of holiness, its songs are the praises of redeeming love, its activities are the sweet obedience of loving hearts? Ask your own conscience solemnly, if you were taken there just as you are, without a thorough change of your affections, would not its very air be oppressive, its services tedious, its employments irksome? Could you sing its songs? Could you shout praises unto him whom you have despised on earth? Verily not! That polluted heart within you would writhe amidst the blaze of infinite purity, and cry out, "This is not my place: I am a stranger to all these persons and enjoyments; I am not adapted to them." Yea, we may all sing in mournfully solemn tones:

> "Had I a throne above the rest,
> Where angels and archangels dwell,
> One sin unslain within my breast,
> Would turn that heaven to hell."

Ah! then the loving, faithful Saviour utters a grand moral necessity when he says to us, "Ye must be born again!" God give you grace to see it and feel it. God grant that you may now be impressed as you have never been before with the fact, that whatever other experiences you may have of joy or sorrow, of prosperity or adversity, you must have this. God grant that the words, "Ye must be born again," may ring in your ears and toll their solemn cadences through every avenue of your being until you cry out, "Holy Spirit! change my heart. Work thy work of grace in me." Then shall it be done, and thou shalt stand up regenerated, redeemed, disenthralled, in all the dignity and bliss of "a new creature in Christ Jesus."

GETHSEMANE.

SPEAK THE TRUTH "IN LOVE."

THERE is sometimes a harshness in presenting truth that effectually obstructs its way in the mind of the hearer. The study of this subject is a most important one, especially since the temptation to impatience is not uncommon among those who, by reason of a clear perception of the peril of the sinner, are earnestly seeking their salvation.

One Sabbath evening in a certain church we lately witnessed the sad results of speaking the truth indeed, but not "in love." Among several penitents bowing at the altar of prayer was a young man evidently awakened by the Holy Spirit to a sense of sin. Some one suggested in a cold, unfeeling way that it was proper thus to prostrate himself; for such a life as he had led sooner or later must end in destruction. Now, while all this may have been true, it was too plainly evident that it was not the truth spoken *in love*, for the tone in which the remark was made showed that the speaker believed the young man insincere. The manner in which the words were spoken could scarcely fail to produce unfortunate results, for an implied censure was betrayed—an unnecessary prejudice thereby awakened. The peculiar tenderness so necessary in the winning worker was sadly wanting. That seeking soul was immediately set back; the lack of the constraining love of Christ in the instruction given vitiated that instruction. Indeed, there was precipitated a needless revolt in the penitent's mind at this, the most critical of all periods. That young man, with but partial views of the Saviour as yet, and in a condition to suffer embarrassment by any opposing circumstances, utterly yielded to tempta-

O Lord, how manifold are thy works! in wisdom hast thou made them all: the earth is full of thy riches

PSAL. 104 24

tion. The sinful self became dominant. Pride and passion once more rallied. The penitents' seat was quickly abandoned.

And even until this day the genuine signs of contrition on account of sin have not reappeared. There is at least a possibility, and we think a probability even, that the same instruction imparted in a different spirit at that hour would have ended in the conversion of the young man to a Christian life. *Love*, burning in the Christian's heart, is absolutely essential to the effective deliverance of the Gospel. Truth, however keen and penetrating, will generally find at least partial acceptance when our words of warning are charged with *all-conquering love*.

LITTLE SERMONS.

ONCE let men see not things alone, but the Divine light and life that stream through them, and then shall every day open new revelations; then shall the bird upon the wing and the flower in the field speak to them of God. Every swelling bud and every grass blade peeping from the cold, bare earth these spring days tell a mute story of resurrected life; speak in their own way of the goodness and mercy of the Heavenly father.

> "Flowers preach to us if we will hear,
> Lichen and moss and sturdy weed
> Tell of His love who sends the dew,
> The rain and the sunshine too,
> To nourish one small seed."

Every flower that pushes its way from the dark mould under the revivifying of the sun's rays and the warm rain utters a protest against the cry, "There is no God," and lifts its petals in speechless astonishment at him who says that death ends all, that the grave is man's final destiny. Every petal that opens to the sun on these bright spring mornings preaches a resurrection sermon, and all the lily bells that swing their waxen tongues in the warm breezes are ringing anthems of praise to the Father and Maker of all.

We too often think of God as only a great and mighty Being, terrible in majesty, awful in power. We see his manifestations in lightnings and earthquakes and pestilences, and think of him only as one who holds the sea in the hollow of his hand. We seem almost to forget that the same hand that created the vast things of the universe, the stars and planets, suns and moons, that poured out the seas and set the mighty cataracts in motion, also painted the leaves of the tiniest flowers, and fashioned their delicate waxen petals, and hung the lilies of the valley in their swinging green belfries in the fields and woods. If we would study the works of God more among the little things of earth, the bright and beautiful things, we might learn more of his love and tenderness than we ever dreamed of before. He who made the flowers of the field to give forth exhaustless perfume, who clothed the birds with plumage of rainbow dyes and tuned their throats to sweet melodies; who fashioned the pearls in the depths of the sea and draped the sunset clouds in glory—such a Being must love the Beautiful, and who can love it truly and not be pure and wise and good? Deaf must he be to every inward calling, and blind to every outward summons, who can go forth in the fields on a beautiful spring morning and not hear and see that God is good. The birds sing it; the leaves whisper it to one another; the flowers speak it forth; in every little thing Nature tells the story of goodness and love.

HOME WITHOUT SPIRITUAL LIFE.

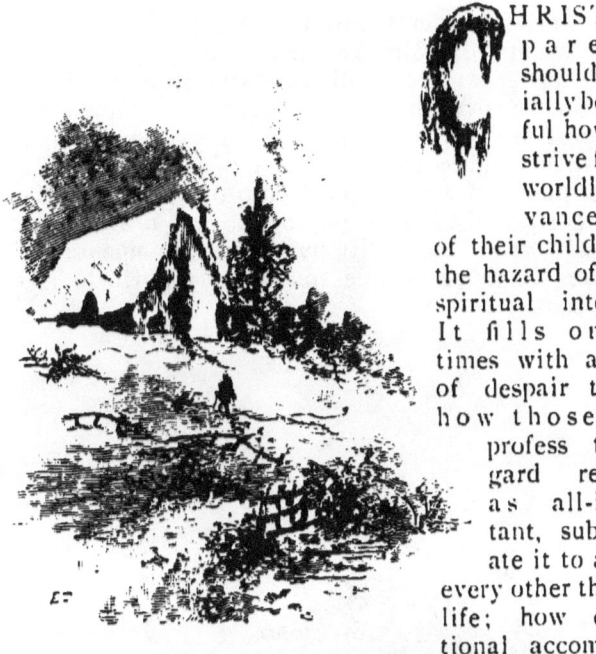

CHRISTIAN parents should specially be careful how they strive for the worldly advancement of their children at the hazard of their spiritual interests. It fills one at times with a kind of despair to see how those who profess to regard religion as all-important, subordinate it to almost every other thing in life; how educational accomplishments, and choice of pursuits, and friendships and alliances, are discussed and fixed without this ever coming into serious view. Were it bodily infection it would fill them with alarm, but spiritual danger is lightly passed by. It is one great reason why Christianity makes so little progress, and why Christian families are constantly melting away into the worldliness around them; while the parents grieve to see their children lost, not only to vital religion, but even to that strength of mind and steadiness of purpose which are necessary to any firm position in life.

Both worlds frequently slip from the grasp in the miserable attempt to gain the false glitter of the present, and the bitter waters of disappointment sweep, like the Sea of Sodom, over the ruins of fortune and fame coveted at the cost of consistent principle. Let the kingdom of God and his righteousness be sought and maintained in the first place; if worldly position follow, it will be honorably borne and usefully employed; and if God do not see fit to give it, there will be sufficient compensation in the pure and imperishable treasures with which he can fill the soul.

FAITHFUL UNTO DEATH.

HERE is nothing in Pompeii that invests it with a deeper interest than the spot where a soldier of old Rome displayed a most heroic fidelity. That fatal day in which Vesuvius, at whose feet the city stood, burst out into an eruption that shook the earth, a sentinel kept watch by the gate which looked to the burning mountain. Amidst the fearful disorder the sentinel had been forgotten, and as Rome required her sentinels, happen what might, to hold their posts till relieved by the guard or set at liberty by their officers, he had to choose between death and dishonor. Slowly, but surely, the ashes thicken on his manly form; now covering his lips, they choke his breathing. But he was "faithful unto death." After seventeen centuries they found his skeleton standing erect in a marble niche, clad in rusty armor, the helmet yet on his head and his bony fingers still closed upon his spear.

After the flight of centuries how the thrilling tale still stirs earnest and true souls! Faithful unto death!

There comes a great comfort to the soul exercising fidelity. He sows his seed, it may be, in weakness. God gives the increase.

We are only commanded to do the best we can, leaving results with God.

In the terrible April gale of 1851, the lighthouse on Minot's Ledge, near Boston, was destroyed. Two men were in it at the time, and a vast multitude was gathered upon the shore waiting, in anxious distress, for the expected catastrophe. Every hour, however, the bell tolled the time, and ever the light pierced the dark raging storm, and bade the sailor beware. No howling blast could silence the one or rising waves extinguish the other. At last one giant wave, mightier than the rest, rose up and threw its arms around the tower and laid it low in the waves. Then alone was the bell silent; then alone did the light cease to shine.

"IF."

ONE of the shortest words in the entire language, but one on which hinges almost every kind of possibility or impossibility. Certainty is something for which mankind would give almost anything at certain times and under many circumstances. But to sift the matter down, because God is infinite and man is finite, the little "if" of our conversation must creep in and occupy its legitimate and unavoidable position in every plan we form, every joy we anticipate, every sorrow we experience.

In all things pertaining to this life and its conditions, the conditional word must be used, but there are joys we may anticipate, and a state of which we may be certain at last upon a few simple conditions; these met and fulfilled, there remains no uncertain "if" to trouble us.

"Whosoever believeth on the name of the Lord shall be saved." There is no "if" here. No condition whatever limits the straight, plain assertion of these words save the one of belief. Though the earth should be removed and the mountains be carried into the midst of the sea, it would in no wise affect the ultimate safety of the believer.

It is strange that with all the lessons of change, accident, disappointment and uncertainty, which attend all worldly transactions, Christians are willing to disregard the only certainties of which they can avail themselves. Contrast the worried, anxious countenance with which the merchant counts on his profits *if* the voyage is a successful one, *if* trade holds secure, *if* the stock remains valuable, with the untroubled serenity and placidity with which the true Christian can speak of his hopes. The world and everything it contains is but dross compared with the riches of the kingdom of God.

THE VALUE OF TIME.

NEVER, until the golden bowl is broken, will we realize the true value of this, one of the richest of all God's gifts to his finite creatures. All material success is born of a just appreciation of the minutes and a proper use of them. A thorough business man acts upon this knowledge, and bases his calculations upon it. Interest is calculated to the day. Railroad time must be adjusted to the second; a five minutes' error may cause the loss of hundreds of lives. Men are discharged for allowing their chronometers any variation whatever. Insurance companies date their policies from a certain hour of the day; five minutes earlier or later may save or lose a fortune. In the realm of mind, we should be equally chary of the moments. Any writer knows if the winged thought is not caught and chained at once, it may be gone forever, or may lose the vital force attending its birth. God is brought face to face with us in such vital utterances. There is a vitality in them that communicates itself to the reader and makes a vivid impression that no mere repetition of words can convey; in short, there is a difference of a living, breathing spirit and a dead letter.

Our spiritual life and work should be possessed of this vitality. How differently the precious Bible utterances affect us from different lips, even though the speakers are equally sincere! The one, believing that time is short and precious, and realizing this belief, works with this end in view, and no arithmetic can compute the measure of his success; the other may believe the facts, but failing to impress himself with the value of flying moments, utters his belief in words so tame that they fall powerless on his hearers. Should a hand appear writing in living characters on the wall of his room, "This day thy soul shall be required of thee," would there not be life and sound sense—the sense of belief—in his expostulations? Would he not forget himself entirely and hasten to the rescue of the souls committed to his care—hasten as did Lot from the burning cities of the plain?

I know of a minister, a good one, too, who, after the introductory exercises of Wednesday evening prayer meetings are over, and his opening remarks have been given, seems to have chilled the entire meeting by the slow, measured utterances of his thoughts. The ideas are right, the language is correct, but there is no life-giving, electrical force in them; the meeting has received a check that some magnetic soul must hasten to avert, or the precious moments will be more than lost. Queen Elizabeth realized in her death-agony the value of moments, when she exclaimed, "My kingdom for an hour of time!" And many another testimony could be added to this. The greatest minds, the most shining examples of culture in every department, can attribute their success, in great part, to a wise disposition of their time. It comes to us but once. Morning, noon, and night are the daily reminders of youth, manhood and old age; each in its time, and but once for each. Seed-time, summer and harvest, and the winter of death. O that we might write on each passing moment some glorious record for eternity—to shine through the ages!

CHRISTIAN SYMPATHY.

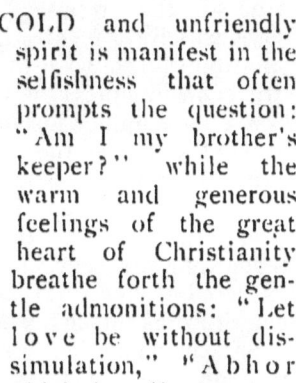

A COLD and unfriendly spirit is manifest in the selfishness that often prompts the question: "Am I my brother's keeper?" while the warm and generous feelings of the great heart of Christianity breathe forth the gentle admonitions: "Let love be without dissimulation," "Abhor that which is evil, cleave to that which is good," "Be kindly affectioned one to another, with brotherly love," even "in honor preferring one another." Christian sympathy, so magnanimously exemplified in the acts of the good Samaritan, comes with her kind words, her balm of consolation, and wipes the tear from the eye of sorrow, binds up the wounds of the suffering, administers to the wants of the stranger, and alleviates the distresses of the neglected poor.

And who that has been imbued with the Spirit can view the scenes of desolation around us without sympathizing with those who are afflicted and distressed; without suffering the tear of compassion to fall, and feeling an emotion of tenderness and sympathy for those who suffer?

Well indeed may we entertain and cherish this divine and generous principle in our hearts, for she is the loveliest of all the beautiful and attractive graces that adorn the chaste and virtuous soul, so much so, that when she takes up her residence in the human heart, she is as a welcome guest from heaven, breathing peace and love into the soul that heretofore was a stranger to such exalted feelings. She throws her softest rays over those blissful regions of immortal delight, without impairing either their beauty or their tranquillity; and sheds her sweetest, soothing balm upon the inhabitants without destroying either their happiness or their repose. Her lily is interwoven with the roses which form celestial garlands, and her drops of consolation mingle with the tears of exquisite delight which glitter in immortal eyes.

She took up her lasting abode in the bosom of the Son of God, and was the constant companion of the Saviour amid the trying scenes of that way of tears and blood, when, looking upon the city, he exclaimed, "O Jerusalem, Jerusalem, thou that killest the prophets, and stonest them that are sent unto thee, how often would I have gathered thy children together, even as a hen gathereth her chickens under her wings, and ye would not!"

She accompanied him in every step of his journey through life, for it is said: "He wept with those that wept," and "in all their afflictions he was afflicted," and "lo, the angel of his presence saved them." She accompanied him even to the scenes of his crucifixion and his death, and at last placed her chaplet of cypress upon his conquering brow when he expired on the cross, praying: "Father, forgive them, for they know not what they do!"

In proportion as we become imitators of the blessed Jesus we shall become the companions of Christian sympathy. She will teach us to bind up the broken-hearted and to pour the oil of consolation and the wine of sympathy into the wounded spirit. O how grand life becomes when it imitates the acts and cultivates the virtues of our blessed Lord and we in spirit become like him!

THE GRACE OF IGNORANCE.

KNOWLEDGE is relative. If we may be excused the seeming paradox, it is only the wise who know when to be ignorant; when to confess and recognize their limitations. There are many things in this life, questions relating to things material and things spiritual, concerning which we must be content to know nothing. In every direction around us there is a point beyond which human wisdom cannot penetrate, depths which it cannot fathom, heights to which it cannot ascend. Granting all that science can do, impelled by energy, perseverance, and enthusiasm, yet this must be acknowledged. All earthly wisdom soon finds its Ultima Thule. We are surrounded by the Unknowable.

> "We have but faith; we cannot know,
> For knowledge is of things we see;
> And yet we trust it comes from Thee
> A beam in darkness: let it grow."

We have such a range of philosophies and sciences, of *isms* and *ologies*, so many books and learned men, we advance a little way into so many realms of knowledge, that we forget how we are playing after all only on the surface of things, only picking up the pebbles on the shore of the great ocean of truth. Every grain of sand has problems too deep for our understanding; every flower has questions to make dumb the lips of sages. The mysterious, the wonderful, the eternal, are almost always before our eyes, whether we lift them to the skies or gaze upon the ground. The earth, our beloved *terra firma*, is full of hidden powers and secret, living impulses of which we can know nothing except in the most superficial way, as they appear in their final and visible results. Our little enclosure of moist brown earth, to the eye cold, motionless, formless, and unlovely, is in reality the most wondrous of laboratories, weaving beneath our feet the curious tapestry of vegetable forms, selecting and sending up the juices fit to nourish each of the hundred different plants, trees, flowers, shrubs, and grasses that flourish on the surface. Who can boast of his wisdom, realizing what he treads upon and what is going on around him in these summer days?

The man of wise and inquiring mind can only be contented with himself when he knows when and where to be ignorant. The trouble is that men are always trying to push their inquiries beyond the fixed and legitimate bounds of human knowledge. They are forever sending down their plummets to measure that which in the nature of things is immeasurable; trying to weigh that which is not to be weighed; to understand that which is not understandable; to see that which is not seeable. It is in this region, just beyond the pale of what is real and actual in human knowledge, that a number of men who think themselves wise are always groping, blind leaders of the blind, full of speculations and theories, of high sounding and boastful talk that begins with nothing and ends with nothing. In this domain lie the questions relating to such unknowable things as the origin and development of life, the being, the mind, and purposes of God, the exact nature of the Trinity, the location and dimensions of the Heavenly, the employments of the redeemed, the whole destiny of man, the plan of the universe, and a thousand other questions akin to these.

In trying to solve these unsolvable problems thousands of men have wasted their lives, wrecked their intellects, and led astray multitudes of their fellow beings. From this region of misty speculations and baseless theories come more than half the doubts, the unbeliefs, the dark errors and false teachings which vex and distract mankind. From thence come the vain philosophies, the oppressive systems, the harsh and cruel creeds which have sown the world with blood and tears.

I will instruct thee and teach thee in the way which thou shalt go: I will guide thee with mine eye.

With respect to these things let us cultivate the grace of ignorance; let us recognize our boundaries, and be wise in those things wherein it is ours to be wise. The field of rightful and legitimate knowledge is wide and curious enough to employ all our powers. Within the realms open to human wisdom and research no Alexander need ever sigh for other worlds to conquer. There is, indeed, within these realms so much that is worth the knowing, so much of beauty and grandeur, so much to fill the mind and enlarge the soul of man that he who goes beyond to tread the impenetrable darkness of unknown and unknowable spaces may ascribe it all to his own folly and presumption if he come at the last to realize that his life has been a hollow mockery, a vanity and vexation of spirit. For all else there is the consolation that many things of which it is not ours to know now we shall know hereafter. Let us be content with what it is possible for us to know under the limitations of our earthly existence, and leave the rest for that time when we shall see no more "through a glass darkly," but with the enlarged and clarified vision of our spiritual and immortal being.

THE CHRISTIAN'S RACE.

THE Christian life is a race, and is expressed in the Bible in this very manner. A mighty race-course is seen stretching away from our feet upward and onward, and that is the place for the Christian, where men strive for mastery, where they run for an immortal crown. We must not stop to look at transitory things, or the glittering prizes of the world, but keep our eyes on the goal lest we should be distanced in the race, and another step in before us. We must look to the end, the glorious crown, the great author and finisher of our faith, and press forward. Mind not the things about us, they are not worthy to be compared with the glory that shall be. "Run with patience," and so run that ye may obtain. As to the conditions and qualities upon which success depends, we can well learn a lesson from the old Grecian games. The racers were in earnest; we do well to emulate their assiduity, their singleness of aim and effort, and the engrossment of every power and faculty in one great master passion to win the race or die. They had but one idea, and everything else was of secondary importance.

That race in which they were to run before the world for a prize was continually in their minds, and it tightened their muscles in anticipation. This was the first grand condition of their success, as it is of all success; for no man ever did anything great with divided energies. We are running a mighty race for an immortal crown; if religion is worth anything it is worth everything; Shall we not therefore emulate the earnestness of those ancient Greeks? The Christian must live for one thing, and one thing only; not that he must renounce all the active duties of life, and spend all his days in meditation, for that would no more make a strong Christian than the close and stifling air of the cave would make a strong athlete. The world is necessary to the true development of Christian character. There must be storm and wind, cares, trials and vexations, and the common business of life in the experience of the Christian to make him strong in the race for eternal life. Every power must be consecrated to God, and every energy concentrated upon his work; then, like an arrow from the bow, like the lightning from the sky, the Christian will spring forward, determined to conquer or die. It is a glorious race to run, and at the goal are the shining forms and loving faces of a great cloud of witnesses, and Jesus, the author and finisher of our faith, waiting to bestow upon us the prize of our high calling.

MARY MAGDALENE'S REWARD.

 MARY MAGDALENE was one of the Saviour's most devoted friends. She had been a deeply afflicted woman, possessed of seven devils. These the Saviour cast out, and ever afterward she loved him with a pure and ardent affection. She clung to him to the last. We often read of her being with him. As he went through every city, preaching and showing the glad tidings of the kingdom, it is recorded that "the twelve were with him, and certain women which had been healed of evil spirits and infirmities,"

amongst whom was Mary Magdalene. She seems to have gone with him wherever it was proper for her to go Not easily could she have torn herself away from him.

When at length the Saviour was taken and condemned and crucified, we find her still clinging to him. Matthew says: "And many women were there (beholding afar off) following him from Galilee, ministering unto him, among which was Mary Magdalene." Gladly would she have alleviated his sufferings had it been in her power. From the cross she followed his lifeless remains to the sepulchre. When Joseph had taken the body he wrapped it in a clean linen cloth and laid it in his own new tomb, which he had hewn out in a rock, and he rolled a great stone to the door of the sepulchre and departed. "And there was Mary Magdalene and the other Mary sitting over against the sepulchre." She was one of the last to leave the place where her dear Lord was laid. As the shadows of evening gathered around her she reluctantly turned away, and "rested according to the commandment."

A long Sabbath day was that to her. But at length it was past and in the end of the Sabbath, as it began to dawn toward the first day of the week, very early, while it was yet dark, we find her with the other Mary again at the sepulchre. They had brought sweet spices and had come that they might anoint the body of their Saviour. To her surprise and sorrow she found that it was gone. Then she announced the sad intelligence to Peter and John, whom she met: "They have taken away my Lord, and I know not where they have laid him." These two disciples, having satisfied themselves of the truth of her assertion, not knowing what to think or what to do, went away again to their own home. "But Mary stood without at the sepulchre, weeping; and as she wept she stooped down and looked into the sepulchre." Possibly she might yet get a glimpse of him. She would at least see the place where her dear Lord had lain. As she looks she sees "two angels in white, sitting, the one at the head, and the other at the feet, where the body of Jesus had lain. And they say unto her, Woman, why weepest thou? She saith unto them, Because they have taken away my Lord, and I know not where they have laid him.

And when she had thus said, she turned herself back,

THE ARK OF THE COVENANT

and saw Jesus standing, and knew not that it was Jesus. Jesus saith unto her, Woman, why weepest thou? whom seekest thou? She, supposing him to be the gardener, saith unto him, Sir, if thou have borne him hence, tell me where thou hast laid him, and I will take him away. Jesus saith unto her, Mary. She turned herself, and said unto him, Rabboni, which is to say, Master." It was the loftiest moment in all her life, a moment never to be forgotten in time or in eternity. She had found her risen Lord. She was the first of all the disciples to whom he appeared. And thus was she a thousand times rewarded for all her love and for all her painstaking in seeking him. And great will be her reward in heaven. Among the nearest of all to her loved Redeemer will she there stand, and most joyfully will she receive the smiles of his approval.

WALKING WITH GOD.

Ah, lovely souls like those we've known,
 Whose lives, one sweet endeavor,
All crowned with beauty and with bloom,
 The hand of death did sever.
Their memory, like the new mown hay,
 Will linger round us ever.

WALKING with God! What a strengthening, comforting, beautiful thought! God by our side, helping us, guiding us, leading us safely whether the way be smooth or rough. We cannot, perhaps, be like the mountains, grand, stately, magnificent, seen from afar and admired by the multitude, but we can be like the grassy dell, beautiful with sunshine and refreshment, fragrant with sweet flowers and jubilant with the songs of birds. The helpfulness in the family circle, if given in a gentle, unobtrusive way, is a training which rapidly uplifts lives. Those are sweet lives which seek to remove obstructing thorns from another's rough path, and there is never a thorn removed from the path without a rose being scattered on one's own. Mild forbearance in regard to other people's faults is a necessity to every sweet life—the suppression of unkind words another necessity.

The sunshine of such lives brightens darkened homes, warms chilled hearts, and illuminates groping souls. It even seems to have the power of opening sightless eyes, Indeed, the power of such lives is wonderful. They point out the right path to the wayward feet and beckon homeward the lost. They hold cups of water to parched lips, and offer the bread of life to human souls. They scatter good seed with generous and never-tiring hand. What a harvest of golden sheaves will be theirs!

THE BLESSINGS AND POWER OF PRAYER

> Prayer is the Christian's vital breath,
> The Christian's native air;
> His passport at the gate of death,
> He enters Heaven by prayer.

GREATEST of God's blessings and benefits to mankind often lose much of their value to those on whom they are bestowed, from the very freedom with which they are dispensed. Water, without which life could not be sustained; air, necessary to the breath we draw; sunlight and rain, without which vegetation could not flourish, or our bodies be fed; these and countless other benefits are accepted too often as a matter of course, and in far too many cases without a thought of gratitude to the bounteous Giver of each good and perfect gift. But greatest of all the privileges with which humanity has been favored, is the rare one of prayer, with its far-reaching influence and almost limitless power. And one great comfort, when thinking of prayer, lies in the fact that application at the throne of grace can never be made at a wrong time. Heaven's doors are never shut; the ear of the Almighty is never so filled with other sounds as to shut out the cry of ever so feeble a plaint directed in faith to his hearing. He that keepeth Israel neither slumbers nor sleeps, and the day and night are both alike to him. No distance so great but it can be spanned by a simple plea poured into the sympathizing ear of the Father who waits to be gracious. There is no such detective as prayer, for no one can hide away from it. It puts its hands on the shoulders of a man ten thousand miles off. It alights on a ship in mid-Atlantic. What a suggestion of power lies in these truthful words! A wayward son may put thousands of miles between himself and a loving mother, but he cannot get away from her prayers; they can follow him to the ends of the earth, and he cannot hide away from them.

To one who is thus dependent on prayer for strength to meet life's varied experiences, a sense of the power is sometimes merged as it were with the consciousness of comfort that lies in continual petitions. It is such unspeakable comfort not only to commend our loved ones to a care which is infinite and all-powerful, but there are so many personal fears to be quelled, so many desires to be presented, so many burdens to be cast upon the Lord. And to one accustomed thus to seek protection, and to present wants and needs, and to seek sustaining grace, the wonder is how any one can live and support the burdens, and meet the varied anxieties and troubles of life, without something stronger and more reliable than mere human aid can supply.

The habit of prayer commends itself to many persons who seldom pray themselves. A thoughtless, frivolous woman will almost invariably teach her child a little prayer to say at night. There is an unacknowledged and perhaps unrecognized consciousness of the power for good which lies in that simple prayer from the lips of a helpless child. Prayer truly becomes the Christian's "vital breath" and "native air;" it supplies courage and fortitude for every event and emergency of life, it quiets the fears and calms the nerves of the timid, it supplies strength to the weak, it makes the dark hours of the night safe with an unseen presence strong to protect, and robs the night of its loneliness. It is all-prevailing, all-powerful, robbing death of its terrors, and opening wide the gates of heaven to all who through its mighty power have learned to know the Lord.

TRUE RELIGION NOT DAMAGED BY ADVERSITY.

MISFORTUNE never harms the Christian. If a man has the right kind of religion he can go through the severest trials and not suffer spiritual loss. Grace in the heart will not rise and fall with his name; faith will not expand and collapse with his business. If it did, then a fire would burn it out, a flood would drown it out, a panic would scare it out. Satan thought that Job's religion would go with his fortune. But witness his amazement at his mistake. He beholds the patriarch's family buried, his flocks wasted, his health gone, his wife scolding, and his life involved in direst misery; but his faith is still strong and his religion beautiful and magnificent as an immovable palace of granite, which the storm cannot shake, though ruins are scattered all around.

The blessings of earth belong to the natural kingdom and are subject to the troubles of that kingdom: redeeming blessings belong to the spiritual kingdom, and are not subject to the tossings and turnings of fortune. You sit in your homes and laugh at the winds that play with the clouds and trees and waves, for they are shut out and you are shut in. But your soul sits in the home of grace, looks out upon the terrors of earth, beholds the distresses and losses of time, sees the storms that play with wealth and fame, and feels serenely safe with God. The tornado cannot invade its shelter. The ruins of the grandest estate on earth cannot bury the soul that fears the Lord.

Goodness of heart is not proof against adversity. A gracious character is no refuge against earthly harm. The church is not an insurance institution against material losses. But the gusts that beat upon the outer heritage cannot beat upon the inner heritage. The building erected out of material gold and silver and precious stones may come down with a crash; but the inherent value remains to all eternity. The calamities of life cannot overthrow it; the river of death cannot overflow it.

The soul that contains Divine grace is the Lord's conservatory. It is his blooming garden fenced about and covered over. The snows of winter may fall; the frosts may flake the fields with the white of death; the piercing cold may bind creation in its glittering manacles; yet the plants put forth their beautiful blossoms in the greenhouse. So with the person that lives in the love of Jesus Christ. The surface of the sea may be tossed with billows, but the pebbles lie quietly at the bottom; troubles may rush over the limitations of the believer, but the pearls of true grace are undisturbed in the depths of his nature. The eagle can soar above the storm; so can the soul on the wings of hope. The whale can descend below the angry waves; so can the soul in resignation. The safe can preserve its treasures in the fires; so can the soul through patience. The oak can gather nourishment from the leaves stripped from its boughs by last year's storms; so can the soul gather strength from every distress through which it passes. The character of the true soul, like that of Florence Nightingale in the Crimean War, grows strong by the very distress and trouble which overcome others.

Calamities help true religion; they add to its vigor, send its root deeper, make its fibres tougher. They fan its coals into flames. Without adversity grace is in danger of smothering under its own ashes. The men who have lived nearest God are they who have seen the vanities of this world through eyes bedewed with tears. Trouble has often caused aching heads to rest on the bosom of

FLORENCE NIGHTINGALE'S MONUMENT, WESTMINSTER.

Jesus for sympathy. Danger has compelled many a hand to clasp hold of the Almighty for protection. Destruction of property has caused many to search after the true riches. The noblest sons and daughters of earth are they who have been purified in the furnace heated many times. The purest of the wheat, the heaviest and the best, is that which is winnowed the most.

Let us grow more conscious of the soul's independence of earthly things. The soul that lives in Christ is not dependent on the products of business. The body is dependent; the present life is dependent; contingencies arise that make daily supplies necessary. But the soul is independent. It can live, and grow strong, and sing praises, whether its income be twenty thousand a year or twenty cents a day. It can find health and joy, whether it stay in a palace or in a prison. It lives not by bread at all; it lives in the Lord.

Let us make our earthly losses our spiritual gains. Let not the strength be wasted weeping over the ruins. Let faith arise as an eagle above the world of desolations. From the charred vanities of earth turn the eyes upon the glory of the other world. Be not too anxious for an increase of prosperity. He who owns a thousand acres of land here, may not have enough ground to stand on in heaven. He who claims a hundred houses in the city may not have a cottage in the other world. Be brave in trial, and sweetly content, and expect your better things hereafter.

GIRDING ON THE ARMOR.

Satan trembles when he sees
The weakest saint upon his knees.

TO be a Christian means a great deal more than believing in certain doctrines, going to church, or even talking about religion. It means living it. It means having Christ in every deed. We cannot leave him out of the most trivial thing. It means we must show the world that we love the Lord, and are serving him. We must show them so plainly that there can be no mistake. As you know the well-tried soldier by his tread, his habits, and endurance the moment you see him, so the world must know you to be a Christian—a real live Christian—the moment it comes in contact with you. You must meet with sinners, as well as half-asleep, careless Christians, and you must live so that your light shall shine clear and above reproach, fearing only, but always, to bring shame upon the Master's name. By your example you must strengthen the weak, and by your unfaltering step and firm hand help the weak-hearted. Let the whole world see the quiet, steady light of your devoted life. Let the perfume of the "white flower of a blameless life" which you wear, scent the air about you till that very perfume will entice those who breathe it to strive likewise to wear one. Let there be no vain glory or striving after praise for any particular gift; but aspire for no other praise (and it is a great one) than that it may be said that your silent example has won many a heart to Christ. Let an assembly be better for your presence. Where you are let it be known it is safe to be.

Above all let your light shine at home. There are many dear ones who would be led astray by the careless life of a professed Christian, or be won by your devotedness. There are no words so eloquent as a well-lived life—a blameless one. Pray that it may be yours. Let your presence be a signal of peace, your very step music to the tired and discouraged.

It may be your sad lot to live with some one who is not at all agreeable; that is, with one so captious that you cannot pass the day without a jar. Try your best, you say, there is trouble; even your kind acts are misconstrued and resented. There are some people with whom it is very difficult to live. You wish your lot had been cast elsewhere, while it may be that your lot was cast just there and nowhere else, because the Lord wants your example and nothing else to bring that wanderer to the Lord. This example may be the particular work sent you. It is hard work indeed, and one the world will never know anything about; but the Master, who knows just how hard the work was, and how patiently and bravely you performed it, will reward you. Trust the Lord. His help is ever present. Be strong and of good courage. Never forget that the responsibility of being a Christian is a very great one; for you not only ruin your own soul if you sin, but you may ruin the souls of those who watch and copy your example.

DON'T BE TOO BUSY.

N this busy age, when the boundaries of life are so enlarged by rapid communications, and action is the rule of the hour, the duty of meditation is often overlooked. People are too busy for meditation, or dreaming, as they call it; they banish meditation entirely from practical life and divorce religion from business. On the contrary, religious life and feelings must go hand in hand with every-day life. Religion is not a creature of the cloister; it is not locked up in the church on Sunday night. We come to church on Sunday to learn religion, to feel its motives, and to deepen all good impressions as well as to gain them. When this is over we have not done with religion for the week; we have been learners, and now we are to go home and practise what we have learned; but this we cannot do if we never think again of the holy lessons of the Sabbath.

Meditation, strictly speaking, is a serious, devout contemplation of divine things. It presupposes quiet and solitude, and such meditation is at once a means of grace and a Christian duty. It is something that no one can get along as well without as with. Dr. Bonar says, "In order to grow much in grace we must be much alone. It is not in society, not even in Christian society, that the soul grows most vigorously." In one single quiet hour it will make more progress than in days in company with others. There is always danger of losing all sense of the value of familiar things by neglecting to consider their merits and their importance to ourselves. Many wonder why the Bible seems so uninteresting to them, and why they cannot throw themselves into it as they can into other books. It would be more wonderful if they could get interested in it, reading it as they do, or taking it up at long intervals. If you treat any other book in that way it will seem uninteresting and dry. Perhaps you read it by chapters with no sense of its connection, or, perhaps you read a few verses in a cursory way. All readers of the Bible should take the advice that Abbé Wenkelman gave to a young sculptor when he sent him to the Apollo Belvidere as the most perfect specimen of art. "Go and study it, and if you see no great beauty in it to captivate you, study it again. If you still discover none, study it more; go again and again; go until you feel its beauty, for be assured it is there." So, readers of the Bible, you should study it well, and if you do not at once realize its beauty you should go again and again, pray over it, study it, meditate upon it, until you feel it, and then it will impress its lineaments upon your soul and become the model of your daily walk and conversation.

LITTLE THINGS.

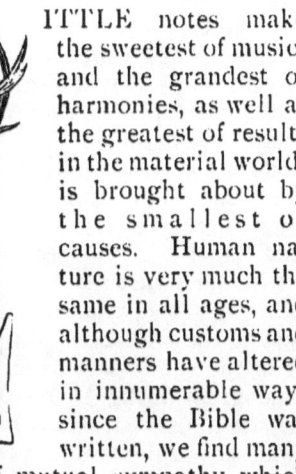

LITTLE notes make the sweetest of music, and the grandest of harmonies, as well as the greatest of results in the material world, is brought about by the smallest of causes. Human nature is very much the same in all ages, and although customs and manners have altered in innumerable ways since the Bible was written, we find many a chord of mutual sympathy which binds us to men of old times. We read of a poor, miserable leper who was actually going to continue to be a leper rather than do a small and simple act to free himself from his leprosy, and that, too, when no doubt he would have done some great thing gladly. It would have seemed to him in perfect keeping with the eternal fitness of things if the prophet had come out in flowing robes, and stretching forth his hand majestically, had called solemnly upon the name of the Lord. He would have liked the cure to be performed with a pomp and majesty in accord with his own fancied greatness and the greatness of the God in whose name it was wrought. But to be told to wash, and be cleansed thereby, was too simple a thing to be thought of. How much of human nature is manifested in that! Men are apt to connect great results with imposing deeds only, while little acts seem too insignificant to effect any worthy results.

We have only to think for an instant to see the fallacy of this, and to find a host of illustrations that prove the value of little things, especially to show that momentous results are often caused by the smallest and most insignificant acts. The simple pressure of a child's finger upon a button caused the explosion at "Hell Gate" that caused thousands of tons of solid rock to burst asunder and fly in every direction. The same force that draws a pin to the floor holds mighty worlds in their places. So simple is it indeed that till a few years ago no one thought to connect it with such vast results.

Strange to say, upon no subject are men so unwilling to trust to the efficacy of simple acts as they are in the matter of the soul's salvation. Men are always willing to do some great thing to be saved. Ever since the fall the despair and dreariness of souls estranged from God, the remorse, perplexity, and fear, have all combined to nerve men to the utmost exertions. They have groped about in the darkness, if, perchance, they might find God. They have touched the door of Eden, and tried its bolts and shaken its fastenings in the effort to return to primitive innocence. They have torn themselves with briers, and cut themselves with stones in their desire to find the narrow way of life. They have slain whole hecatombs of animals, and waded through seas of sacrificial blood for their souls' salvation. This way and that they have groped for every way but the right way, and all in vain. Eden's doors are fast closed, and the lofty peak of sinlessness is inaccessible. When all is done man is no nearer God than he was at first. What is the trouble? Simply that we are not bidden to do any great thing; God never laid down such a command. So men have made a mistake, and failed to find the way of life because it is so simple. They have tried to do some great thing, when all that God wanted was a childlike faith in Jesus Christ. Until men have learned this lesson, and have utterly abandoned all hope of saving themselves, they are far from salvation. I believe there are but few people in this world who do not appreciate the blessing of salvation, even though they may not have availed themselves of it, and who do not mean to be Christians some day and go to heaven; and yet because coming to Christ is such a simple

CHRIST BLESSING LITTLE CHILDREN.

thing that the youngest child can do it, they hold back and search rather for some great thing.

And how often do those who are professing Christians leave neglected the small, homely duties which should make up their life while they search for some great deed that will better show their love to the Saviour. The little things seem so trivial that they are hardly worth doing, and they do not call for the energy and sacrifice that greater deeds do. And yet it is just these little things, done faithfully as unto the Lord, that make up a life of consecration and devotion to the Master. If love inspires us to our work, the simplest act, the most trivial duty becomes a part of our worship.

> "That the full glory may abound, increase,
> Until Thy likeness shall be formed in me
> I pray. The answer is not rest or peace,
> But charges, duties, wants, anxieties,
> Till there seems room for everything but Thee,
> And never time for anything but these.
>
> The busy fingers fly, the eyes may see
> Only the glancing needle that they hold,
> But all my life is blossoming inwardly,
> And every breath is like a litany,
> While through each labor like a thread of gold
> Is woven the sweet consciousness of Thee."

Our God is too great to need great deeds. If we do our duty just where he has placed us to work for him, it will make no difference whether we labor in an obscure corner of the vineyard where no great harvest will repay our labor, or whether our works are seen and known of all men. The little things "that most leave undone or despised" are great enough to glorify God if we do them for him.

THE LOVE OF GOD.

OUR ideas of religion and of God have changed somewhat since the days when our grandmothers handed down through the lips of our mothers the idea of what religion is, and ought to be, and of what the dear Lord, who loved us so much that he sent his only and well-beloved Son to die for us, for you and me, is to us. Then he was a king whose subjects might not even touch the lowest stone at his feet, a judge who sat upon the judgment seat to condenm the sinner rather than to take him in loving arms and say to him, "Go thy way, sin no more."

Now that we have learned to read the precious words of the Bible more from the standpoint of God's love, with a light from heaven's own blessedness shining into and through our eyes, our God has revealed himself as a Father who pitieth his children, who reasons with them, who says, "Son, daughter, give me thy heart." And when we cry out in the discouragement of our hearts, that the delight of our heart is ceased, our joy turned into mourning, we hear a gentle voice whispering in our ears, "I am God, even thy God—in the day that thou callest upon me I will answer. All that the Father giveth me shall come to me; and him that cometh to me I will in no wise cast out." And the voice of love calls: "Art thou weary, heavy laden, come to me and find rest."

With eyes full of tears we look around and see nothing, it may be, but a stormy sea, a dark and starless night; our bark is drifting helplessly, we are discouraged because of the gloom; but in the sweetest, calmest tones, Jesus, our Saviour, says to us, "Why are you fearful! it is I, be not afraid."

A Christian who really loves God should never doubt the love that our Father gives us. We are helped through nine troubles, and when the tenth comes our faith fails and we are sure that there will be no further assistance for us, and that being left alone we must perish. Jesus may be asleep in the vessel, or you may think so, but it is only that he is feigning unconsciousness to see if your faith will take you to him for help.

Our Father loves us, is patient with us, is anxious to help us, and is even more ready to give than we are to ask.

> " A Father's hand we felt,
> A Father's heart we knew,
> With tears of penitence we knelt
> And found his word was true.
>
> " We told him all our grief,
> We thought of Jesus' love;
> A sense of pardon brought relief,
> And bade our pains remove."

When he really becomes in very truth our Father, the world, its pleasures, trials, and troubles become so very different. What was hard to bear becomes easy, because we know the Father's hand never causes his child one needless tear. When the dear Saviour's hand takes the weight of our burden from us, and we find ourselves at last among the chorus of the redeemed in heaven, our glad voices will have no minor notes to jar the melody, as we at last, "safe at home," sing the praises of our Saviour's love.

NOT INCOMPLETE.

MANY good people, even the best of Christians, misinterpret God's acts of kindness to us in calling us home. Almost invariably it happens that we mourn the death of a good man, who is often taken out of the world just when his life is in full blossom of beauty; and we are liable to sigh and groan over what at first thought appears to be a premature removal. "But there are no premature removals, no incomplete lives." The death of Henry Ward Beecher perhaps called out more response from the press, and from Christians generally, than that of any other man during the last century. Some mourned that he could not have been spared to complete his Life of Christ, which was left in an unfinished state. But God, who knoweth all things, and ordereth all things, knows best at what time to call his own. Mr. Beecher's life work, although ended in one sense with his death, still was far from complete as to its results here.

No good man's life is incomplete, because stilled on its earthly side. There is a heavenly side, and it still grows on in beauty and symmetry.

To the eye of faith the broken column in our cemeteries is a sentimental falsehood. No Christian life is broken short off so, but rises in a symmetrical shaft, and its capital is garlanded with amaranthine flowers in heaven.

Apelles, the Grecian painter, when asked why he touched and retouched his pictures with so much care, answered: "Because I paint for eternity." A real, living Christian works for eternity, and if it is God's will that he should go higher, even while in the midst of a noble work here, his life still goes on. No matter how many broken shafts are reared above his coffin lid, he would say if he could speak "Thy will be done." He would echo Dr. Preston's dying words: "Blessed be God, though I change my place I shall not change my company; for I have walked with God while living, and now I go to rest with God."

"FIRST PURE."

"The wisdom that is from above is first pure, then peaceable, gentle and easy to be entreated, full of mercy and good fruits."—Jas. iii. 17.

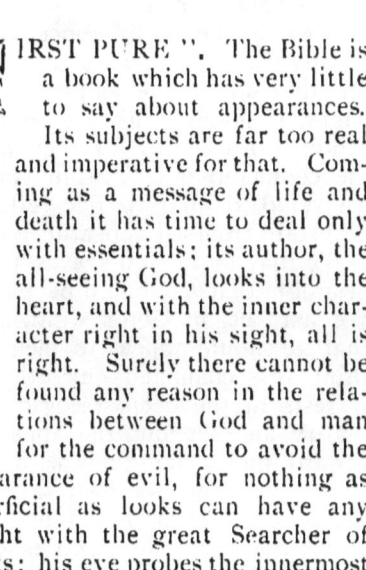

"FIRST PURE". The Bible is a book which has very little to say about appearances. Its subjects are far too real and imperative for that. Coming as a message of life and death it has time to deal only with essentials; its author, the all-seeing God, looks into the heart, and with the inner character right in his sight, all is right. Surely there cannot be found any reason in the relations between God and man for the command to avoid the appearance of evil, for nothing as superficial as looks can have any weight with the great Searcher of hearts; his eye probes the innermost depths of character, and finds there all the material for judgment, either acquittal or condemnation. Man, however, cannot do that; all he sees is the surface, the appearance, and his judgment must be formed from them.

As Christianity, then, is a system placed in the world to commend itself to mankind and be received by them, and as the Christian is a man among men, seen, known and judged by them, in these facts lies the reason for this exhortation. The inner character is everything in the sight of God, but that is not all. We are not alone in the world, so for the sake of humanity and those around us, we are to abstain from the appearance of evil.

It will make no difference in our standing in the sight of God if any one thinks us dishonest or untruthful, but for the sake of example, of morality, of religion, we ought, if possible, always so to act that others cannot think ill of us. As far then as our relations to God go, the command is, "Abstain from all evil," but so far as we stand related to our fellow-men, the command is, "Abstain from all appearance of evil."

We may be in God's eyes pure in heart, but it is also desirable that we should be pure in outward appearance. We may be, in God's sight, sincere, but it is desirable that we should appear to men to be so. We should not think this command unworthy of divine inspiration, for it rests in the deepest logic. Appearance is one thing, reality another, but the appearance of evil will go far toward familiarizing one with the reality.

So much for our own sake, and in regard to others there is the example. Whether it be right or wrong to do so, the world does, and is going to, judge of religion by Christians. The appearance is what they see, for they cannot look deeper, so it will be little advantage to the cause of Christ, no matter how consistent we may really be, if we do not seem to the world to be so. The Christian's mission as a light in the world depends largely on his care in avoiding what looks wrong. This is not hypocrisy. The Christian must walk on a higher level, and live in a purer light than others; while thinking most of the heart, he must not be indifferent to the exponents of the heart's life and purposes and aims. Without making the outer life the main thing, we must yet try to keep that outer life blameless and without reproach. There is no grander, nobler spirit for any one to regulate his conduct by than that of Paul in his resolve, "If meat make my brother to offend, I will eat no meat while the world standeth."

We should not be discouraged if we find that we are not always successful in our efforts to abstain from the appearance of evil, for it cannot be denied that this is

THE WILD PALM.

an uncharitable, censorious world in which we live, with
a strong sympathy with what is evil, and a desire that
everybody above its level should be brought as low as
itself. There are persons who, like the tarantula, suck
poison from the sweetest flowers; there are malevolent
spirits among men who do not care for the good and
noble, but, like wasps which fly at the incipient decay of
the ripest fruits, seize on the least appearance of imperfection. There are many who study human nature as old
Zoilus searched the poems of Homer, simply to find out
the defects and errors.

It is far nobler and better, with magnanimous generosity, never to form a bad opinion of an action if it is
possible to construe it as good; unfortunately those who
are able to do this are the exception and not the rule.
The vast majority are too much like the restless sea,
liable to be ruffled by every gust of passion, open to all
impulses; and many are prone to take even the good and
speak evil of it.

What then is our line of duty? It will not do any
good to denounce these uncharitable judgments as wrong,
unjust, and unworthy of notice. We all know that they
are wrong, but that does not prevent them, so we must
take things as we find them, and with an eye to God's
glory adapt ourselves to them. We ought to care in some
measure what the world says, and if the cause of the
adverse judgments be something indiscreet in our conduct, something in appearances that is against us, then
though all may be right within, we ought to abandon our
evil appearances. Whether we realize it or not, the cause
of Christ is bound up in us, and when we suffer from disregard of appearances, the Church of Christ suffers too.

We err when we speak indiscreetly, or act imprudently,
or allow appearances which are liable to misconstruction,
for by all these things we may injure the cause we love.
There is great need of humble, prayerful, earnest effort,
not only to be right, to be holy, to be beautiful within,
but to let that inner light shine so brightly upon the outer
world that there shall be no occasion to suspect evil,
because there shall be no appearance of it.

"THEN PEACEABLE."

IT was said in our hearing not long ago, of an excellent and useful Christian woman who had just passed away, that "she lived such a quiet life—she did so much good in a quiet way." She was, indeed, one of those gentle, patient, earnest workers who come and go in their appointed ways like those beings of light who wait upon God's children, but of whom we cannot even hear the rustle of a wing. They speak to our hearts, yet not in words; they touch our lives and guide us by the hand, and yet we hear, we see them not. Yet God knows all the quiet lives that are lived for him. He marks them with his eye as he marks the sparrow's fall. No kindly deed, nor act of love and charity, is unnoticed by him who seeth all things, "even the secret and hidden things among the children of men."

For the highest example of gentleness we have only to look to him who went up and down among the hills and plains of Judea eighteen centuries ago healing the thronging multitudes, and blessing even those who touched but the hem of his garment. From the manger at Bethlehem to the cross on Calvary, it is all the record of a meek and quiet life. We can never think of our Saviour in any other way than as one whose every word and deed was gentleness itself. We cannot but think of him, sometimes, as moving in and out and among the multitudes, and up and down the streets and by-ways of the land, so gently and noiselessly that the sound of his footsteps was scarcely heard upon the ground. We know that on more than one occasion he passed out of the midst of a multitude when they knew it not. We know that he walked upon the waves of Galilee, while rash and faithless Peter sank beneath. We know also that when the Scribes and Pharisees tried to draw him into a noisy disputation a few quiet words from him put their sophistry to flight; and when he was reviled, he reviled not again. And in all his wonderful works Christ never sought publicity. Again and again he charged his disciples and those whom he had healed that they "should tell no man." He taught both by precept and example that "when thou doest alms let not thy right hand know what thy left hand doeth." Jesus was indeed a King, but no heralds went before him to trumpet his appearance; he was a Conqueror, but no triumphal arches were erected in his honor: he was "very God," but he never spoke in Sinai thunders, nor transfixed the hearts of men with the bolts of wrath.

The greatest forces in nature are the quiet ones. That mysterious power called gravitation, which links the universe together as with a mighty chain, acts as noiselessly as thought itself. The sunlight falls upon the earth as softly as a dream, and yet it draws the sea into its embrace, and makes the earth throb with life. The atmosphere silently eats its way into the hearts of rocks, and crumbles down temples and pyramids. The most stupendous works of the Almighty swing in their orbits without a jar or tremor. And so with the most wonderful works of human hands. The mighty Corliss engine moves with more apparent ease than the noisy little clock upon the mantel. It is everywhere the quiet things that serve the highest purposes.

We should not, then, complain because our lives must needs move in quiet channels. It is not the roaring, dashing, impetuous streams, but the deep and silent rivers that bear the ships to the sea. It has been said that the quiet power of a serene and holy life is the greatest power in the world, next to the might of God. Who has not known, and been blessed by knowing, some of those gentle souls whose very presence seems a balm to wounded hearts, whose voices fall upon the ear like a benediction from heaven, and whose hands, laid upon an aching brow, seem to woo to themselves the pain. It was of one of these gentle, loving natures that Whittier thus writes:

> " The blessing of her quiet life
>   Fell on us like the dew :
> And good thoughts, where her footsteps passed,
>   Like fairy blossoms grew.
>
> Sweet promptings unto kindly deeds
>   Were in her very look ;
> We read her face as one who reads
>   A true and holy book.
>
> And half we deemed she needed not
>   The changing of her sphere ;
> To go to heaven, a shining one,
>   Who walked an angel here."

"GENTLE AND EASY TO BE ENTREATED."

PITY is one of the strongest elements of Christ's character—compassion for the wants and sorrows of others. It is said that the artists who have represented the Saviour's face have given us the picture of a man burdened with his own sorrows. That is just where all such representations fail, and must fail. If it were possible to put on the canvas a true Christ, it would be preeminently a gentle, sympathizing Christ, divinity trembling through lines of finest sensibility, with a mouth shaped by words of compassion, and eyes fathomless with unutterable pity.

Until such things are possible to the brush, all pictures must be failures, and we must draw our devotion from the word pictures of inspiration. The Saviour was always specially responsive to the sufferings of mankind; perhaps it was on the principle that those who are whole need no physician, that the most touching and the truest of the revelations speak of his pity. We know that he was far from irresponsive to human joy, and the occasion of his first miracle was one of happiness—a wedding feast in Cana of Galilee—and the miracle itself was one tending to promote the enjoyment of the feast. We may be sure that he always rejoiced with those that rejoiced as well as wept with those that wept; and we can imagine that his presence on a festive occasion gave a better and holier zest to enjoyment. Nevertheless his mission as the Saviour of the world seemed to place him naturally among the burdened and distressed, for he no doubt saw, as no man could see, that there was some lack in every pleasure, that laughter is not always the echo of happiness.

Suffering appeals more powerfully to all sympathies than joy, and if we feel suffering to be the strongest of the world's appeals, how much more would Christ? Would he be indeed the Christ, the Saviour, if the cry of distress had not reached his ears more quickly than the laughter of the gay? We expect to find him just where the evangelists place him most often, bending over the sufferings of mankind. Sometimes in the house of joy, when there was a holy purpose to be served by his presence there, sometimes in the retirement of the mountain top when the weariness of the flesh demanded solitary communion with his Father, but for the most part with his eyes fixed steadily on the suffering before him.

A thousand years had passed since David sang the beautiful shepherd's Psalm, when another was born in the same town of Bethlehem who was like David, his type, the good shepherd, but his sheep were men. His heart was full of the true shepherd pity, when he looked on the multitudes, infinitely better than sheep, which congregated in the cities and villages, worse off, perhaps, in some respects than the flocks which were pastured around Bethlehem, beneath the shepherd's watchful eye. All who had come before him were false leaders who gained admittance to the fold that they might kill and destroy, and great had been their execution. The true Shepherd had compassion on the multitude; he showed it as he went through the villages, telling the good news of the kingdom of God, healing all sickness and disease among the people. They were a woefully neglected flock upon which his eye fell as he went to and fro. He saw their suffering everywhere, on the couches of the sick, the beds of the diseased. They lined the streets where he passed, and were let down from the roofs where he was, and they were spread upon the seashore where he taught. Physical ailment, bodily infirmity, it was that ailed; but none the less did it touch his pity, for this compassionating Shepherd took in the whole range of suffering, the distressed body, aching brow, and weary limbs.

Besides their bodily distress, he saw their soul trouble; they were as sheep having no shepherd; under that he saw the great spiritual meaning. Why did they wander to and fro along hard and thorny roads, up rugged mountains and down into dark valleys? It was the unrest within them, the longing of sheep for a shepherd, the inevitable longing of the homeless for a shelter, the restlessness of a soul seeking its God. Multitudes were scattered abroad in the weary search for rest and peace, without a shepherd's guidance.

He is moved with infinite compassion as his thoughts go out to a wide world, composed of such as these, and because he pitied, he delivered. And not only those who suffered outwardly did he pity, for oft-times the heaviest sorrow is borne in silence, and hidden within the bosom, and no sound betrays the secret grief. Others, too, were claimants on his pity who did not know their own need of compassion, who were content with their barren lives, and heeded not the call of the shepherd. The all-searching eye of the Saviour penetrated this abject contentedness, and then his pity was most profound, since they realized not their own need and would take no steps to fill their empty hands. Sometimes it is not the greatest but the least sufferers who are the most to be pitied; the distressed and starving may have currents of spiritual life flowing through them, but there is a poverty of heart and soul infinitely more pitiable.

Over all these forms of suffering and want the Saviour's pity brooded tenderly, even as it does to-day over his fold, and we need never fear that we are in any distress too deep for his loving pity to succor and rescue us.

"FULL OF MERCY."—FORGIVENESS.

> "Let bygones be bygones;
>   Your heart will be lighter
> When kindness of yours with reception has met;
> The flame of your love
>   Will be purer and brighter,
> If, God-like, you strive to forgive and forget."

LOVE and forgive even your enemies. "I can never forgive him," is a remark we so frequently hear that we often do not realize its awful significance. Some one beautifully and truthfully remarks: "He that cannot forgive others breaks down the bridge which he must pass himself; for every one has need to be forgiven." Thomas Adams says: "The angry man is like a ship sent into the sea, which hath the devil for its pilot." How easily forgiveness could be granted if anger were not allowed to burn too deeply in the soul. It is an easy matter to stop the fire that is kindled only in a little chaff; but if it once have taken hold of matter that hath solidity or thickness it soon inflames and consumes the entire building.

One might naturally suppose that the anger of mortal

man should be mortal like himself. But with many, it is a question whether they or their anger die first, or whether death takes away both together. Our Saviour taught the doctrine of forgiveness of enemies. So contrary is this spirit to the natural inclinations of the unregenerate heart, that when one of our venerable missionaries read to a number of Hindu youths from the Sermon on the Mount the passage, "I say unto you, love your enemies, bless them that curse you, do good to them that hate you, and pray for them who despitefully use you and persecute you," so deep and intense was the impression produced on them, that one exclaimed in ecstasy: "Oh! how beautiful, how divine! This is the truth!" And for days and weeks he could not help repeating: "Love your enemies, bless them that curse you," etc.; constantly exclaiming: "How beautiful! surely this is the truth!" Nor could he rest until he had renounced his false gods and their senseless worship and accepted the truth as it is in Jesus.

Another example illustrating the same truth is found in an incident which occurred in the seventeenth century. A Turkish grandee in Hungary made a Christian nobleman his prisoner and treated him with the utmost barbarity. The slave, for such he was, was yoked with an ox and compelled to drag the plow. But the fortune of war is changeful; and the Turk fell into the hands of the Hungarians, who said to their enslaved fellow countryman: "Now take your revenge upon your enemy." This was in accordance with the custom of the age, and the Turk, supposing as a matter of course that he would be tortured to death, had already swallowed poison, when a messenger came from his Christian slave, telling him to go in peace, he had nothing to fear. The Moslem was so impressed with this heavenly spirit, that he proclaimed with his dying breath, "I will not die a Moslem, but I die a Christian; for there is no religion but that of Christ which teaches forgiveness of injuries." A forgiving nature is the direct result of the teachings of Christianity.

"What can Jesus Christ do for you now?" said an inhuman slave-master when in the act of applying the lacerating whip to an already half-murdered slave, "Him teach me to forgive you, massa," was the beautiful reply learned at the feet of the blessed Master.

We should forgive our enemies even as Christ forgives us, quickly, freely, fully. "As we forgive others their trespasses" so shall we be forgiven. Forgiveness is the characteristic symbol by which the true Christian is known. Every sincere follower of the Master will feel at all times a readiness to forgive others: and by this the Christian may know that God hath sealed the forgiveness of his sins upon his own heart.

"AND GOOD FRUITS."

WE may be exceeding punctilious in all the outward forms and ceremonies of a Christian life. We may attend church regularly, and even pray morning and evening during the week—the Pharisees did as much. If it is form, and form alone, if there is not in us a living Christianity; if the fruits of our profession cannot be found in our daily lives—take care, Christian! God judges by the fruits. Professing to serve him here on earth will not avail you at the bar of God. There will be many at the last day who will cry, "Have we not prophesied in thy name, cast out devils and done many wonderful works?" Then shall he say unto them, "I never knew you. Depart from me, ye that work iniquity."

It thus behooves us as true followers of Christ to look well to our daily life, for there we shall find the evidence of our hope. If we are truly Christians, trusting in Christ alone, and striving to do his will, we cannot hide our Christian profession. "No man lighteth a candle and putteth it under a bushel." If our hearts are enlightened from on high, the flame will burn brighter and brighter, continually shedding light upon our pathway; and our companions and those round us will take knowledge that we have chosen the good part that cannot be taken away from us.

With every such man, it matters not where he may be placed, or what may be the environments of his daily life. He may be rich, or he may be poor; he may be well, or languishing on a bed of sickness; he may have one talent or ten—it matters not; nay, he may even now be bowed down with the infirmities of old age, and already beginning to cross the river; still he will be sustained by a firm and sure hope, and be enabled to look up with confidence and cry: "Though I walk through the valley of the shadow of death, I will fear no evil, for thou art with me; thy rod and thy staff, they comfort me."

Happy for us, if we can thus look back upon our lives, feeling in our inmost souls that our purposes and desires have been right before God; that we have striven to do our whole duty, and preserve a conscience void of offence. Then are we ready and waiting for the coming of the Master, and can feel the blessed assurance that "We have fought a good fight; we have kept the faith; and that henceforth there is laid up for us a crown of righteousness, which the Lord, the righteous Judge, shall give."

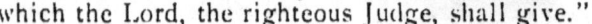

BREAD UPON THE WATERS.

TRAVELLER going to China at the right season of the year would doubtless be interested in their method of planting rice in that country. They sow it in the mud, and then immediately turn on a flood of water, so that the whole field becomes a shallow pond. One might think that the seed was drowned. But let him wait a few weeks and then go and view one of these artificial lakes, and from all its surface he will see the green shoots sprouting, and day by day growing taller, till at last the water is no more seen, and the shallow pool has been transformed into a field of rich, waving grain. Casting bread upon the waters expresses this Oriental method of planting, and sometimes it is actually their bread they sow, for even when the spring comes on and finds their supply scanty, instead of eating it all they will rather cast it upon the lake. They may go hungry for weeks and live on a pittance, for the bread which they cast into the water in the spring causes the crop on which they are to live next autumn and winter, and they are content to cast it into the water now, being sure to find it after many days. In Egypt they have a river which by its spontaneous overflow saves men all the trouble of irrigation. There the Nile has from time immemorial been rolling down its rich deposits of earth, making the land fertile enough to fill the granaries of the East. There they scatter their seed upon the still submerged fields, leaving to nature the harvest. It is a precious deposit that they cast upon the waters, not seed merely, but bread. A portion of every harvest must go back to the soil, if there are to be any harvests in the future. It is so much abstracted from that which would be made into daily bread, and it is therefore equally precious. There is always a risk involved in returning it to the vicissitudes of the season, and the uncertainties of the soil. We do not know surely whether it will prosper; nevertheless, to keep it is to waste it. If the husbandman would have increase, he must sow his seed with faith in an ever-watchful Providence. The law of the harvest is so well understood that no one ever grudges the seed, precious though it may be.

It is strange that we cannot reason thus with regard to spiritual sowing and reaping. How hard it is for many to cast their precious bread upon the waters! If it were only seed, something that could not be used except for sowing, it would be far easier, but bread has its distinct value, it stands for that which is useful to one's self. This point marks the limit of too many people's beneficence and charity. They give to the point where they begin to feel it, and then straightway stop. Can that be called generosity, in any true sense? In the way of contributions to the Lord's cause, to the various departments of Christian work at home and abroad, what real sacrifices do we make, what luxuries do we deny ourselves that we may offer something to the Lord?

In the far west and in foreign climes are men who have given up all the comforts of life in the midst of civilization, and all the pleasures of Christian society that they might preach Christ to the ignorant and degraded. Have we ever cast a single precious thing, something that required self-denial, upon the waters of home and foreign missions? Where is the bread that we ought to cast upon the waters? Have we been casting only crusts and crumbs upon the stream, have we been offering to the Lord that which cost us nothing, only what we did not need ourselves? Then we have determined our own har-

THE ANNUAL OVERFLOW OF THE NILE.

vest. The waters will subside some day, and when we look for abundant increase we shall find only a harvest of crusts and crumbs for ourselves.

True, the water seems an uncertain receptacle of our bounty, but nevertheless we are commanded to sow. A common plea for neglect is this uncertainty. The expression has been converted into a proverb for uncertainty, and an excuse behind which many take refuge. " Like sowing upon the waters " has come to mean fruitless efforts. Men say we can't see the result of our efforts, we can't see where our beneficence goes, therefore we will do and give nothing. But God's command is to do and give if it is uncertain. Cast thy bread upon the waters, never mind seeing where it goes, leave that to God. All sowing is to a certain extent committing ourselves to uncertainty, but in sowing upon the waters the uncertainty is indefinitely increased. The soil is hidden, and we cannot tell where the waif of the waters will settle.

No doubt we like to see and select the place where our seed is to grow, but if the Egyptians insisted upon that they would starve to death. Moreover the prudence of the agriculturist may be praiseworthy, while the same thing in a spiritual worker may be blameworthy. It is a lamentable want of trust in God to do nothing but that of which we can see the good. In whose hand is the bread cast upon the waters, in whose hand but His who holdeth the waters in his palm? He who guides each grain sown over the fields to its prepared place under the water, and cares for and cherishes it till it grows, can he not guide and direct each Christian effort to a noble determination?

It is often the duty of the Christian to give, even when he cannot be certain of results. Loyalty to God and faith in God's providence makes this a duty. In the Master's field the soil is often hidden, and always has been to a greater or less extent; the Christian therefore has no right to confine his efforts to what he considers hopeful cases. Whatever the work of love, it is sure of its reward, and if at any time it seems to be all sowing and no reaping, and you grow discouraged, remember the sure promise, " Thou *shall find it* after many days."

WHAT IS PRAYER?

WHAT is prayer? It is the lifting of the heart, the human heart—so full of wants, so anxious and troubled about many things, so full of regrets for the past, so burdened with cares of the present, so over-burdened with the necessary and possible wants of the future—the asking, craving, agonizing for things whose name is legion. God is not only the hearer but the answerer of prayer. He is not like the earthly father whose child comes to him asking for what he wants, but who is too busy or too indifferent to attend to his child's wants.

Far different is it with the dear Father above. He

hardly waits for his child to speak, so ready is he to hear. He says, in sweetest tones, "What is it, my child? Is the burden too heavy for you? Are your shoulders aching from carrying it? Does your frame tremble from the exertion of steadying it? Listen! I loved you before the world was." He knows all about that burden; it was tested by him according to your strength. Nor was any of it laid upon you until he knew that you could carry it —nay, he holds the corners thereof, so that the weight may not fall upon you. And now bring it to him, and he will help you to carry it, so that it will be light. Have you a heavy cross to carry? Do not look about you to see if there is a lighter one than yours, for rest assured that, if you ask, he will help you to bear it. Is it a cross of sorrow, poverty, loss, the absence of health? Ah! there the minor chord is sounding, that means that truth compels you to admit that with such a thorn in the flesh evil is ever present with you; that your life is a burden, that the sun is dark at noonday, that the moon gives no light at night, that courage is gone from you, and like Jonah (when his gourd, that had become dear to him, withered) you are ready to exclaim, when you are faint with the heat, "It is better for me to die to than to live."

But the answer that your Heavenly Father gives to you is, "My child, lean more upon me. Come to me. Ask in prayer for help, and I, the Lord, your Father who loves you, will make the cross so easy, will rob it so greatly of its power to hurt, that you will no longer be loth to bend beneath it, but will go singing on your way toward Heaven." It is good to remind ourselves that such help can be obtained; it is good to remember that Jesus taught us to say "Our Father"; to ask for daily bread, and that we may love God's will; to ask forgiveness for our sins; deliverance from temptation; to be shielded from evil, and finally to be brought into full view of the everlasting glory.

Does your finite mind think that to be answered it must be according to your dictation? Ask the myriads of those who have so earnestly prayed in years gone by for what God in love withheld, if the answer was not received over and over again in the utter thankfulness for not having been gratified, not having the gourd; because now they

WHAT IS PRAYER?

can see where the worm would have come up to destroy the pleasure that they might have hoped for.

But more than this; while a large part of prayer consists of petitions to our Heavenly Father to grant us those things that we need: *true* prayer is more than this. It is not mere petition; behind and besides this, it is the feeling that is down deep in our hearts that prompts the desire; it is the spring from which bubbles up the fountain of yearning for God's blessing; it is the coal that kindles the fire upon the altar that will waft the incense up into the very presence of God; it is the outcome of the heart full of love that is precious in his sight.

> "Have you no words? Ah, think again!
> Words flow apace when we complain."

Take your sorrows, your joys, your trials right to God, whose ear is never closed to his children's cry, and take it in the accents of *true* prayer. Do you ask where to take it?

> "There is a place where Jesus sheds
> The oil of gladness on our heads;
> A place than all besides more sweet,
> It is the blood-bought mercy seat."

THE ANCHOR OF THE SOUL.

FROM many noble ships which leave port in strength and beauty no tidings of safety are ever heard. Some incoming vessel may report a signal of distress heard in the darkness, and a fruitless search; or perhaps a letter may be found in a bottle, but that is all that is ever known. Upon some beach is a broken wreck, the sport and plaything of the breakers, all that is left of the stately ship which sailed away so gallantly. But what is a wreck on the beach to a wreck on the shores of eternity? The ship may go down with all hands on board, and yet it may be well with them. The ocean may be for them the gate into the heavenly city whence they shall go out no more, but this wreck of the soul is a hopeless thing, and yet so easily accomplished. It seems only necessary to let a soul alone and let it drift, and by some terrible tendency in itself it will dash upon the rocks. You need not touch the tiller, but some magnetic attraction will draw it swiftly into danger.

If you add the winds of temptation and sin to accelerate its speed, it seems to fly on its destructive course. Surely amidst these perils we need a sure and steadfast anchor, and this we have in hope. As the huge anchor goes down into the great deep and fastens its iron tooth upon the moveless rocks, holding the ship like a giant arm, so the Christian's anchor of hope goes up into the heavenly sanctuary and fastens itself upon Jesus, and we are held safely forever, sure and steadfast. Hope is desire and expectation, and if we are hoping for some great earthly good or pleasure in the near future, it helps us greatly to bear present pain or evil. All pain that is not perpetual is attended with consolation in the thought that some time it will be over, so we can see the cheering power of hope. Thus the Christian hope acts. It reaches up to heaven and whispers to the soul, this light affliction is

but for a moment, then comes the great good; heaven will atone for all sorrow here. God's people meet adversity with courage, one trial after another, shock succeeding shock, because they are anchored safely, and have trust in God, and a sublime hope in his present favor and his future blessing.

It is a glorious thing to have this anchor of the soul, but we must not expect wrong or impossible things from its use. For one thing we must not fasten it to visible things. That floating log, the world, will not hold. You must not throw it on the deck of any passing vessel or together you will go to shipwreck. Our anchor must fasten upon the invisible things of God. Hope that is seen is not hope, but the unseen things are eternal. Let us hope in God, in Christ, in heaven, and never fasten our soul to the passing things of time and sense. Let go the anchor, let out the chain far out of sight down to the immovable rock, believing in him whom we have not seen, and this hope we shall have as an anchor of the soul both sure and steadfast, which entereth into that within the veil.

IN THE SHEPHERD'S CARE.

IN familiarizing a little child with what would be otherwise incomprehensible to it, we tell a little story that illustrates the truth we desire it to learn. So Christ was wont to fix truths in the minds of his followers by using such facts as were common to their everyday life. In St. John x. 1, we have a true and beautiful allusion to the sheep and their shepherd. In the Holy Land, where he was talking, flocks of sheep were then and are now seen. Such flocks of sheep consist perhaps of a hundred or more sheep and lambs. The shepherd has a name for every one, and his peculiar way of calling them, and they follow him; but a stranger's voice frightens them and they run away. Sometimes a little lamb thoughtlessly skips here and there until it wanders away and is lost. But the shepherd knows the number as well as the name of each one of the flock. So he leaves the ninety and nine with the dog who is trained to care for them, and goes to seek the lost one. When it is found, tired and frightened, how tenderly he takes it up, and opening the front of his loose gown or frock, with what gentle tenderness he puts the little lamb inside against his warm heart; and its bleatings cease, and the weary eyes close in sleep.

God's will is worked out in a way that often astonishes even those who serve him. When Joseph's brethren, to get rid of him, sold him into bondage in Egypt, they little thought that they were thereby providing him a home. For Joseph's sake, and because they were a thrifty race, Pharaoh invited them through him to settle in Egypt. And Joseph told them to ask for the land of Goshen, which was a goodly land, and as shepherds were an abomination to the Egyptians, he knew it would be granted to them, and it was. And there they kept their sheep, as their descendants did in the days when Christ was on earth; when he was their shepherd and they were the sheep. Abel was a shepherd, for when the firstling of his flock was accepted he lost his life. That shows us that even before the time that the sons of Jacob kept their sheep in Goshen there were shepherds and sheep.

The Messiah is often called a shepherd. Isaiah speaks thus of him: "He shall feed his flock like a shepherd; he shall gather the lambs with his arms and carry them in his bosom." And in another place we read: "Awake, O sword, against the shepherd and against the man that is my fellow, saith the Lord of hosts: smite the shepherd, and the sheep shall be scattered and I will turn mine hand upon the little ones." Paul writes to the Hebrews, calling Jesus the "great shepherd of the sheep." And St. Peter tells the elders of the churc that "when the chief shepherd shall appear, ye shall receive a crown of glory that fadeth not away."

So the dear shepherd, Jesus, cares for the sheep, not only for the strong ones, but the tender lambs, those whose feet easily tire; who faint by the wayside; the very ones who wander away into strange fields, and for whom the shepherd has to seek. Is it not a pleasant thought, that we belong to him? Will it not be safe to be folded when the night of death comes, by one who knows each one by name? Is it not now worth while to learn to know and obey that gentle voice that in the

IN THE SHEPHERD'S CARE.

day the sheep are divided from the goats will say: "Come, ye blessed of my Father, inherit the kingdom prepared for you from the foundation of the world." And is it not the highest wisdom so to live that we may be among the number who shall then go into life eternal?

"The Lord is my shepherd, I shall not want; he maketh me to lie down in green pastures; he leadeth me beside the still waters." What a joyful home heaven will be when, having found all the lost sheep that he came to save, the shepherd shall bring them rejoicing to that blissful place, into which we are assured that there shall in no wise enter anything that defileth, neither shall there be any need of the light of the sun, for the light of our blessed Saviour's countenance will fill the whole place with joy and with light.

THE WHEAT AND THE TARES.

HARVESTS are the result of seed sowing. Good harvests can result only from sowing good seed and by properly preparing the soil. Every farmer knows that he must plough, and perhaps subsoil, before he can reasonably expect a crop. The earth gets tired of producing, and by running the subsoil plough deep into the clay and turning it over, he is opening up ruts into which the rain will fall, and which the snow will cover, and that when the spring days are here, the ground will be so invigorated that it will bring forth abundance for the harvest.

So the seed is sown in good time. The sun by day and the dew by night fall upon it: it has to die to live; the seed germinates, the blade appears, and springing up, the wheat forms heads; they fill, they swell, they turn to a golden yellow, and lo! the time for the harvest is near. The farmer's toil is rewarded when his men, swinging the cradle to the monotony of their harvest song, lay great swaths of wheat in even rows up and down the field. Then the binders come and bind the grain, stacking the wheat that it may be carried to the barn where the grain is threshed, and the wheat separated from the tares, which are burned.

Is there no lesson for us in all this? Christ said that the field is the world, and Christians were compared to the wheat; and among the wheat Satan sows tares. Day follows day; the weeks, months, years roll together, and the Christian life is being developed. The love of Christ is at first only as the little wheat grain, but if the germ of sincerity is in it, it will at last come to the full fruition of the life eternal.

It is a great comfort to know, when Satan desires to sift us as wheat, that the Saviour has prayed for us that our faith fail not. How is it, are the tares springing up among the wheat? Are you fearing that when "his fan is in his hand, and he will thoroughly purge his floor, and will gather the wheat into his garner," you may be found as the chaff? Has Satan sown the tares of sin in your heart, so that the good seed is well nigh choked? Weed them out before they are well rooted. Ask the dear Lord to help you, and never grow weary until they are burned.

> The path is rough, my father! Many a thorn
> Has pierced me; and my feet all torn
> And bleeding, mark the way. Yet thy command
> Bids me press forward. Father, take my hand.
>   Then safe and blest, O lead to rest,
>   Lead to rest, lead to rest,
>   O lead to rest Thy child!

GOD'S SPECIAL CARE.

GOD'S special care extends over all his works and to each one of his creatures. We can begin at the lowest point, and trace his care up to the highest creations. Not even a sparrow falls to the ground without his notice. We may pluck a daisy from the midst of a meadow full of them, or we may gather a hundred, and we shall find each one of them as carefully shaped and as complete in all its parts as if it were the only object of God's creation. May we not then trust his care for us? Untold myriads of just such perfect flowers are created and die every year in solitudes where no human eye beholds them, not only beautiful and perfect, but under the microscope showing a delicacy and care of construction which, while it increases our wonder, shows that God has bestowed his direct care upon each. We may look at the animal kingdom, the thousands of beasts and birds which never knew human care. They are every one the special objects of God's care. The sparrow chirping on the hedge during the stormy winter does not fall to the ground without our Father's knowledge. He feedeth the young ravens and the young lions which cry for lack of food. He giveth them their meat in due season.

And then, rising to the rational creation, to man, he careth for each one of us. Jesus spoke of God's care in clothing the flowers and feeding the animals as a proof of his special care for human beings. We have been made capable of knowing and loving him, and we need his care. Whoever we may be, whatever our circumstances, we may be sure that God cares for us, not only in the mass, but individually we have his regard. He calls every one of us by name, and distinguishes each by special dealings. Every soul has an individual life, and an individual history; then, as we are each a separate creation, so we are each a separate care to God. We are shut out from fellow creatures in the seclusion of individuality that we may be shut in more closely with God. We differ from others that God may deal with each of us personally, that he may know us, love us, watch over us individually. God gives us special care, because he needs various workers.

Each of us is sent into the world to do some particular work in some special place, and the very specialty of each one's experience brings things to him in an aspect which cannot be exactly the same to any other. What a thought of precious comfort, that each one of us is the object of God's care as much as if we were the only being in the universe. Surely it is a balm for every sorrow, to think that we may cast ourselves and our burdens upon God's infinite care.

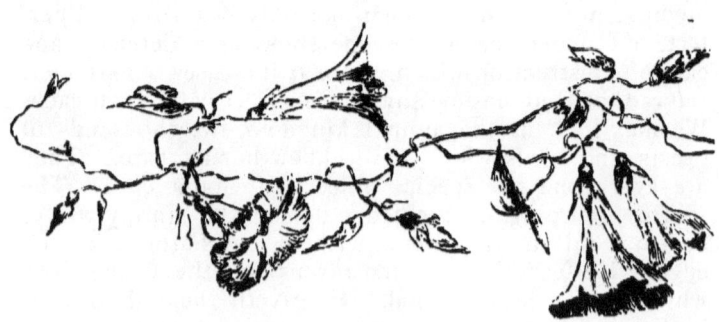

THE CHRISTIAN'S POSSESSIONS.

PAUL says "All things are yours." And when we consider the matter it would seem as if there were nothing on earth or in heaven, in time or eternity, to which the Christian cannot lay claim. Estimate religion as a matter of profit and see if it does not pay. Test it, weigh it, measure it, learn what is in it, and see if godliness is not profitable. Is it degrading to religion to appeal in this way to selfishness? Not altogether, though it is not of course the highest motive, but it is an appeal that we often meet in the Bible. Salvation is called the pearl of great price; the hid treasure; the one thing needful. Godliness is profitable; all things belong to the Christian. When men ask, What is religion worth? is it profitable? will it pay? Religion takes her stand on that level and says, I give all things to those who buy me.

What do we find in the catalogue of Christianity's treasures? We find not only death and things to come, but also the world and life and present things; it gives promise of the life that now is as well as the life that is to come. We are surprised when we see that the world is mentioned first in the list of the Christian's possessions. Are we not to give up everything for Christ, and what have we in the world? Here we are mistaken; it is only our sins that we must give up, so there is nothing in the world which does not belong to the Christian, save that which is a bane and an incumbrance; and for everything that he gives up he receives twofold more even in this present world. Life and all that makes it good and joyous and glorious belongs also to the Christian. He will never ask, with the wearied pleasure-seeker, Is life worth living? His life is linked with the infinite, is full of fresh joy, is sacred to earnest work, and goes on into eternity. The Christian's life has a side that satisfies the soul. All who are busy by day and weary at eventide need the bright radiance of salvation, a true spiritual religion which will enter into every relation and transaction of toil, and not only regulate them, but give energy of heart and strength to fulfil them.

The present life is the Christian's in the noblest, highest sense, and will be until it is merged in the Sabbath life of eternity. Death, too, is the Christian's, for to one whose life has been hid with Christ in God death is an ally, a servant, a ministering spirit who comes to open the radiant gates of an eternal world to the immortal soul. Death is gain to the Christian, for it ushers him into the joys of things to come. The treasures laid up in heaven, they, too, are the Christian's. When mortal life is ended, with its scheming and its planning, the things to come are his eternal reward, and we cannot put in words the meaning of this climax nor sum up the value of the inheritance of the saints in light. All things are ours, through Christ.

BURDEN-BEARING.

GOD will let us bear our burdens all by ourselves, if we are determined to do so. He has promised to sustain and help only those who cast off on him their troubles and cares. Those of us who will not heed this promise, but prefer to go about laden down with griefs and perplexities, will be permitted to do so. This thought is one which should prove of great value from its truthfulness and sound sense. God, all merciful and kind as he is, is not going to force us to accept the gracious promises of his word. The Word abideth forever, and every promise is sure and steadfast, but it is only whosoever will that can be benefited thereby. The will and purpose of the individual determines whether in each case the comfort can be applied and divine aid accepted. Many a sufferer from physical disability, after having tested the healing power of some potent remedy, has been heard to declare, "Had I dreamed of the virtue contained in such medicine, I might have experienced this unspeakable relief long ago; but I had no faith in its efficacy until driven to give it a trial." In many cases God allows his children to be brought into places where they must exercise some faith, or sink in despair. At such times, how repeatedly faith has proved itself indeed an anchor to the soul; yet the wonder and the pity is that such lessons can be forgotten, and the old habit is continually resorted to of trying to rid the shoulders of burdens too heavy to be borne, in some other way than by casting all our care on him who careth for us. The Bible is not taken literally enough, even by staunch believers in its doctrines. So cramped and hampered is the human heart and understanding by earthly and everyday-life surroundings, that it would seem as if an impression existed that the all-powerful Father in heaven was hampered too, and his power bounded by natural events.

It is a helpful, wholesome thing to let the mind dwell on the limitless power of God. Keep the thought by you, that God is always a very present helper. Do not wait until the stress of some extreme experience forces you to think of faith and trust as a last resort. Here is comfort and help for every day's needs, freely offered, and ready to be bestowed if you will only *will* to avail yourself of the blessing. In time of trial think to yourself, "Well, now, how useless to attempt carrying this heavy burden unaided and alone, when God Almighty waits to be gracious and wants to assist me." Only a personal test of what is meant by "divine assistance" can ever prove its great value. The lamentable tendency of many of the lax doctrines of the present day is, undeniably, to weaken a literal acceptance of many of the truths of the Bible. Christians cannot be too watchful, lest through too general and impersonal views they fail to apply the promises of God when and where their help is most needed. Prove these things for yourselves; "taste and see that the Lord is good." Make an honest, prayerful effort to cast your burden, what ever it may be, on the Lord, and your heart will be filled with gratitude at finding how divinely you will be sustained.

A SPIRITUAL ATMOSPHERE.

"The feeble soul, a haunt of fears,
Forgot his weakness in thy sight."

SERENITY and spirituality go hand in hand. The theme, as given above and as we wish to present it, has no relation to atmospheric conditions in our natural world, either in its ordinary phases of the air we breathe, or in its phenomenal appearances. It was suggested by the story of an experience that comprehends that last change which awaits us all. This story was of a brave soul—a faithful, earnest, inspiring minister of the gospel—one who had a message, and who felt the "Woe is me," until he delivered it. That man battled for his life against the advance messengers of consumption. Repulsed again and again, he fought like a hero, until at last his strong spirit was obliged to recognize the truth that further resistance to the law of decay must be useless.

Then, from the sharp agony of the acceptance of the fact that he could never hope to stand again in any pulpit to hold up Christ to needy souls, could not hope to extend his earthly love and care over a large family of children through their years of development, came to this brave soul a beautiful and rare experience. He began to cast his spiritual eyes over toward the fair country of sure ease from care and pain, and he saw things there that he described not in words, for they were to him, as to that vision-seer of the long ago, *unspeakable;* but he had so taken them into himself that they became a part of his personality, so far that it created an atmosphere for even his family.

"I do not understand how a fond wife has strength to bear the trial of seeing such a husband gradually fade before her eyes," remarked one to whom the story was told. "The secret lies in being able to get into this spiritual atmosphere," answered the other. "Ah, yes!" answered one who had listened; but there was a tugging at the heart-strings as she remembered how her own loved one had at one time been for weeks at the border-land of this mysterious country, and had looked over, and how she herself had not been able to recognize the atmosphere, if, indeed, it had surrounded him. Her loved one had not died, he had been saved, it seemed under protest, yet saved to her longer. After the caller had departed, her words with regard to this spiritual atmosphere lingered with the wife, and she said within herself, "I'll ask John about it when he comes."

When John at last came in he seemed to bring a fresh breeze with him, and taking his seat by the side of the window where his wife sat, waited for a word from her. After a long silence from the little woman, John looked steadily into her face, and noticing her in a brown study, asked: "Has anything serious happened, little wife?" "Oh, no, John," the wife answered, "only—only I was thinking about an—atmosphere, that was all."

John opened his eyes and gave a long look out of the window, where everything seemed sombre and gray under the influence of the gathering forces of the storm. It was plainly to be seen that John was very far from conceiving of the altitude of his wife's vision. Turning his eyes again to her face, he caught the perplexed, far-away expression that rested there, and remarked: "I really do not understand you, my wife." Then she told him all she had heard with regard to the atmosphere which the dying man had made in his home, and added: "I have been a little puzzled, John, when I remembered that there seemed no such atmosphere in your sick room when you were very near to death, or was it that I could not get into it?"

"I am sure that there was no atmosphere of this kind, my wife. This brave man of whom you speak has nothing more to do with the world's work, his interests lie *now* on the other side. Whilst he was fighting for his life his energy made an atmosphere peculiar to itself that inspired others with courage; now that his rest awaits him, he lives in anticipation of it. He is really tarrying in the land of Beulah."

Among our memories there is one of a New England town whose leading church was an exceedingly proper church, its standard of propriety being as old as its edifice. To this church, for many years, one had ministered according to a flawless theological code, as the church members regarded it, and had never once preached a sermon that had shocked their sense of propriety. But there was no spiritual atmosphere in that ministry. Never had the people been bidden to tarry whilst the good man went up into the mount. To be sure they had never been left to the temptation of making idols after their own devising. But, in the end, would it not have been well if they had been left for a time, and been shocked by finding their own weakness, if the thunder and lightning from the mount could have been heard and seen by them, and, at last, the good old doctor could have come back, not the *proper* minister that went up, but a man with a shining face, an inspired man, bearing the law—a sacred mission—that he had received from the Lord himself? The preacher let things take their course because he disliked to disturb the old order of things by a new atmosphere.

After his removal by death a young man without much experience in the ministry, but with a spiritual experience daily deepening through communion with the Master, came to minister to this people. Those who, hungering and thirsting, had been waiting for the revelation of God, breathed a new, deep life; but those wedded to traditions began to feel uneasy, and to compare his preaching with the old standard, first to find fault with his *theology*, and at last with his *motives*, until this man with a needed message found it best to leave the church, where so few seemed to be able to breathe in the atmosphere which he created; but his atmosphere remains for the benefit of those whose spiritual lungs were healthy—until this day.

Through all the callings of life the true worker distinguishes himself by a power that creates an atmosphere—too rarefied often for those who are diseased, yet it is not his to question whether the majority will feel exhilarated by it. It is his to ask only: "Is it the Spirit's bidding?" Such an one, obeying this spiritual necessity, can never ask whether his words and work will make him popular, never can speculate whether his singular life will place him on the side of failure, as the world has it; and when he sees worldly friends turning away because of the "atmosphere," he may, in the loneliness of his own soul, cry out, as did the great spiritual Teacher: "Will ye also go away?" Yet if he persists in faithfully declaring the whole truth, he will finally stand forth victor and king, in the highest realm of conception, and receive his crown and reward hereafter.

A GOOD NAME.

OF a truth "A good name in man or woman is the immediate jewel of their souls." Strange how often the jewel is bartered for a mess of pottage. Happy is he who makes choice of a good name at the beginning of life and keeps it to the end.

Mackenzie writes, "As a rill from a fountain increases as it flows,—rises into a stream,—swells into a river, so symbolically are the origin and course of a good name. At first its beginning is small; it takes its rise from home, its natural source; extends to the neighborhood, stretches through the community, and finally takes a range proportioned to the qualities by which it is supported; its talents, virtue, and usefulness the surest basis of an honorable reputation."

"I had a good name until I became so greedy for gold," wept a young man in his prison cell, and his cry might be echoed over the length and breadth of the land. Bacchus once offered Midas his choice of gifts. He asked that whatever he might touch should be changed to gold. Bacchus consented, though sorry that he had not made a better choice. Midas went his way, rejoicing in his newly acquired power, which he hastened to put to the test. He could scarcely believe his eyes when he found that a twig of an oak which he had plucked became gold in his hand. He took up a stone, it changed to gold. He touched a sod, it did the same. He took an apple from a tree you would have thought he had robbed the garden of the Hesperides. His joy knew no bounds, and when he got home he ordered the servants to set a splendid repast on the table. Then he found to his dismay that whether he touched bread it hardened in his hand, or put a morsel to his lips it defied his teeth. He took a glass of wine, but it became liquid gold. In consternation, fearing starvation, he held up his arms to Bacchus and besought him to take back his gift. Bacchus said: "Go to the River Pactolus, trace the stream to its fountain-head, then plunge your head and body in, and wash away your fault and its punishment." Hence Midas learned to hate wealth and splendor and to prize a good name only.

So we say to those who have chosen gold or anything else rather than a good name. They will surely yet regret their choice. The only remedy is to go to the fountain-head, Christ Jesus, and there be washed whiter than snow.

GOD'S DISCIPLINE.

A WELL-KNOWN artist once described the sensations with which he witnessed the burning of a lawn. To his practiced eye the grass was a picture of verdure as it swayed to and fro in the brisk spring breeze. True, there were spots where it was not quite as even as it might have been, and despite its general greenness small patches of brown showed here and there. Yet the whole effect was one of freshness and beauty, and it seemed unwise to burn to the earth so much that was pleasant to look upon. The artist ventured a remonstrance.

"My friend," said the gardener, "if you come this way in the summer, I shall be glad to show you the effect of to-day's scorching and withering along the lawn."

"And," added the artist, "I did visit the spot in the summer, and I never trod a turf of such velvet softness, such perfect evenness and such living green before." The man acquainted with the imperfections and needs of the soil understood perfectly what the effect of that scathing process would be, and his art, seemingly so unwise to the untaught, was that of an expert, and the wisest possible.

Who of us has not been interested and amused in watching the methods of a mother bird, in teaching her birdlings how to fly. It often becomes necessary for their tender little mothers to push the helpless creatures from the nest in order to force them to use their wings, being unconscious of possessing such things until forced to discover and use them. The lessons imposed upon the young during school days, and the restrictions of parents and teachers, are often seemingly arbitrary and needless. But who would desire to witness the conduct of an undisciplined child? If discipline is necessary in forming the outward conduct, how much more in forming and perfecting the Christian character!

The Scriptures from beginning to end form a continuous story of the fiery discipline God exercised over the people and nations of the Bible times. But the results invariably justify and prove the wisdom of the measures employed.

Paul, in his fatherly exhortations to the Hebrews, charges them not to faint when rebuked of the Lord. Christ tells his followers plainly that in the world they shall have tribulation, and tribulation and discipline we understand here as synonymous terms. Trouble and trials are sure to yield the peaceable fruit of righteousness to all who are properly exercised thereby. Out from every form and kind of discipline comes renewed and pure enjoyment to the child of God. The great training school of God's providences yields many rare and valuable prizes. There are many sweets along the way. Discipline is merely temporary, and is strictly discipline, not punishment. Accept it as a good soldier—and many times before the final crown of victory adorns the brow, there will be flowers and sunshine to reward the patient endurance.

A PREPARED LIFE.

T is such an overwhelming comfort to know that our life with its flashes of happiness, its vicissitudes, its cares, its sorrows and perplexities, has been prepared for us by the dear Father, who alone knows what is best for us. Trusting him, we cannot be surprised on the turning of any corner by meeting any emergencies beyond our power to endure; for with the emergency comes the grace that we need, the fitting of the back to the burden.

From the cradle to the grave our life is one of progression; we cannot stand still, for as the shuttle flies, so our days and weeks fly past us, carrying their record with them, as we keep on to the close. We make many mistakes, great and small, and there is left many a gap in the symmetry of our lives, but the Father is quite able to weave out of them a beautiful whole; we make plans but do not finish them; we commence to build but are not able to complete. We sit before the wheel, and as the shuttle flies, dragging the threads of warp and woof through the loom, sometimes a thread breaks, and the fabric is imperfect, and although it may be so joined together as to be imperceptible to the unpracticed eye, yet the break is there, and makes a blemish.

God's work is without wrinkle, or spot, or any such thing. He gathers up the ravelled ends, smooths the disjointed work, and we become complete in him who died for us—our Jesus, our Saviour, our Friend.

Our life is manifestly a life of faith. We believe in the God we see not, yet love. Jesus says: "I am he that liveth, and was dead; and behold I am alive forevermore." What a comfort it is to believe in a living Christ—not one that was crucified, buried and lost, but one who lives and reigns forever. Thomas was not with the other disciples when Jesus came to them after his resurrection, but he was glad when he saw Jesus, because he could put his finger in the print of the nails which had suspended him from the cross. To-day our Lord is risen, and sits by the right hand of the Father, and we are glad to hear echoing down through these thousands of years the words, "Blessed are they that have not seen, yet have believed."

Our prepared life has many rough spots in it; we are not promised any full tide of prosperity on which to float to heaven; we cannot expect to be carried upon flowery beds of ease while we await our Lord's coming, so that we can go in to the marriage supper. Stop a moment and think! Would we choose, would we prefer such a life? In ordering the golden vessels for the tabernacle they were to be of beaten gold. The ore was to be melted, beaten, burnished, worked, until it was strong and beautiful. What does an uncultivated garden produce but weeds? What good would a life that was inert, unproductive, undisciplined, do for character? We know that "character groweth day by day, and all things aid it in unfolding." That little word "all" holds a vast amount of meaning for us: it means our cares, little troubles,

slips, mistakes, trials, joys; and every one of them aids in unfolding character—our character—that will never be fully developed until in heaven we no longer see darkly. In the light from the throne we shall also see that every trial is allowed by the gracious love of the Father, who in preparing our life filled it full to overflowing of mercy, help and love.

We will not then regret the blind eyes that now trouble us, and if we could return there would no longer be any cry upon our lips except, " Lord! that I might receive my sight to behold the wonderful things that thou art ever showering upon the path of our prepared life." Beloved, now are we the sons of God, and it doth not yet appear what we shall be: but we know when he shall appear, we shall be like him, for we shall see him as he is.

A CITY OF REFUGE.

IN the Bible we are told that when a man accidentally killed another, God ordered Moses to furnish him with a place or city of refuge to which he might flee and where he might remain in safety.

Of such cities there were three on each side of Jordan, as can be seen by Joshua xx. 7. On the west Kedesh of Napthali, Shechem and Hebron; on the east Golan, Ramoth-Gilead and Bezer. These cities of refuge were not only for the children of Israel, but for all strangers who resided in the country. It was not contrary to God's will that the injured should seek revenge. Moses says: "An eye for an eye, a tooth for a tooth." He did not therefore forbid the desire for redress, but provided a place of refuge to which the accidental slayer could run. It is said by some writers that good roads and sign-posts were made to facilitate the escape. After the escape revenge is said to have been sought upon some member of the slayer's family; and thus feuds were kept alive for thirty and forty years.

Among the nations of antiquity the temple, especially the horns of the altar, were supposed to be guarantees of safety; but in some cases the Hebrews in violation of this dragged the culprit even from the altar and put him to death.

When Joab was flying from King Solomon he "caught hold upon the horns of the altar." But there at the king's command he was slain.

We have not perhaps killed any one, but sinners as we are, do not we need a city of refuge to which we can flee? In Heb. iv. 18 we find that a refuge has been furnished for us. Wherefore, "that by two immutable things, in which it was impossible for God to lie, we might have a strong consolation who have fled for refuge to lay hold upon the hope set before us: which hope we have as an anchor to the soul, both sure and steadfast, which entereth into that within the veil."

What more can we want or need? Christ overcomes the law, stands between us and an avenging God, and with his dear arms shields us from every harm through time and eternity.

"WATCH!"

SHORT and emphatic as is this command of our Saviour, it involves a whole volume of caution and warning. To make it the more impressive he extends the injunction to make it reach and apply to all readers of the Scriptures for all time to come. "And what I say unto you, I say unto all, watch!" This watchfulness was not meant to be put into practice merely at an hour when the thief or when death might be expected, but it was to prove a safeguard at all times. The exact time of peril is rarely known, so the only safe way is to be continually on guard. But the watchfulness of which the Saviour speaks is far more comprehensive, we take it, than would at first appear. The caution is one not only for the time of danger, of death, but should stand by as a kind of watchword for life. Years ago a teacher wrote in our copy-book at school a motto which has followed one pupil, at least, through life thus far: "Learn to live as you would wish to die." This involves a rule which if followed will make life worth living, will rob death of all terror, and rid the mind of all forebodings as to the future.

A life of watchfulness is a life of safety. There is a very strong lesson for parents to be found in this brief, sharp text of Scripture. Parents often wonder where their children have learned certain things they have never taught them, and where they have acquired certain habits and tendencies never learned at home. The old alarum, the "watch" of the Bible, has been mated to a degree by the phrase "eternal vigilance" of late years. And if eternal vigilance, which is only a longer term for the word watchfulness, is the price of peace and safety in a worldly sense, the same conditions apply in matters of vital and spiritual importance.

The trouble too often is that parents relax a strict watch over their children before they have sense enough to discern just what is right and what is wrong, and before they have strength to resist temptation. If only every mother blest with the care of little children would take time at night to ask a few searching questions, it would be a great help toward keeping the little feet in the right path. Ask a child gently and lovingly at bedtime if it has said or done anything during the day which it thinks mamma would be sorry to know. Try it. Night is an impressive time to susceptible childhood, the hour favorable for frank confessions and tender confidences. It very often would be a great relief to unburden the heart of some little conscious sin. Get at the child's heart and have it in your keeping, then keep over it an eternal watch, that is, in so far as the word eternal can apply to the bounds of time.

As the children grow older try to know just where they spend their time when out of the house. Make the attractions of home so great that when evening comes it will be the rule to stay in, and the exception to go away from home in quest of entertainment or pleasure. And then— a matter of great importance—know what they are reading, and be sure to know who is the author of the books they read. It will take time to give the mind a taste for the right kind of reading, but a relish once formed for only good books will almost invariably prove an abiding one. Watch at every point and at all times. Watch even as you would pray, without ceasing. Watchfulness is not peevish anxiety. It is not a restless prying about with troubled eyes. It should be a calm, never-ending vigilance, an earnest, persevering effort to see and judge wisely our own desires, motives, and deeds, and also those of the children committed to our care. It is to adopt as our motto the watchword given us by Jesus, our Master.

GOD'S INSTRUMENTS.

GOD uses very humble instruments to carry out his great works. Gideon had but an empty pitcher and a lamp, yet he put to flight with them the host of Midian. With an oxgoad Shamgar defeated the Philistines, and with a rude sling David slew the giant Goliath. Simple instruments these to accomplish such great results, and by a no less simple instrument God works out the salvation of mankind. By the foolishness of preaching he saves them that believe. What has the preacher? Only a small vantage on the side of God, after people have been exposed for six days together to the full weight of the world's temptation. Only a short hearing for a matter of life and death—but some thirty minutes to get at the separate hearts of men, to convince them of all their weaknesses, to shame them for all their sins, to warn them of all their dangers, to try by this way and that to stir the hard fastenings of those doors where the Master himself has stood and knocked, yet none has opened, and to call at the openings of those dark streets where wisdom herself has stretched forth her hands and no man regarded.

Who is the preacher? an angel? No, though he might have been. Every Sabbath morning the windows of heaven might have opened, and into every sanctuary of earth a shining messenger might have been sent into the pulpit, and when he had veiled his glory with his wings, might have taken up the wondrous theme of Jesus and his love. Gladly would the angels do it, if commanded, for such is the work they love. Rather than fill the highest earthly throne, an angel would feel honored to fill a pulpit and tell the story of the cross. But such is not their mission. While they are deeply interested in the success of Christ's cause, while their wondering eyes are upon the sinner who can resist the Saviour's love, while they make heaven's arches ring with triumphant songs over one sinner that repenteth, rejoicing in the salvation of a soul even more than mortals do, yet their interest is at best only the watching of spectators.

Crowding the corridors of heaven they look down with eager eyes and beating hearts as the battle rages here and there, Satan and his forces on one side, men and the cross on the other. As we fight against principalities and powers and rulers of darkness, they love to see us buckle the armor tighter, grasp the sword more firmly, and lift up the cross more valiantly. But they are not permitted to lend a hand to help, else gladly would they leave the heights of heaven, and, lighting on the sanctuary, sound a trumpet note of encouragement which would thrill the pulses of the languid, and inspire new life in the wounded. Eagerly would they raise this or that fallen brother, tenderly would they bind up wounds where the arrows of the adversary had struck, and zealously would they enlist new recruits, furnishing them with the helmet of salvation, and putting in their hands the sword of the

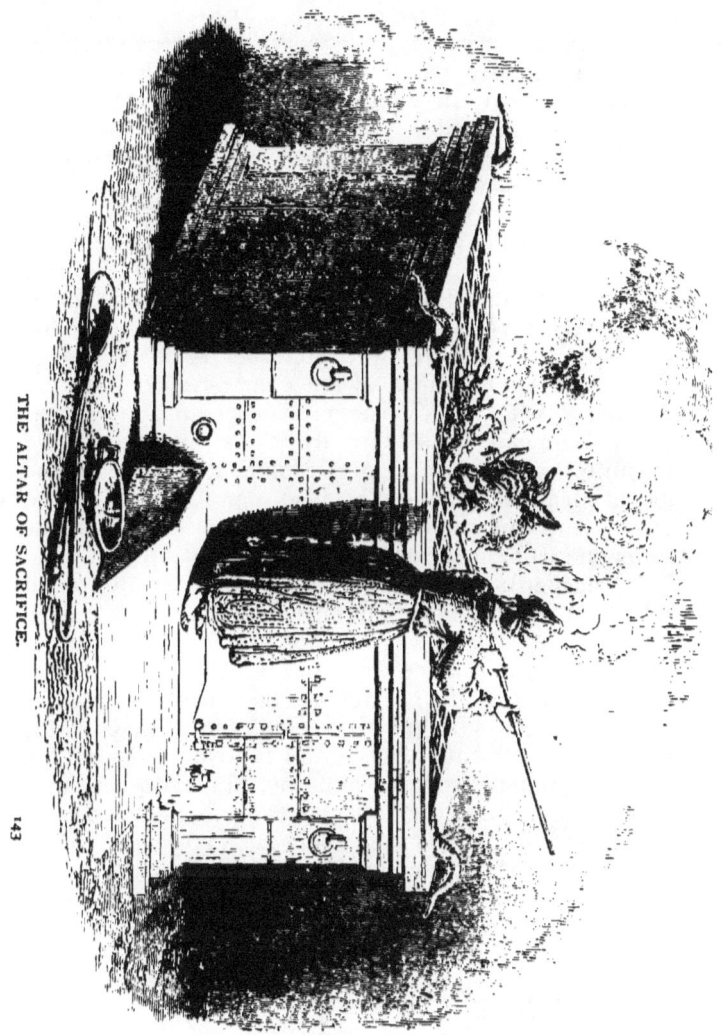

THE ALTAR OF SACRIFICE.

Spirit. Yes, gladly would they do the preacher's work, and honored would they feel to be sent visibly to watch with folded wings beside a sick bed.

Surely this work of preaching were worthy of an angel's power and eloquence and knowledge, and would seem to demand angelic messengers. But instead of this, in the pulpit is placed a poor, frail, dying man, tempted and tried and sinful, living the same life his hearers live, beset with the same infirmities, needing the same salvation. Surely this is an humble instrument which God has chosen; the treasure of the Gospel is committed to earthen vessels, sometimes of the coarsest clay, rude and misshapen. Yet God's wisdom is never so apparent as in this. Who can speak more truly of sin than a sinner? Who can tell so rapturously of pardon as a pardoned man? Who can plead so well for Christ as one for whom Christ pleads? And who can tell so touchingly the story of the cross as one who has been weeping beside it himself?

The preacher must needs be a man. Those white-robed angels never felt the misery of sin; how could they preach like those who have had experience of guilt, have felt the serpent's sting and have fled to the Rock of Ages for peace, and joy, and life? Men are best fitted to preach a Saviour, to plead with men for God, and with God for men. Truly God hath chosen the foolish things of the world to confound the wise, and the things of earth that are weak and despised, he hath chosen for his instruments, and they accomplish his great purpose no less truly than if he had sent angelic messengers to fulfil his will.

IS LIFE WORTH LIVING?

ALAS, how often the old question comes knocking at the door of our tired souls! How many weary, overburdened souls have answered it with a terrible negative by peremptorily summoning death without God's sanction. Such awful presumption sends a thrill of horror over even a worldling. But Christians take a different view of life from the fact that they believe in love and intelligence at the helm, and even as rowers in a boat turn their backs to the shore and trust to the man whose eye is fixed upon it, so should we proceed in duty through life—turning our backs from our anxious cares for the future, and leaving the guidance of them all to God, who is at the helm. Had these tortured souls, who found life unendurable, trusted in God, they would have been guided safely until the Lord, in his own good time, had called them.

The root of tne trouble may be, and often is, that people forget that happiness is *not* the end of life. If one could remember in life's emergencies that adversity is the true touchstone of merit he might hope to rise above it.

We can answer without pausing for thought that some lives are *not* worth living. If every storm weakens us, every breath of wind chills us, every thorn in our path discourages us, every blast from the furnace shrivels, we are faint and weak indeed. One might appropriately compare such lives to that of those unhappy victims where the prisoner is put in a cell, which, at the first entrance, presents an air of comfort and ease; but after being a few days confined, he observes the dimensions of his chamber beginning to contract and day by day the sides draw closer, till the hapless inmate at last is crushed to death.

Lives are worth living, if they answer the purpose for which they were given. And such lives, how ineffably sweet and fruitful they are! God's smile beams upon them, and all humanity is conscious of the fact. Some of them, perhaps most of them, are quiet lives—no ostentation, no bustle and stir, only earnest, faithful, and conscientious doing of whatever their hands find to do. But "tiniest insects build up loftiest mountains." Broad bands of solid rock which undergird the earth have been welded by the patient, constant toil of invisible creatures, working on through the ages, unhasting, unresting, fulfilling their Master's will. On the shores of primeval oceans, watched only by the patient stars, these silent workmen have been building for us and for themselves the structure of the world.

We ought to begin life as at the source of a river, growing deeper every league to the sea; whereas, in fact, thousands are like men who enter the mouths of rivers and sail upward, finding less and less water every day; and in old age they lie shrunk and gaping upon the dry ground. If youth is still yours, thank God and build the foundations strong, so that you may be able to give an earnest affirmative to the question heading this article. No regret, nor grief, nor remorse, nor desire can regain a lost youth— there is only one spring-time in the year. But whether young or old, we can solve the problem whether life is worth living only by doing all God requires of us, offering our "bodies a living sacrifice, holy, acceptable unto God." The Psalmist answers "Yes" with a chime as sweet as that of silver bells when he says, "The righteous shall flourish like the palm tree; he shall grow like a cedar in Lebanon. Those that be planted in the house of the Lord, shall flourish in the courts of our God. They shall still bring forth fruit in old age."

CHARACTER.

IT has been truthfully said, that character is what a person is, and reputation what he seems to be. Now we are all something, consequently we all have character; we all seem to be something, hence we all have reputation. Each one of us has been endowed with a will-power, enabling him to choose for himself what he will be. One of the last recorded acts of Joshua was to assemble the tribes of Israel at Shechem and say to them, "Choose ye this day whom ye will serve," thus asserting that power of choice rested with the people. This power of choice rests as much with the people now as it did then. Good and evil are in the world; we may choose between them, and according to our choice so will our character be.

It is of vital importance to ourselves that we choose the good. A good character will tend to give us a good reputation; and the wise man said, "A good name is rather to be chosen than riches." It will also keep us from doing much that is wrong, and cause us to do much that is right.

A good character is also of importance to others, for it makes one a friend to be relied on when fortune frowns as well as when she smiles. If by any means you chance to be in need, this friend will ever remain firm and ready to lend a helping hand.

In the formation of character, the study of the Bible and a realization of the truths therein contained, is of the utmost consequence. Train up a child in the way he should go, says Solomon, and when he is old he will not depart

CHARACTER.

from it. Even the most favored man meets with many difficulties in this life. There are trials to withstand and temptations to overcome; and if the enemy sees himself about to be vanquished he will be ready to effect a compromise. But a man needs the stability of character which will enable him to meet all such proposals with an immediate and unconditional refusal.

Christ is the great example to be followed. He was firm. After fasting for many days, when he must have been suffering the extreme pangs of hunger, he was tempted of the devil to turn stones into bread; then he was taken to a pinnacle of the temple and tempted to cast himself down; and then he was taken up into a high mountain and shown the kingdoms of the earth, and promised them if he would fall down and worship Satan. But Christ resisted all temptations. He had so great stability that his character could not be overturned, neither by Satan nor all the powers of darkness.

The broader we make the foundations of our character on the bed-rock of truth, and the lower their centre of gravity, so far as anger, hate, jealousy, and other wrong emotions are concerned, the greater will be their stability. And if the foundations are very broad and the centres of gravity very deep, there is but little danger of our character being injured by Satan or any one else. The fifteenth chapter of the Apostle Paul's first letter to the Corinthians closes with these characteristic words, "Therefore, my beloved brethren, be ye steadfast, unmovable, always abounding in the work of the Lord, knowing that your labor is not in vain in the Lord."

THE TRIBUTE MONEY.

WILL IT PAY?

THE question of gain or loss is one that is always uppermost in men's minds, when they are undertaking any new scheme or engaging in any new pursuit. "Will it pay?" is the question that arises involuntarily, and if the question is answered in the negative, it almost invariably decides the fate of the undertaking. It is not strange, therefore, that when we come to the consideration of so solemn a question as that of the soul's salvation this thought comes to our mind. Centuries ago Peter asked the self-same question of our Saviour. "Behold we have forsaken all, and followed thee; what shall we have therefore?"

It was not much that the disciples had left, only their nets and boats, but it was as much to them, and just as hard to forsake, as the great wealth of the young man who turned away sorrowfully because he could not bring himself to give it up. They had given up their all, their life and livelihood, and the associations of their youth. They loved the water as all who have lived by it do; the smooth stretches of Gennesaret formed the dearest spot in the world to them, yet at a word from Christ they had forsaken home and family and occupation: the question now was, What shall we have therefore?

It is a question which more than one disciple has asked, and a question which stands squarely across the threshold of the Christian life. If we become Christians must we really renounce all the world, and turn aside from all its gains and pleasures? We stand here on ground that must place where Christ meant us thus to stand, but on either extreme, the right and the left, there are places of danger. On the one side is a marsh which will sadly hinder the feet of a disciple, on the other side is a Vanity Fair where heedless pilgrims are beguiled until they forget the race that is set before them.

If we look over the one side we shall find a motley throng of hermits, their homes in the dens of the earth; and of pillar saints, raised high in their isolation; of religious beggars, denying themselves, to live upon frugal charity. These are the products of bygone ages, but they are reinforced in these later times by a sad sort of Christians, who think if they love Jesus, they must by just so much cease to love their home and family; who are constantly making close examinations to see whether they love their dear ones better than God, and are continually going through a process of getting ready for the wife, or husband, or children to be taken away, which renders them constantly melancholy and sad. But surely this is a mistake. We know that if the ascetics and hermits and their kind of Christianity had continued, the whole world would be wrapped in heathendom to-day, and we know that God ordained the family relation, and implanted human love in the heart. If there had been so great a conflict between these things and himself, he would not have endowed us so richly.

God gave us our possessions and comforts, and meant us to enjoy them. Is it reasonable to suppose that because one is a Christian, a follower of Jesus Christ, the very Son of God, he has thereby forfeited all the comforts of life and thrown away all worldly gain? Is it true that every one except Christians can have gold and silver and pleasure, and they cannot have them, because they are heirs of heaven? Does God give all his bounties to his enemies and reserve none for his children? This is absurd reasoning, and any healthy mind can see the folly of it at once. So far from this being true, the fact is that love for God intensifies all our lawful affections, makes husband and wife dearer to each other, renders children more loving, and hallows and sanctifies all possessions.

Of course we cannot expect to accept the Gospel without some loss, but let us see what it is that the Christian must give up. Upon examination we find that the Christian need give up nothing which his new heart would want to keep, or would think worth having. He takes with him everything which one's senses have a right to enjoy, and besides this he gets everything that it is possible for the soul to experience, and in the possession of this quickened energy and power, can look over the world and say, " He gives me all things richly to enjoy."

Then what does the Christian sacrifice? Only the things that he is far better without; some pet sins and indulgences perhaps, to which his heart clings. But he is far better off without them. You know there can be more of a man when there is less of him. When pride and selfishness and intemperate desires are abandoned, that which remains of the character is greater and better than the whole mass was before. It costs an effort at first to give them up, but these things must be sacrificed with a ruthless hand, for they are only blemishes upon a life after all. It is a blessing to get rid of them, even though it cost sacrifice and, struggle, and self-denial.

When we stand in the great hereafter we shall not be disposed to look back upon or think much of what we have given up for God; we shall see that the gain is infinitely greater than the sacrifice. Against every self-denial and sacrifice that goes down on the debit side, we may put to God's credit the daily and hourly preservations, the mercies new every morning and fresh every evening, and the goodness and mercy that have followed us all the days of our lives.

"PEACE, BE STILL!"

VERILY, of the height and depth and breadth of God's love no one can fully know. If Christ dwells in our hearts and they are thus rooted and grounded in love, through faith, they will become strong to apprehend the love of God. Storms of sorrow may come, waves of distress may beat around us, but the dear Lord, who never causes his child a needless tear, knows all about it, and even though we may think that Jesus is asleep, he will say to the waves, "Peace, be still."

God's love covers all our sins; it hides us in the hollow of his hand; restless and careworn as we are, it shields us beneath the wings of the dove of peace. It brings rest to the weary, the entering into the rest that remaineth for the people of God, not after death only, but now, as soon as we choose to claim it.

God's love abides with us not only now, but always and forevermore; not only for time but eternity. What has God's love done for you? Are you hiding in it from the wrath that belongs to the children of disobedience? Is God's love the precious boon that you crave above all else? While it is unfathomable, is it also so interwoven with your desires that darkness is made light?

Do you owe the dear Lord anything? Has he given you life, health, strength, your home, your daily bread? Is it because of God's love that Christ has died for you, that though your sins be as scarlet they may be washed as white as snow? Does he abide with you in the house, walk with you by the wayside, live in you? Get low down before God, forget self, learn to see only Jesus, and then say,

> "Take my love, my God; I pour
> At thy feet its treasure store;
> Take myself; and I will be
> Ever, only, all for Thee.
> All to Thee, all to Thee,
> Consecrated, Lord, to Thee."

CHRISTIAN CHEERFULNESS.

MUCH of the success of life is due to Christian cheerfulness. There is no one whose history is not sprinkled here and there with vexations, disappointments, and trials; but then, a cheerful spirit helps wonderfully in bearing them. Suppose when the troubles come, you go about with a long face, moaning over what hurts you, constantly fretting about your losses, disappointments, worrying about what is inevitable. How much do you gain? What is there at the end of the turmoil of mind that you have raised, but an hundredfold more of trouble than you had before?

If you so lament and worry, is your life a benediction to any one? Are you a help to any one who is trying to get on in the Christian life? Do any of God's little ones find strength and renewed courage from being with you? Are the burdens that are borne on men's shoulders any easier to carry because you try to lift even the least little corner of them?

But, you say, "I never harm anybody. I never add to any one's cares. I never hold any one back who is trying to get on in the Christian life." Stop a moment and think. Do you exist in a little world that is made for you alone? Then, if you do live in a world of God's creating, a busy world in which every life touches every other, where men and women are striving for daily bread, where the wail of the poor, the hungry, the sinful, is arising in an awful, solemn chorus to the ears of the dear Father of us all, is it nothing to you? Can you afford, with the realities of eternity staring you in the face, to say, "I am not my brother's keeper?"

There goes a sad, weary one whose life is full to the brim of anguish, who has not a place in which to lay a tired head, to whom even the sun is veiled in shadow; and sometimes, when eyes ache with looking for something better, they are turned upward to heaven to see if even there a ray of comfort may come to pierce the lowering clouds. And when no answer comes to the ears not attuned to the whispers of the still, small voice, they turn to look at you, and seeing only a gloomy brow and heavy eyes, they are not bettered by the minor chords of your voice, nay, judging from your own lack of cheerfulness, they are persuaded that religion is as comfortless and useless as anything they have tried; and they become reckless, hopeless, and discouraged.

Go to some of the many missions in the city that are established to help the helpless; see how eagerly they watch those who have a word to speak for Jesus; and above all, see how even for the moment a cheerful face reflects upon their own. A religion which can bring cheerfulness and happiness is surely worth seeking. And so you come to realize what a blessed thing cheerfulness is. It is the reality that puts into every trial and every disappointment the blessed "Lord's will," that makes them so much easier to bear.

Cheerfulness must be genuine, not put on as a mask that can be removed at pleasure; it must be the outcome of a healthy soul, the shining forth of the light that is within you, the real, actual cheerfulness of one who is not insensible to the troubles and trials of this life, but who lives above them and endures them with cheerful patience because he is true to his convictions of Christian life beyond.

"HE SAITH."

IT seems easy enough to understand that one's life may reach such a degree of anxiety that there is a hopeless outlook as to unravelling it. On every side plans are hemmed in by the *pros* and *cons;* one reason points to a decision in one direction, another reason in another; friends advise one course, when our own judgment recommends another; and in a weary, hopeless way we sit down, and wish the mists would clear away that hide the light for which our hearts, as well as our eyes, ache, and we despair more and more as to what is best.

In such seasons of deep and sore trial, the Christian has a secret pass-word which robs them of all power to harm beyond what we are able to bear. It is the precious words, "He saith it is best."

The darkest part of the night is just before the dawn. "Sorrow may endure for a night, but joy cometh in the morning." It is well to look at it in this way, to remember that after a few hours of night, of trial, of suffering, there comes the eternal day.

At the marriage of Cana in Galilee, when Jesus turned

water into wine for the needs of the feast, the mother of Jesus said to the servants, "Whatsoever he saith unto you, do it."

The substance of this comforting thought is thus not only "He saith,"—but "whatsoever he saith." Are you to do the whatsoevers of his loving commands? Will you say:

> "Saviour, I weary of this ceaseless mind,
>   That needs must spin and spin its tangling thought;
>   That needs must weave what thou dost bring to naught.
> Rest I would find!
>
> "Not thoughts of thee, but thine own self impart!
>   Ever I learn thy precepts and thy way,
>   Yet know not how to follow and obey.
> Teach thou my heart!"

A STRANGER AND A PILGRIM.

THE Psalmist said of himself: "I am a stranger in the earth." And this world was to him a scene of perpetual warfare. In some sense, and really in the highest sense, this is true of the Christian. Every Christian may adopt the language as his own. We are all strangers here. If we were to cross the ocean and to mingle with the people of some foreign land, not only would the faces of all be unfamiliar, but they would all be to us of a "strange speech," and in vain should we seek to communicate with one another. We should be strangers in a strange land.

And in yet another important sense we are strangers in the earth. For the most part we are strangers to the inner life of others, to their thoughts and feelings, their joys and sorrows, and they are alike strangers to ours. "Every heart knoweth its own bitterness." The world within ourselves is for the most part known only to God and to our own hearts. It is but little comparatively that others know of our inner lives, our trials, our secret sins; and our efforts to overcome them are known only to the all-searching eye.

But not only are we strangers in the earth, but we are also pilgrims here. The world is not our home. We are on the march rapidly passing through it. We are hurried on from one stage of the journey to another, and shall soon be gone, and done forever with all earthly things. Truly may we all say: "We are strangers before thee, and sojourners, as were all our fathers; our days on the earth are a shadow, and there is none abiding." Nor would we have it otherwise. The true Christian can truly say—

"Heaven is my home."

Nor shall we be strangers there. We shall know our best friend, the Lord Jesus Christ, and dwell forever in nearness to him. We shall know the holy angels, some of whom were ministering spirits to us whilst we were strangers here. And we shall know all the millions of the blood-washed saints, amongst whom will be many whose names and lives have already become familiar to us, and whose examples have proved so helpful and so dear to us while yet here in the house of our pilgrimage. In no true sense shall we be strangers there. Most delightful will be our converse as the everlasting years shall roll on. We shall compose one great, happy family, and we shall all fully know each other, and in like manner be known.

GOD "OUR FATHER."

OUR FATHER.—There is nothing sweeter to the Christian than this. We are not like children who must go out from our Father's house in the morning, to spend the working day away from him, and only to come back to him at evening. No; we are with him, and he with us, all the day through. We never leave his presence; he is beside us through all our work, our weariness, our perplexity, our worry, all the day. And we may tell him what we want, and how we are feeling—not stiffly and formally, twice a day at morning and evening, but as often as we please. He will not weary of listening to us, if we do not weary of speaking to him. We need not limit ourselves to morning and evening prayer. Twenty times, and far more than that, as you go through your day's work, the eye may look up for a moment, the heart may be lifted up; the brief word may carry up to God's ear the story of your need and of your trust in him.

Sitting down to your desk and taking up your pen, if that be your work, O you do not know how much better you may do it for just covering your eyes with your hand for a minute and asking God's blessing in prayer! Or, dealing with your fellow-men—some of them impracticable and wrong-headed enough—some of them sharp-set and low-principled enough—some of them provoking and stupid enough—how much better you will keep your temper amid the provocations of business; with how much clearer head and kinder heart you will treat your fellow-sinners for a word of silent prayer! If you desire to influence any for good, remember how wisely it has been said that the shortest road to any human heart is found by God, and explain to your heavenly Father all you wish to do. Every little pain will be better borne and every little joy enhanced by a moment's silent mention of them to God. You can, alone with him, speak of a host of little things which really make a great part in your thoughts and in your life, yet which are less suitable for speaking of in united prayer with other people.

FAITH OF WOMAN.

THE intuitions of woman are more spiritual than those of man. His slower nature enables him to reason more logically perhaps at times, but he often climbs laboriously to the mountain top and finds a woman there before him who has reached the same altitude without such effort. She simply used her wings of faith and they carried her even more safely and speedily than his reason ever could carry him. Emerson says: "All I have seen teaches me to trust the Creator for all I have not seen." Here is an expression of the value of faith from one who thought profoundly. Paul says: "Faith is the substance of things hoped for," and especially to woman has this spiritual substance been largely given. A good woman has more faith than a good man. It is natural for her to trust with confidence in a higher power, and in this respect, as in many others, she is far superior to her husband.

But without faith woman is a wreck. If old-time standards are swept away, she seeks to formulate a religion of her own, and she worships idols of her own creation. She becomes a cynical, despondent creature, dependent upon some human love it may be, as in the case of George Eliot, who, after the shipwreck of her faith, sank into the very depths of despondency. The voices that come to us from beyond the walls of Doubting Castle have always in them a moan of pain, especially if the voices are those of women. In the breast of woman is the well of tenderness, whose waters keep the world pure. Worship is to her a necessary part of living. She must worship at some shrine, and when God gave the command, "Thou shalt worship the Lord thy God, and him only shalt thou serve," it was not that the act of worship could benefit the Creator, but the created. In the earlier ages of the world, when human beings were in their infancy, it was necessary to say, as to wilful children, "Thou shalt!" or "Thou shalt not!" but, like older children now, we learn the goodness of our Father in leaving us no choice but to obey.

God will more and more reveal himself as a God of love, as the world advances, because the time has come when love has a greater influence over mankind than fear; and one evidence of the truth of the Bible is its eternal adaptability to human needs. Am I troubled about the doctrines of the Bible? about its system of rewards and punishments? While my little child is unable to comprehend my first benevolent thought toward her, she must be taught by the only system she can understand—a smile her reward, a frown her punishment. She is restrained by a command as she older grows—she may not understand why the command is given—yet obedience is required for her own perfect development It is only when in the maturity of powers, after childhood has passed away, that the parent will be able to take the child into his counsels and tell the why and the wherefore, and show that love lay deep at the root of every command.

SEEKING RELIEF IN PRAYER.

"In every joy that crowns my days,
In every pain I bear,
My heart shall find delight in praise,
Or seek relief in prayer."

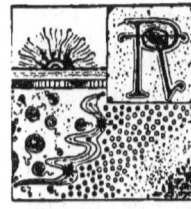ELIEF we all seek in our troubles and trials, but not all in the same way. Some resort to the intoxicating cup and seek thus to drown their sorrows. Some seek to divert their minds by foreign travel. Some fly to scenes of pleasure, to the ball-room or the theatre. Some plunge more deeply into the business and cares of life; and others engage more eagerly in literary pursuits. Almost numberless methods are tried. The only true method, and that which will give permanent relief, is that

suggested by the heading of this article. It is by telling our griefs to God, and seeking his grace.

The little child is an example to us in this regard. In its troubles, it runs to its parent. It flies to its mother, and freely tells her all its sorrows. The child of God, in all his trials, should always resort first of all to his Heavenly Father. Turning away from all other sources of relief, he should go at once to the "God of all comfort." This is his precious privilege. Here we are all invited to come, and with the assurance that we shall not come in vain. "Cast thy burden upon the Lord and he shall sustain thee." "The Lord is nigh unto all them that call upon him, to all that call upon him in truth." He is graciously nigh unto them to hear their cry and to help them. Such is the testimony of thousands. Such has been the experience of all who have made the trial.

They have thus tasted, and seen that the Lord is good, and can say with the Psalmist: "I called upon the Lord in distress; the Lord answered me, and set me in a large place."

And when you have prayed to God about your distresses, and cast them upon him, learn to be silent and be at peace. Your affairs are his affairs. If you have tried to live as his servant, and to do all things to please him, he is your partner in business, and the real head of the firm. He can protect you from misfortunes; but if he wants you to serve him in trouble, it is because he can make trouble do more for you than prosperity. "Rest in the Lord." The great life you live in him is your true life, and none of the uncertainties or accidents of your external condition can touch it. An inward peace is possible to you and me while surrounded by agitation, and our hearts may rest while we are maintaining a strenuous conflict with difficulties. Be a child again; God is your father. Rest in him; his love is wonderful, his power is wonderful. The life he lives is beyond the reach of storm and of peril, though he cares for us in all our cares. Think of him, if you can, rather than of your wrongs. Think of him, if you can, rather than of the calamities by which you are menaced.

DESPONDENCY.

THERE seems to be a natural tendency on the part of some people persistently to look upon the dark side of things, and to look forward to the future with gloomy forebodings, no matter how bright and unclouded the day may be.
Almost every phase of human nature was represented among our Lord's disciples, and the despondent disciple was by no means wanting. Thomas always looked upon the dark side of things, but the Saviour had no harsh reproof for him; he seemed rather to pity than to blame him. For his own sake he wished that Thomas could rise above his gloomy tendencies. So it is with all desponding Christians. Christ does not rebuke them. Very patiently he puts the truth before them, tries to dispel the gloom and bring them out of the shadows, and make their hearts glad.

There are many causes of spiritual despondency, and as often as not they may be physical causes. The body may affect the mind. Ill health, unpropitious surroundings, continual over-work, may darken the horizon of the mind until not a star is visible. It may be a hereditary disposition, or the result of many and keen disappointments, or of sad and bereaving providences. It may, too, be a natural desire to exact demonstration for the foundation of faith; any or all of these things may cause despondency, and he who knows our frame and orders all our circumstances takes all these things into account. He remembers that we are but dust, and deals very gently with the despondent.

Yet he tries to lead them, as he did Thomas, into a larger, brighter place. There are too many disadvantages connected with despondency to let it go on unhindered. There are disadvantages to the persons themselves; they miss great peace and serenity of mind and are apt to become captious and irritable. Despondency takes the heart out of a person, and though he may go on with Christian service, it is with a burdened feeling.

There are positive disadvantages, too, to the church. Despondent people take the heart out of others. If this were better, or that were remedied, there might be hope of better things, they say, but there are so many things that are wrong that they can hardly see any good. Every Christian should be loyal to the church of his choice. If there are evils they cannot remedy, they should not blazon them abroad. Speak only of the good things, uphold them, and be loyal to your own church. But close contact with the Master is, after all, the great remedy for despondency. If we cannot look on the bright side of things we should go and look into Christ's face. The case of the despondent soul that is not saved is far sadder than that of the despondent Christian. One who despairs of salvation, who has grown spiritually desperate and says, "There is no hope for my soul," is in the saddest of all conditions, and needs comfort most deeply.

One of the causes of such despondency is the judgments of God, the severer dispensations of Providence with which the Almighty sometimes visits people. The real meaning of all afflictive providences is that our Heavenly

Father still loves and cares for us, and tries by these calls to bring us to himself, but oftentimes they are misinterpreted into intimations of wrath, and crush out all hope.

Sometimes the discovery of one's sinfulness produces deep hopelessness. Such was the case with the disciple who betrayed his Lord. When Judas realized the crime he had committed, and found it was too late for reparation, his heart stood still, appalled. Like an icy chill the thought stole over him, "There is no hope," and out into the night he went to end by voluntary death his wretched days. Any one who is brought to deep conviction of sin feels somewhat of that great despair.

Then, too, not only the discovery of our sins, but a long unsuccessful struggle against any one of them, may produce a feeling of despondency. If any one begins the conflict with some easily besetting sin, be it great or small, the love of strong drink, or a hot temper, or an ungovernable tongue, and in that conflict proves unsuccessful for a time, then there comes over his soul a dark cloud.

This despondency may be a Satanic suggestion. If the enemy can get us so fast in the castle of despair, that we make no efforts to escape, he counts us as his own. Feelings of despondency, however originated, are apt to produce different effects. Sometimes they produce utter misery. A profound melancholy seizes the soul and embitters every moment, but a more common result is that of recklessness. Like a nerve that has ached itself to death, the soul may get past feeling and smile into insensibility. One may believe in a measure all the threatenings of God's law, and yet feel them no more than a stone. Utter indifference and insensibility take possession of the mind, and the old life is pursued with careless apathy. Sometimes recklessness follows despondency, and this is the saddest of all results.

But there is really no cause for spiritual despondency. There is no human being, however straitened his spiritual circumstances, who may not, while he draws the breath of life, turn unto God and be saved. The will of God, the promises of God, the power of God all forbid despondency, and bid despairing souls turn to the One who is mighty to help.

BE NOT WEARY IN WELL DOING.

BE not weary in well doing. We are not to work always, and even when we are at work we learn that many things do not follow our bidding, and we must wait upon theirs. More and more we learn this truth as years interpret to us our own limitations, and the force of the great tide upon which we and all things float. Our patience is quite as much a measure of our wisdom as our enterprise; nay, what folly stamps every enterprise which is not begun in the patience which can bear delays as well as in the courage that can dare risks! Children of time, when we are doing our best we must wait God's hours for opportunity in our special aims; and, above all our special aims, we must lean upon Him to carry us forward in the one divine way which earthly power may accept but not control. Blessed is the office of true patience in relation to time. Vast is the loss it saves by keeping for efficient action the time and thought saved from fretting and struggling against what cannot be helped. Vast is the gain it secures by keeping the soul calm before God, accepting the allotments of his providence, and watching wisely the lessons of the events which it cannot control. Are there not twelve hours in the day? said he who consecrated them alike by his waiting and his work, whose crowning sacrifice, alike in its act and its sufferance, illustrated the worth of time, and leaves upon its track the alternate footprints of labor and patience to mark the way of eternal life. Blessed are the hours to us, when calmed by his patience as well as quickened by his fidelity.

AFFLICTION AND TRIBULATION.

SORE trials and deep afflictions are often the portion of the Christian's heritage here. Often, like the Prophet Elijah, we are inclined to be despondent therefrom. But affliction is frequently the fire that consumes the dross and separates it from the finer metal. So essential is this that the all-wise Father has seen fit that every redeemed soul shall pass through some fiery furnace of trial in this life, and the fact that one's way is beset with much affliction and many temptations shows that it is the highway that God has ordained that his children should travel as they journey heavenward. What does he say? "In the world ye shall have tribulation." And in Hebrews, "For whom the Lord loveth he chasteneth, and scourgeth every son whom he receiveth." Peter writes, "Beloved, think it not strange concerning the fiery trial which is to try you." And Paul adds, "For verily when we were with you, we told you before that we should suffer tribulation, even as it came to pass and ye know."

But the afflicted may ask, Why is this? Let us see what James says: "Blessed is the man that endureth temptations, for when he is tried he shall receive the crown of life which the Lord hath promised to them that love him." And Paul exultingly cries, "Yea, for our light affliction, which is but for a moment, worketh for us a far more exceeding and eternal weight of glory," and he goes on to say: "For I reckon that the sufferings of this present time are not worthy to be compared with the glory which shall be revealed in us." Again he says: "If we suffer, we shall also reign, with him." And in Revelations we read: "These are they which came out of great tribulation, and have washed their robes, and made them white in the blood of the Lamb. Therefore are they before the throne of God, and serve him day and night in his temple, and he that sitteth on the throne shall dwell among them. They shall hunger no more, neither shall the sun light on them, nor any heat. For the Lamb which is in the midst of the throne shall feed them, and shall lead them unto living fountains of waters, and God shall wipe away all tears from their eyes."

LABORING IN THE VINEYARD.

"Hast thou not agreed with me for a penny a day?"

HOW much has been written and said about this parable! It is impossible to explain it by any worldly reasoning, but how easy to understand when we grasp the real meaning!

The Lord of the vineyard is the great head of the Church. He sees fit to call many in infancy and youth to labor in his vineyard, to be his children by covenant, to call him Abba, Father. Others heed the summons in early manhood or womanhood, and put their hands to the plough. Again, some (very few) are obedient to the Master's call for laborers when old and feeble, perhaps unable to do any great work. Still, when evening comes, when death calls to rest, or the laborers stand before the judgment seat, each will receive the same, "a penny," in the words of the parable, eternal life in the deep meaning of the story. The Master can give neither more nor less than eternal life to his disciples. He gave every man a penny.

Now, would those who have sought and found Jesus in early life, who have labored in the Church all their lives, exchange places with those who followed the prince of this world for many years? When the end comes and we all stand before the throne shall we regret one day or one hour or one minute spent in doing God's work in his vineyard? It is true that those who remained outside, blind to the Master's call till life was almost over, will receive just the same pay in one sense, but think of all they missed—the sweet communion, solemn feasts, delightful labor, and daily intercourse with the Master! So we will not complain, nor grudge them their pay, though earned late, by little service. Only let us be sure that we are hired, and the recompense is sure to be adequate and satisfying.

SUFFICIENT UNTO THE DAY.

WILL men ever learn that the Bible means what it says? Modern adage has added its weight to the wisdom of the Scriptures and assured us there is no use in attempting to cross bridges before coming to them. If only fear of the future, dread of coming evil, could be stricken out of life, much of the pain and suffering endured would be stricken out at the same time. But after all, there is much of pathos in this timid shrinking, which it cannot be denied arises from what has been endured of adverse fate. If "a burnt child dreads the fire," so one who has met and been overcome by misfortune can never forget the discomfiture of the sad defeat. Yet does not fear become a misfortune of itself? Many may have read the old legend of how Fever appeared before the king and asked leave to slay a thousand victims. Permission was granted him, but when the given time for his ravages to cease had arrived, ten thousand men lay dead. The king at once summoned Fever to his presence. "How is this?" he asked; "I gave consent to your conquering a thousand, and lo! ten thousand men lie slain." "I slew but the single thousand granted me to," Fever replied, "but Fear killed the other nine." Even so, work kills a victim or two at times, but does not worry slay more than work? One of our religious papers revived recently an old saying as quaint as it is brief and simple, "Do the next thynge." And strive our best, that is the most that can be done.

Fear and Worry stand deplorably in the way of many a Christian's progress. It would seem that in vain the Saviour counselled His followers to take no thought for the morrow, and our course too often implies doubt as to the truth of the assurance that the morrow shall take thought for the things of itself. The concluding words that sufficient unto the day is the evil thereof do not necessarily mean that only evil will come with the day. One of our most reliable commentators says with regard to this passage: "We shall indeed find that sufficient unto the day is the evil thereof, and have no need to anticipate pain and sorrow. We shall also find that the day will bring its comforts and supports with it."

There is one verse of the Bible which promises exemption through one strong power from much of dread and worry—"Perfect love casteth out fear." Fear indeed has torments. What spectres a timid imagination will conjure up! What untold misery and depth of painful apprehension a licensed fancy will create! What greater torment need a poor mortal suffer than that which arises from a morbid, faithless, nervous fear of future events? All the teachings of Holy Writ enforce the chief need of human beings and point to the source of supply. Simple love for the Saviour, perfect love for him, a firm reliance on his strong, powerful arm, will disarm all fear, dispel all apprehension, vanquish each spectre of evil. The very simplicity of the remedy, like that once prescribed of old, seems to detract from its efficacy to poor, short-sighted man. It takes great faith, unfaltering resolution, and indomitable courage to meet life in a worthy, manly way. It requires but an unwavering belief in the Saviour and his precepts to realize that sufficient to each day will be its evils and its conflicts, its comforts and its blessings, but free to every soul of man is the perfect love which casteth out fear.

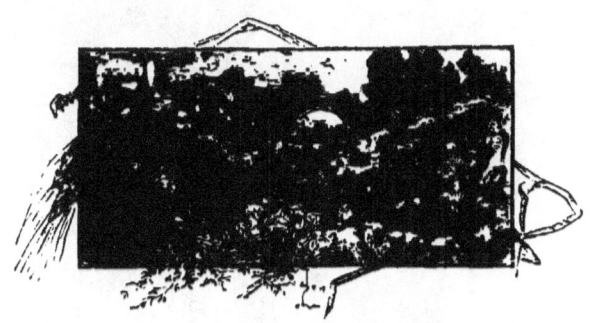

THE SEA OF GALILEE.

A BELOVED DISCIPLE.

IN the Sea of Galilee a father and his sons were fishing. All night long they had toiled and had caught nothing. They seem to have been men in good circumstances, for they were able to minister to the wants of the Saviour; but having been out in their boat all night and having taken no fish, they were weary and left off trying to catch fish, and were washing their nets. But at Jesus' command they took in such a draught of fishes that their boat began to sink.

How like that is to ourselves in our striving so hard to obtain success, and when it is granted to us we do not know what to do with it, but cry out for help! No doubt John expected to be always a fisherman as his father was, but Jesus often has other work for us to do besides that which we may have chosen, and when he calls us, as he did call John, we must forsake all else.

One does not need to be old before being able to do the Lord's work, for John is supposed to have been the youngest of all the disciples, yet he was beloved. At the last supper, as they reclined upon their couches to eat, according to custom, Jesus, about to leave his disciples, told them that one should betray him. The Beloved Disciple, leaning back on Jesus' breast and looking up into the face which he so tenderly loved, asked, "Lord, is it I?" Long years afterwards, when he was grown too old to say much, and had lost the power to walk so that he had to be carried to the assemblies of the people, he would reach forth his hands and say: "Little children, love one another;" and when they did not understand why he would not talk more to them, he added that if they obeyed the command of love they had the whole of the Gospel of Jesus Christ.

Are we *beloved* disciples? In the day that "He shall sit as a refiner and purifier of silver," when the jewels are fastened together will our souls be a part of the crown of rejoicing? And when the years are too heavy upon us to admit of our doing the Lord's work, shall we not as beloved disciples spend our time talking of the love that in our state of life is teaching us to take our part in the new song that will be sung before the throne by the redeemed?

PUT YOUR HEART IN IT.

THIS quality of *heartiness* is what makes all the difference between poor work and useful work, between what is real and true and what is hollow and superficial in the purposes and deeds of men. To put one's heart into anything means to put one's self into it, and when was ever anything noble, or great, or useful in the highest or the lowest degree, performed in this world, that did not involve the putting in of self? The famous saying of one of the old masters, that he mixed his paint with brains, is but another way of expressing a great general truth, applicable to all master work, whether it be in painting a canvas, or writing a poem, or building a house. It must be done with the mixing of brains, or with what is the same thing, a mixing of heart, a mixing of self. The average man, to say the least, is not a very strong or a very wise or great being. Measured by the standard of the Infinite, his noblest endeavors are weak and puny beyond comparison. Measured by the standard of Nature's handiwork, the results of his skill and craftiness are insignificant.

How then can a man do less than put forth the best there is in him, since that falls so far short of perfection? And this always and everywhere, whether the thing to be done calls for the exercise of brains or hands, whether it is carving a statue or digging a ditch. Heart, heart, heart, is what is needed for the world's work of every kind, be it such as is called great, or such as is termed menial. And most of all it is needed for spiritual work, for the saving of sinners, for the regeneration of men. Want of heart here means failure from the beginning, utter failure and disaster. The sermon, the prayer, the exhortation, the spiritual counsel, the teaching, that does not have heart in it, the spirit of a sanctified heart, is devoid of the very thing that carries the sermon, the exhortation, the counsel to the consciences and souls of men. Words of counsel that do not come from the heart are like arrows made of pith; however finely formed and beautifully finished, they fail to carry to the mark; they have no weight, no momentum. A man may succeed very well in some kinds of mechanical work even though it is done in a listless, careless, indifferent manner, but when it comes to working for God, to soul-saving, there can be no success without the merging of the whole being in the work, the putting in of self.

It is a very easy matter to shuffle over religious duties with a loose and careless spirit; but to work from the heart and with the heart in earnestness and seriousness of purpose,—this costs an effort. One may work, after a fashion, with hands or feet or brain or tongue, while the heart itself is engaged in matters far away, or in pursuits entirely foreign to those before them. But such work is not the best work; it is superficial; it is of little real value. The heart must work with the hands, or the results will be poor and unsatisfactory, both to ourselves and to others who seek to benefit by them. Heart work demands concentration of purpose, definiteness, and singleness of aim. It demands a gathering of all the energies into one line of action; a united effort towards one end. It presupposes self-control; an ability to curb vain and profitless thinking, and bring the mind into constant and serious attendance upon one thing. And this heart service is the only kind of service that is acceptable to God. We may work for others with only our hands, and receive our wages in due season, but if we do God's work we must work with the heart or there is no recompense for us: we shall be counted as unprofitable servants, unworthy of our hire. We serve a Master who "looketh upon the heart," who knows its secret motives and purposes, and all mere outward show of zeal and devotion is mockery in his sight. Heart work is true work,—the noblest, highest, and best service which man can give, and the only kind that will insure a heavenly and eternal reward.

CALLED AND CHOSEN, AND FAITHFUL.

THESE three adjectives describe the character of Christ's followers. The first two belong to God's part and the last to ours. It is by a Divine call that we are made partakers of the benefits of redemption. The influence of the Spirit by which we are translated from the kingdom of darkness into the kingdom of light is a calling. In the spiritual world a nation or individual becomes by the call of God that which he intends them to be. God forces no one into his kingdom, he compels no recruits into his army, he drives no workmen into his vineyard; he simply calls, sometimes very gently, and those who are his own obey. To all alike comes the call, and the only difference between a sinner and a saint is that one is deaf to the voice, and the other gladly hears and answers it.

That God's people are not only called, but chosen, is to many anything but a pleasing thought, for it seems to them to close the door of mercy to some, perhaps to themselves. But God never refused any one who came to him for salvation; he has pledged his word that whoever cometh to him shall in nowise be cast out. It is easy to decide whether or not we belong to the number of the chosen. If we love religion and spiritual things, God has chosen us to receive them, for unless God had given us that desire and that love, we would never have had them. God has chosen his people to be holy; if any one believes in the Lord Jesus Christ he is elect; if any one truly desires to leave sin and live unto God there is mercy in store for him.

No decree passed in the unknown ages of eternity will keep any one out of heaven if he is growing in holiness, but without holiness no one can see the Lord. This is the character of the chosen ones. By patient continuance in well doing they seek for glory, honor, and immortality; and the vast multitude now rejoicing with the Lamb bear witness that this is the way to obtain eternal life.

The third characteristic of Christian followers is that they are faithful. This belongs to our care. Called and chosen we are by God, but faithfulness is the task committed to us. To be faithful to Christ is our work. Many of us have made solemn vows, that are registered ineffaceably in heaven, to devote ourselves to him. Upon all of us lies the obligation to be his, whether we recognize it or not. Let the pulse of heavenly affection beat strongly and steadily in us, let our love to Jesus burn like the sun. As his devotion to us was unchecked by the indignities he endured and the agonies he suffered, by the grave he entered, so let neither life nor death, nor angels, nor principalities, nor powers, separate us from him. Let this above all be our motto, faithfulness to our Master. Then, when he comes bringing our rewards with him, he will give to every man according to his work, and will say to those who are faithful, "Blessed are they that do my commandments, that they may have right to the tree of life and may enter in through the gates into the city."

ONE RESTFUL DAY.

IN the midst of the mad rush of life, jostling at elbows with our fellow-man, hurrying hither and thither through every wakeful hour, agonizing to reach the goal on which we have fixed our eyes, filled with plans of the present and the future to get our daily bread, or grasp success in this venture or that, what a boon one restful day is!

What is a *restful* day? Is it the attainment of our wishes, the culmination of our plans, the acme of bliss that follows our having placed our feet upon a pinnacle of happiness, the intoxication of pleasure from an overflowing cup, the having wrung from possibilities the all but impossible success?

Philosophers cannot give it to us; wise men of all ages cannot show us how to possess it. The loveliest cloudless day that ever dawned is not all that we crave, for if there were no night to follow it, we would never see the stars that twinkle in the sky. If we had not sailed upon the rough seas, we would never enjoy to the full the fair haven of rest. If blessings fell thick and fast, there would be no thankfulness for deliverance from crosses. If there were no planting through weary hours, there would be no gathering of fruit and flowers.

The foundation of all rest comes from what is within ourselves. A soul satisfied of God, a heart at peace with itself and the world, brings rest. Not only beyond the confines of life, not only on the other side of death the rest remains, it is ours now, to-day, this moment. Will not one restful day condone for the weary weeks of the labor that never seems to diminish—will not one day with Jesus rest us? You remember that when Moses and Elias vanished there remained "Jesus only." Is anything else needed to bring rest? Whether of the twain shall be given to us, Barabbas, or Jesus which is called Christ? If we have the dear Saviour with us, if he is so near that we can whisper to him,—

"Saviour, I weary of this ceaseless mind,
That needs must spin its tangling thought,
That needs must weave what Thou dost bring to naught,
Rest I would find.

"Not thoughts of Thee, but Thine ownself impart!
Ever I learn Thy precepts and Thy way,
Yet know not how to follow and obey,
Teach Thou my heart."

—what else can we need to bring rest? Does Jesus turn a deaf ear to our cry does he permit us to be driven away? Ah! no, very gently the hand that was pierced for us is laid upon our heads, and the sweetest voice that angels ever heard is saying, "Peace be unto you;" and behold he is in the midst!

Do we long for only *one* restful day? The soul that is satisfied is always at rest, because it has gone to the fountain and been cleansed from sin; God's will is ours; whatever befalls us comes from the hand of One who never errs; not one needless tear can fall from eyes that are fixed upon him; not one cross is too heavy for us to carry, because before it was laid upon our shoulders he measured it to our strength; and then, lest it might be too heavy, he held the corner of it. Christian had upon his shoulders a big burden that caused him to fall into the Slough of Despond; but when he had climbed a hill he saw a cross, and when he reached the cross his burden fell off. Then he said, "He hath given me rest by his sorrow, and life by his death." So we learn that at the cross the burden of life falls away, and through Jesus we obtain life, rest, and peace.

THE JOY OF THE MORNING.

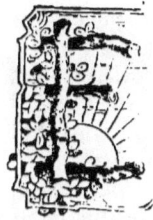
ACH day the sun rises in the East, and sends his light into every home. He does not seem to be stationary, as is the fact, but as if he came up out of a sea to come up higher and higher from the horizon; shooting great flecks of golden splendor into every cloud, gilding the mountain tops, touching every leaf on the trees with light, and laying beauty alike upon the homes of the rich and the abodes of the poor.

In yonder small house, at the corner of the lane, as you turn from the highway to go to the mill, a mother has been watching through the darkness of the night the fitful slumber of her sick child. As the weary hours crept on she felt so sad, so utterly discouraged, that it seemed as if hope had died in her heart; she never heard the crickets chirp; she gave no heed to the whirr of the night birds; she did not notice the fact that the wheel at the mill had been stopped; she forgot that to some people daylight was past the dawning; she never looked out to see the myriads of stars in the sky; for her there was nothing but the blackness. There was not much in the world that she could call her own, but the child was hers, and its sickness made her rebellious; for the time she lost faith in God, her fellow-man, herself. Over the whole world there was cast an impenetrable pall; it was night, dark night, till the sun should rise in all its glory and bring forth the joy of the morning.

In grander solitude a lone man sits in his prison cell; the walls are of stone, not so hard, though, as the hearts of his judges; the one window through which light and air could come is barred; the door is locked, and when he shakes it he only bruises his fingers, in his efforts to escape. Outside the last streak of daylight has faded, twilight has deepened into night, and the stars, that have been called the "forget-me-nots of the angels," have studded the sky. He sees them twinkle, but they only make the darkness more perceptible, and he paces his stone floor, weary of night, waiting for the morning.

Out upon the angry sea a vessel rocks, now rolling, then pitching; now wave-swept, then rising as if it were a ball to be tossed here and there. Sad eyes look up from that vessel to see if it is possible that through any rift in the utter darkness even one ray of light may penetrate. But although there comes the swift thought of the little child who said that "if the wrong side of heaven is so beautiful, what must the right side be, the star-gemmed firmament holds no beauty for those eyes, for the stars are set in the darkness, and that to them means sadness, sorrow, despair.

But lo! in the East there comes a light; the sun arises, and through the small windows of the little house in the lane his beams peep, transfiguring the well-worn carpet; and across the face of the sick baby the mother sees the flush of returning health, and falling upon her knees she breathes out earnest thanks for the joy of the morning. That joy floats in through the grated window of the prisoner's cell; and as he opens his anxious eyes, into them is cast the golden light; forthwith the new life seems to cry out to him to take courage, that hope is not dead, only sleeping; and that before long the coveted blessing of freedom will open the iron door and send him forth a free man. And the light beams around and over the waves and shows the sailor where to find a safe harbor.

"Watchman, what of the night?" The morning cometh. Are we so weary of the little self-denials, the little crosses which the dark side of life brings, that we cannot comfort ourselves as the gloaming gathers about us with the same thought that yet there will surely follow a bright, happy, God-given sunshine on the morrow? The joy of the morning will repay us for everything that seemed to shut out all hope; and beyond the river there will be the "many mansions, the city that hath foundations, and the Lamb who is the light thereof."

OUR TENDER SHEPHERD.

THERE are many lessons taught us in nature, whose significance, as applied to Christian things, is more deeply impressed upon the mind than much that is said or written. While sitting upon the broad veranda of a beautiful home on the north shore of Long Island, this charming Sunday morning in June, we are reminded as never before, by scores of sheep grazing about the fields, how frequently they were employed as figures to express the peculiar care which our Lord feels and exercises for his people. This symbolism is often announced with special strength, as if he would assure his followers that in the sacrifice he made he would be always the good Shepherd giving his life for the sheep!

In the Eastern world, doubtless, the force of this passage is more clearly seen than here. We can hardly appreciate the feelings of the shepherd for his flock. Even though he has a vast number under his care, he knows every feature of every sheep. He gives names to each of them, and they know him, too, and come at his call, "whithersoever he goeth." In danger they fly to him for protection, and feel safe when near him. As he would guard his own fireside, so he defends them, and the little ones, nursing the feeble and even laying them in his bosom as he would his own child.

Now all this is a most apt and beautiful figure of Christ's care over us. It almost ceases to be a figure, and becomes a sweet reality when we think of the exceeding force of the illustration. Does he not say, "I am the good Shepherd, and know my sheep, and am known of mine?" And how comforting to feel that we are of his flock, that he has chosen us for his own—gathered us into his fold—set his mark upon us, and trained us to know and follow, obey and enjoy him. He is so good to us. Oh, how sure we are of this! Does he not show it daily, hourly, yea, every moment of our lives?

He saw us wandering far away, and came to seek and save us; when we were perishing took us in his arms, laid us in his bosom, brought us home to himself, and nurtured us with more than parental care; and how he guards us from danger, foes within and foes without, seen and unseen. Our enemies are many and mighty, and their wiles so deceitful that we should fall into snares and be lost, if the same grace that rescued us did not care for us on the way!

He feeds his sheep, too! The finest of food is theirs! He calls them to the storehouse, and throws its doors wide open, to enter and be filled. He brought me into his banqueting house and his banner over me was love—his mercy to those who fear and love him will endure forever! "The good Shepherd giveth his life for the sheep." This crowns the evidence of his matchless goodness,—"greater love hath no man than this, that he lay down his life for his friends!"

"But while Christ died to have us reconciled to him in God, how near this great condescension on his part brings us." What a privilege to look to him as lambs to a shepherd, who will not only feed, defend, and save his flock, but give up his very life for them rather than suffer one to be plucked out of his hand! Do we think enough of this, and our relationship to him, and above all, of the infinite obligations that rest with us? These are ties that, made strong and holy by his love and sacrifice, should draw us nearer and still nearer to his feet, causing us evermore to trust in him for safety, for strength, for daily food, for the bread that perisheth, for the bread that cometh down from heaven and for life everlasting.

Surely he is our "tender Shepherd," our great High Priest, our living Saviour, Prophet, King! These may be common metaphors, so common that we need sometimes to have our attention called to them, to take in their true significance as on the Sunday morning in question it came to us. If in our deep experience of life, amid the thorns and flowers that grow along the highway, we can only regard the Saviour in this light, happy will it be for each of us. Let us think of him as our good Shepherd, and of ourselves as his sheep, bearing his name, known to him, and following "whithersoever he leadeth" through this hard travel of life, which at best is short and weary, and gathered at last into the great fold, "to go no more out forever."

> "Then shall we find a settled rest,
> While others go and come,
> No more a stranger or a guest,
> But like a child at home."

LESSONS OF THE DAY.

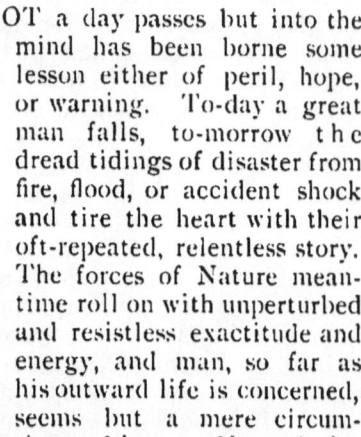NOT a day passes but into the mind has been borne some lesson either of peril, hope, or warning. To-day a great man falls, to-morrow the dread tidings of disaster from fire, flood, or accident shock and tire the heart with their oft-repeated, relentless story. The forces of Nature meantime roll on with unperturbed and resistless exactitude and energy, and man, so far as his outward life is concerned, seems but a mere circumstance of creation, subject to Nature's inexorable and despotic rule.

Of but one thing can mortals be certain: everything in the realm of Nature dies. The leaves fall, the blossom decays, and in process of time the tree itself suffers blight and death. But in the Spring the great lesson of life's renewal is taught. The sun grows warmer day by day, the frost is oozing from the softened, expectant earth, and already in the country the moss is showing green and fresh close to the bosom of old Mother Earth. The pussy-willows are sprouting gray and furry on the parent stem, and very soon the green grass and cheery little crocus will refresh the eye with their glad appearing. Progression becomes the order of the day, and ere long, responding to Nature's irresistible call, field, orchard, and garden will burst into spontaneous bloom. In the garden will be certain plants on which special care has been bestowed. By dint of ceaseless nurture and patient cultivation a degree of culture is reached, making the stately rose-tree a very marvel of loveliness amid the other beauties of the rose-bed. And as with the plants, so with the human mind in its superior growth and intelligence.

The question has often been raised as to whether or not there are degrees in heaven, places to which the soul attains at once on entering, having been fitted for such placing while on earth. Pray, how could it be otherwise! A great soul has just gone forth from the midst of us. The eloquent preacher, the powerful orator, the best type of a representative American citizen of ripe scholarship and advanced age, has passed on to fulness of life, the life everlasting. What incalculable heights of bliss and spiritual advancement is that soul capable of entering upon and appreciating now! Is it not worth while making all possible progress while on earth, that the greater may be the capacity of the soul for the enjoyment of the delights of heaven?

At the appointed time the inexorable decree of Nature asserts itself and the body suffers decay even as the grass or the flower of the field, but what matters it that the shell crumbles back to earth while the soul lives on to countless ages of—what?

Ay, that is the great question for each to determine for himself. But how piteously the great consideration is overlooked and evaded. Moses, the servant of God, deploring the indifference of the people of his charge concerning these things, exclaimed: "O that they were wise, that they understood this, that they would consider their latter end!" For the end is but the beginning. When the harvest, which is the end of the world, shall come, the spring-time of the soul is at hand. Heed the lesson of the day. Strive so to live that at the last it may be said of us as of a wise man lately departed, "a great soul has entered into eternal life." The true life has just begun.

EVERY-DAY CHRISTIAN LIFE.

IT is our every-day life that reveals exactly what kind of Christians we are. We cannot always form a proper estimate of Christian character by seeing others now and then, or passing a day or two in their society at intervals. We are generally thrown into the society of friends upon pleasant occasions. We meet them upon life's holidays oftener than in the usual routine of daily duties. We greet them upon social occasions when they are prepared to meet us with pleasant words and loving smiles.

It is easy then to smile and speak kindly. It is easy to wear a cheerful look when the burden and task are put away from them, and when free from the influences that chafe and fret the body and soul.

Divine grace is not always required upon occasions like this to win the good opinion and approval of others. There is often enough natural goodness about human beings to bring to the surface of their lives those genial graces which charm other eyes and win the respect and confidence of those with whom they come in contact. But these can scarce hold good in the every-day life. Divine grace alone can sustain the soul when the burden is heavy, and care and troubles appear at every step. There is not enough moral strength in the natural heart to sustain it when the body is weary, and the poor weak arms are just ready to let fall the burden.

When trial, discouragement, and disaster all combine to

EVERY-DAY CHRISTIAN LIFE. 193

render the life-path dreary, then the blessed faith in Christ alone can hold those unpleasant influences in check, and still the troubled waters. With the abiding Comforter in the soul, it is as easy to smile and appear cheerful in adverse circumstances as for the worldling to be happy in the hours of peace and prosperity.

It is this every-day life that builds up our Christian character. If we overcome the daily annoyances we grow strong and heroic, and it soon becomes, if not a pleasant; at least a cheerful, task to do, bear, and suffer. The service of Christ is one that grows lighter and more pleasant as the years go by. It never galls or inflicts needless wounds upon those who are engaged in it.

It is this that exerts a lasting influence over the world. It is this that tests the value of religion, and proves to others that it is pure gold, and not a mere profession. It weighs and measures the golden treasure in a way which proves its great worth, and the sceptic himself stands confounded and silenced.

PERFECT TRUST.

A MOTHER was awakened in the still, small hours of the night by the touch of her little boy's hand. He said, "Mamma, I don't know what is the matter; I can't sleep, and I've tried ever so long." She took him up, laid his head upon her breast, and folded his hands in hers; in a few moments he was sleeping the sweet sleep of happy childhood. Mother's embrace and touch of hand, with his implicit confidence, brought repose. I wonder why we grown-up, restless, faulty children cannot in our troubles cast ourselves thus confidingly into the "everlasting arms." It cannot be that we doubt God's ability to care for us, for we know that he is omnipotent and able to do all things. It is not that we doubt his love, for every day evidences that, and we have his word that though the mother may forget her child, yet his love will never fail us. It must be our unreasonable want of trust, whereas we should ever feel perfect confidence in our Father.

The way may be dark, the body very weary, and the feet sore from the thorns in the path, still we should remember that all our trials are disciplinary—no atonement through suffering is worked out by us, but by our sorrows our characters are rounded, polished, and perfected. This trustfulness of little children should often reveal a loving Father to us, even in this world, and when "the leaves of the judgment book unfold," how clear will be the revelation—all in love.

OUR OLD ENEMIES.

WE lift up our eyes and see our old enemies, like sly, crafty foxes, pursuing our footsteps. We shall assuredly find no help or mercy in the direction of the pursuing enemy, but the outlook is full of hope if we only glance in the right direction. Moses told the Israelites that they should see no more again forever the enemies who were pursuing them. That blessed assurance will come to us some day. It may not be now, nor to-morrow, nor for weeks nor months, but some day, constant resistance will bring us the consciousness that our easily besetting sin is dead, that it has lost its hold upon us forever. Where is our strength? Behind us are the hosts of sin; our strength surely is not there. We gauge our own puny strength and wisdom, it is insufficient; we look upon ourselves and see how weak we are, but when we cease to look at our enemies and ourselves and lift our eyes above, there moves the angel of our deliverance, none other than Jesus. When we hear the tramping of temptation and the discords of warring elements, the angel of the Lord moves behind us and comes between us and the enemy.

The chosen Israelites were in bondage in Egypt, and so are many of God's chosen ones. The state of Israel in Egypt was one of severest depression; at every point they were overborne and were under the lash of a tyrant; if their manhood tried to rise and assert itself, a blow in the face was the response. This is the condition of those who are in a state of sin. Some of God's freemen have been many years under the lash of Satan; they may boast of their liberty and think themselves free, but sin is slavery and continual oppression. At last the children of Israel escaped from Pharaoh, and by a strong hand and a stretched-out arm God delivered them. Suddenly they turned to look behind them, and behold the Egyptians were after them, their old enemies were close upon their heels. This is just the experience of Christians; old enemies pursue them, years of sin are behind them, and old associations are hard to break. Satan is close behind them, making special efforts to reclaim them as his own.

We ought not to expect to escape from all our enemies at once; one cannot throw off his past as he would throw off an old garment. Old slaveries, old tyrannies, old recollections, old habits will assert themselves in one way or another. It is more than a step from sin to holiness, it is a long way from evil to goodness, from darkness to light, from the depths of nature to the highest attainments of grace. There will be many a struggle, many a reappearance of the old self. Judas was cast down in the dust by his sin and there he stayed. Peter fell as deeply, but looked at Christ and rose again. So every true Christian will rise stronger than before, and look more at Christ and less at self. It is our chiefest blessing, that we have not a human judge to stand before. God does not expect us to step from Egypt direct to his throne; he leads us through the Red Sea and the wilderness and the long wanderings and daily discipline, but he only asks that at each day's close we should be a little stronger, a little nearer, a little more devoted.

Like the Israelites we are in a wilderness; but ours is a wilderness of sin. We have left Egypt, but not yet gained Canaan; we have had long and bitter experience

"HE THAT IS WITHOUT SIN AMONG YOU, LET HIM FIRST CAST A STONE."

of sin, and it has made us weak; we have been under a powerful and remorseless enemy who has never spared us, but has been very severe with us, but we have been redeemed by a gracious and Omnipotent Saviour, and so though our old enemies are pursuing us as if they would never give us up as long as there remains a single chance of winning us back to their old allegiance, we are safe if we look unto Jesus and lean upon his strength.

While we remember the fact that our own enemies are still pursuing us, let us not be uncharitable and censorious to others who are just beginning the Christian life. Let us remember that they have just escaped the grasp of their enemies, so it is not strange if now and then, in spite of their best efforts, they are overtaken and fall. There are always people ready to condemn and crush them. There are thousands of men who never notice the stars swinging in order and beauty in their appointed places, who do stop and mark the falling star. There are many who pass over a hundred moral victories without a word of praise, who glory over one fault. Because a Christian cannot step from the world to heaven, they exaggerate and hold up to criticism every fault, all that is unworthy a Christian, and exult over it, forgetting that old enemies do not bid a new-born soul Godspeed in the way to heaven, but pursue them hotly even after they have started out towards the promised land.

MORAL BEAUTY.

VIRTUE, wisdom, and goodness, those graces of character which constitute moral beauty, like the loadstone, never lose their power of attraction. The beauty that shines forth from a pure and sweet-tempered Christian soul far transcends, in all those qualities which command and hold a worthy admiration, the transient charm of mere outward adornment either of nature or art.

Purity of life and character is one of the essentials of this type of loveliness. Good thoughts, good motives, good companionships, are the influences that help to mould the mind into a form of real and lasting beauty. Evil companionships frequently lead to an impure heart—a foul and diseased imagination that discovers itself in the outward features, in spite of all that art or skilful dissimulation can do. There is nothing more repulsive or hideous than a corrupt, sin-disfigured character brought into sharp contrast by the weak, shallow disguises of outward show and gaudy attire. Meekness, patience, kindness, charitableness, a self-denying spirit—these are the vestments of the highest type of beauty—the kind which commands not only the admiration of the best of men, but is admired by God himself.

> "Beautiful faces they, that wear
> The light of a pleasant spirit there,
> It matters little, if dark or fair."

WHAT ARE WE DOING?

IT is a very serious question, and one which we should often ask ourselves, What are we doing, you and I, for the dear Saviour who has redeemed us, bought us with his blood, paid such a price for us? If we can only give a cup of cold water to one of his little ones, if given in his name, it is something for him. Said an aged disciple:

"I have reached the borderland and am only waiting for the summons to meet my Lord. As I look about me to-night I see new faces, few, I was about to say, for there is only here and there one face that met with us in this place of prayer fifty years ago — ay, twenty-five years — and how many changes even in ten! The nearer we live to the dear Lord the more he will show us, if we ask him what we can do for him, and I must say from my experience that none ask in vain.

"If you really wish to do something for the dear Lord he will show you how and when to do it. He will teach you to speak a loving word of comfort to some weary pilgrim, footsore, struggling on in life's journey through toil and hardship; or to give of your substance as he hath prospered you in furtherance of the cause of Christ. But withal do not forget to implore the blessings of the dear Lord on all your efforts, and you may be certain he will be sure to hear and answer your prayers. Try it and prove it; you will find it true."

Few who heard Father Payson's remarks that evening ever forgot them or his appearance as he stood like one of the patriarchs of old leaning on his staff. The very next morning as the day was dawning the village church bell tolled for one of eighty years. The news soon spread far and wide that Father Payson was dead. When they went to call him in the morning his Bible lay open on the stand by his bedside, his spectacles lay on the open page, but Father Payson "was not, for God took him."

"NO GOD."

THE celebrated astronomer Kircher, having an acquaintance who denied the existence of God, took the following method to convince him of his error. He procured a very handsome globe, or representative of the starry heavens, which he placed in a corner of the room to attract his friend's observation, who, when he came, asked from whence it came and to whom it belonged.

"Not to me," said Kircher; "nor was it ever made by any person, but came here by mere chance."

"That," replied his sceptical friend, "is absolutely impossible. You surely jest."

Kircher, however, seriously persisting in his assertion, took occasion to reason with his friend on his own atheistical principles.

"You will not believe," said he, "that this small body originated in mere chance, and yet you would contend that those heavenly bodies, of which it is but a faint resemblance, came into existence without order or design."

Pursuing this train of reasoning, his friend was at first confounded, next convinced, when he cordially confessed the absurdity of denying the existence of a God.

To a thoughtful mind it seems incredible that any intelligent human being could deny the existence of our King of Kings, could refuse, dare refuse to do him homage. What but omnipotent power could plan and keep in motion such a world as ours? While I am writing it is winter. Looking out of my window I see snow and ice, the leafless trees in their cold shrouds; but is this picture to continue? Ah, no! the ice and snow will pass away when the Spring comes with its balmy breath. The trees will bud and blossom, the grass will spread its velvet mantle, the buttercups and daisies will spring up by the wayside, and the violets in the meadows. The streams will be loosened from their frosty prison, the birds will sing their songs of thanksgiving, the browsing cattle will lap the clear water from the running brook. Everywhere will be life and growth and beauty; did it all come by chance? Truly it is only the fool who hath said in his heart, "No God," for to prove it, one would need to be himself a god and to travel abroad over the surrounding universe till he had exhausted it. He must search backward through all the hidden recesses of eternity; traverse in every direction the plains of infinitude; he must sweep the outskirts of that space which is itself interminable, and then bring back to this little world of ours the report of a universal blank, wherein he had not met with one movement of a presiding God. For man not to know of a God, he has only to sink beneath the level of our common nature, but to deny him, he must be a god himself; he must arrogate the ubiquity and omniscience of God himself.

CAUSE AND EFFECT.

YOU stand beside some great artist as he paints. Every color glows, every line is alive, every touch is true, and under his skilful hand the canvas becomes a counterpart of nature and the landscape stands out in wonderful perspective. You wonder at his skill which prevents all mistakes and makes the picture true in every detail; you could not do it, nor could he, if he painted for the first time. The skill he exhibits is a sum total, the effect of a long series of causes. It began years ago in the schoolroom, and from that it has grown until the present. Let us watch the effect of wrong-doing. A young man takes an intoxicating draught. It is a simple act and may not be attended with any very serious results in the present; but that act is a cause, and every cause will have its effect. We would not consign him to degradation and a nameless grave now, but the probability is that that cause will act until in after-years the strength of manhood will break under the burden of disease, the open, cheerful countenance will become the bloated face, the free, springing step will give way to a swagger, and the bright, quick intellect will become beclouded and dull.

Let us look at the effect of goodness. One has faith in the Lord Jesus Christ and in the reality of spiritual things; he is shaping his life on the great principles which the one perfect model laid down; and who can doubt but that such a one will become a son of God and enter into an inheritance incorruptible, undefiled, that fadeth not away?

Causes produce their own effects, legitimate effects, and as one sows, so he shall reap. As travellers are descending through the pass of St. Bernard they are cautioned by the guide not to utter a single word, as the very vibration of the voice may loosen some part of the overhanging snow, which will result in an avalanche, sweeping everything before it. Who would think of an effect so formidable from a cause so small? The voice loosens only a small piece of snow, but that in falling becomes a cause for a larger fall, until the glacier is moved and the mountain is shaken to its foundation by the avalanche. Who can tell what moral effect a single word may have? It is a cause which starts a series of causes, and thus progressing the effect becomes tremendous. But few pay any regard to such effects; they seem such a long way off that they cannot affect us, and yet they are the most serious things in the universe. However indifferent we may be, these causes are at work and will bring about their results. Beware what causes you set in motion, lest the effects bring you and others life-long sorrow!

GOD'S OMNISCIENCE.

LONG ago when our Saviour was upon earth it was said of him that he needed not that any should testify of man, for he knew what was in man. How wonderful a thing is this part of God's omniscience! It is a knowledge at once to us sad and joyful. It is so far from being possessed by man that it cannot even be said that we know ourselves, much less any human being around us. Much often depends upon our knowing the motives, the hidden springs of action, the sincerity and real purpose of another. How differently we would act sometimes if we could really see below the surface, and know what is in man. All are not what they seem! Some wear masks, sometimes over their faces, and more often over their hearts; it is universal experience as well as an inspired declaration that "the heart is deceitful above all things." It would be a great amount of knowledge to see all of a man's actions, to tear aside the veil from the hours when he is alone, to note every motion and attitude, and leave no part of his life unaccounted for. Simply to know all external acts in every moment of life would be knowledge far beyond human capacity, and yet it would hardly begin the real knowledge of the man. Perhaps not a hundredth part of a man's character ever takes outward form, and what is in man is an unexplored realm. It includes all the past history of the race and encompasses all the future: it enters into every detail and takes account of every day, every position, and every circumstance. Only the omniscient One knows all that is in man, and it is worse than folly to attempt to hide anything from his all-seeing eyes.

Our past life has been full of sin; he knows it better than we do. Why try to hide it? Why not rather tell it to him and gain his pardon? We can be sure that we tell our story in an appreciative ear when we whisper it to Jesus, for as very man as well as very God he knows what is in man. He knows and pities; he knows and saves.

THE FATHER'S WAY.

HAVE you a heavenly Father—is there a Being to whom you can go as children go to a parent, and with the simplicity of a little child of whom the Saviour said, "Suffer them to come"—can you look up, though it may be with tearful eyes, and say, "Father, not my will, but Thine?" Do you feel that no matter what happens, no matter what is contrary to your desires, no matter how untoward circumstances may be, you can still love the hand that smites? Even when the chastening for the present seemeth to be grievous, can you still say, "Not my will, but Thine?"

Life under such circumstances becomes all peace, and contentment, and satisfaction. Though seas of trouble are rough, and sometimes threaten to engulf you; although your roses with their perfume carry many thorns; although the sun smites your gourds; although the almond-tree shall fail, the grasshopper become a burden, and desire shall cease; yet you can still cry out aloud, "I desire to be, to have, to know nothing, but what is best; all that I desire to have is only what is according to the Father's way."

THE WAY OF PEACE.

GOD'S CRUCIBLE.

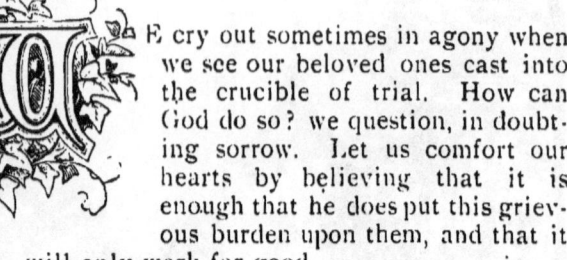

WE cry out sometimes in agony when we see our beloved ones cast into the crucible of trial. How can God do so? we question, in doubting sorrow. Let us comfort our hearts by believing that it is enough that he does put this grievous burden upon them, and that it will only work for good.

"I want to take that likeness home with me," said a lady to an artist. "But, madam," he expostulated, "it is out of the question; it is not yet finished." "Not finished!" in surprise. "Why, what more can you do to it?" she asked, looking at the lovely pictured face of one of her darlings. "Ah," he said, "it must be touched and retouched before I shall allow it to leave my studio."

It is so with God—the divine artist. To us our friends—some of them at least—may seem to be perfect, but the Omniscient knows they are not. He will not rest, nor allow them to rest, until they are "refined" unto the utmost limit of which they are capable.

> "Great Master! touch us with Thy skilful hand,
> Let not the music that is in us die.
> Great Sculptor! hew and polish us; nor let,
> Hidden and lost, Thy form within us lie.
> Spare not the stroke; do with us as Thou wilt;
> Let there be naught unfinished, broken, maimed;
> Complete Thy purpose, that we may become
> Thy perfect image, O our God and Lord."

FULL AND FREE FORGIVENESS.

THERE are shrinking, introspective natures, who must always look back upon sins committed, remorsefully regarding them as determining the final estate of the soul. They are so constituted that they never can, of their own selves, without help, see the absolution offered freely and fully from the Father upon repentance. It may be the result of an unbalanced mind, or of peculiar circumstances, or of defects in training, but there are those who thus sit in sackcloth all their days—the wine of life turned to poison, the energies of mind and heart rusted, life not worth living, sorrowing always over the past.

To deal rightly with one in such a condition, the priest of absolution must be wise and true and tender, having his hand, as it were, upon the key-note of the Father's love and justice, and being informed by an experience, personal and deep. He must possess an unerring spiritual insight, and, while tender and sympathetic, must be a surgeon for the soul that will not allow the searching probe to stop short of the bottom of the diseased spot.

There are some natures so constituted as to make them in the highest sense priests of absolution. A true mother, with insight sharpened by love, and with sympathies kept alert for her child's needs, when she gathers the weeping penitent one to her heart and whispers, " Dry your tears and think no more about it. You are sorry, I have forgiven you, and I am sure God, who is even more kind and sympathetic than I, forgives you too "—she perhaps is the highest type of this priest. Those of us who have thus received absolution, do we not think so? It is a great blessing to thus possess this rare gift of leading repentant, despairing souls so close to the Master that they may touch his garment and feel conscious of his forgiving power.

LITTLE SINS.

MOST men who fail to obtain salvation are brought into a state of misery by prevaricating with themselves, and not living up to the judgment and resolves of their own knowledge. They miss their way to heaven, not because they do not know it, but because they know it and do not heed it. They deceive themselves by some false hope; they are allured here and there by some shadowy form of doctrine or belief that offers nothing better to them in their hour of bitter extremity than blank despair and unavailing regret. How many fly in the face of their convictions of right and duty simply because they think that somehow in the future the wrong will be atoned, and they will escape the punishment justly due them for their folly and impiety. They run blindly toward destruction, thinking that somehow God's restraining grace will interpose to save them before they reach the fatal hour that hurls them from time into eternity. "Surely," they say within themselves, "this is a little thing." And then the downward course begins. The "little things" grow to be great things, and what was at first a slight swerving from the path of rectitude becomes a wide divergence. The self-deceiving power of sin—how it blinds men's eyes to their own highest and truest and best interests! promising them bread and giving them a stone; mocking them at last with the pangs of remorse, and the accusations of a conscience whose warnings they have so long ignored. Let every one consider the truth of the words: "Be not deceived; God is not mocked, for whatsoever a man soweth that shall he also reap."

CROWNS.

CROWNS or garlands were given to the successful competitors at the Grecian games. These were made of parsley, pine, and oak, and although they soon perished they were highly prized by those who gained them. Our Saviour was crowned with thorns in mockery by the Roman soldiers, an especial insult. It is said that the *Spina Christi*, although abundant in the neighborhood of Jerusalem, cannot be the plant of which it was composed, because its thorns are so strong and large that it could not have been woven into a wreath. Probably some thorny shrub is meant; possibly, and we think quite likely, it may be the Arabian *nubk*, whose round branches are flexible and pliant, and can easily be woven into a crown and whose sharp thorns inflict painful wounds. In color this resembles the triumphant ivy-wreath; and that would add to its ironical purpose.

For us there remains a crown of glory which, unlike that of the winner of the race, fadeth not away. Our race may endure for a long time, but at the end, if we keep our eyes fixed upon the goal, which is heaven, we shall receive the crown of life which the Lord hath promised to those who love him.

"Be thou faithful unto death, and I will give thee a crown of life."

WHAT IS REST?

IN a book of Persian tales there is a beautiful legend about Rabbi Judah and his brethren, who, as the seven pillars of wisdom, sat one day in the Court of the Temple at Jerusalem disputing about rest. One said that it was to have attained sufficient flocks and herds, yet without sin. The second, that it was fame and praise of all men. The third, that it was possession of power to rule the state. The fourth, that it consisted only in a happy home. The fifth, that it must be in the old age of one who is rich, powerful, famous, surrounded by children and children's children. The sixth said that all were vain unless a man keep the ritual law of Moses. And Rabbi Judah, the venerable, the tallest of the brothers, said, "Ye have all spoken wisely, but one thing more is necessary. He only can find rest who to all things addeth this: that he keepeth the tradition of the elders."

There sat in the Court a fair-haired boy, playing with some lilies in his lap, and, hearing the talk, he dropped them with astonishment from his hands, and looking up said, "Nay, nay, fathers: he only findeth rest who loveth his brother as himself, and God with his whole heart and soul. He is greater than fame, and wealth, and power; happier than a happy home, happy without it, better than honored age; he is a law to himself, and above tradition." The doctors were astonished. They said: "When Christ cometh, shall he tell us greater things?" And they thanked God, for they said: "The old men are not always wise, yet God be praised that out of the mouth of this little one has his praise become perfect."

"MY PRESENCE SHALL GO WITH THEE."

WHAT a comfort this is! No burden is too heavy if we are thus favored. No disciplinary tests will fail to produce their intended benefit. No schemes of evil, though formed against us with consummate skill, will succeed. More than this, God's presence with His people is an infallible sign of the truth of religion.

The outpouring of the Holy Spirit upon a church is, for this reason, the most effectual means of exterminating all forms of infidelity and vice in the community. Moses said, "Wherein shall it be known here that I and thy people have found grace in thy sight? is it not in that thou goest with us?"

How are we to live so that this benign, invisible presence will evermore be our portion? This question has but one answer, namely, the voluntary and habitual exercise of believing prayer. The Psalmist said, "I have set the Lord always before me: because He is at my right hand, I shall not be moved."

PLANNING AND DOING.

EVERY ONE knows there is a very wide difference between planning and doing, but how few gain practical wisdom from the knowledge! One rises in the morning after a night of refreshing sleep, and in the fresh vigor gained from the rest makes great plans that are to be carried out before the shades of night gather once more over him. Yesterday just as many plans were made, just as great things were to be accomplished, but then—ah! but they were not done. The plans of to-day will be just as ill-matured, and those of to-morrow will follow in like manner.

The young are ever hopeful; they sneer at the idea that they may be unable to do great things. What if they had thought to accomplish more than was possible; life is long and life is gay, and to-morrow will do just as well; the blossoms of to-day fall, but the buds will be blossoms to-morrow, and perhaps far more beautiful; and if they do not bloom with to-morrow's sun there is the next day, and time enough. Hope may not be quite so reckless in middle age, but hope still lives. The farmer plants his seed to-day to reap it in one of the to-morrows, and he does it. The merchant, the man of business, the head of the house—they are all alike, sowing to reap, over and over again.

It is pretty much the same with the Christian. He sees a little corner of the Lord's vineyard that needs to be cultivated, and he says in God's name that he will do it; but does he *do* it—does he not plan without performing? Was not his plan formed in an idle, careless way, without feeling the great wrong of which he is guilty in not doing all he can to pay the vows he has made? Do we realize what we are doing when we deal thus with the dear Lord who is so patient with us, when we promise so much and perform so little?

After the heyday of life comes old age, and how different all is then! The days become so short, the noon-day sun comes so soon after the dew of morning, and in the twinkling of an eye the evening stars are shining. There is less planning and more doing then, but the "keepers of the house" begin to tremble, the grasshopper is a burden, and the "years draw nigh when thou shalt say, I have no pleasure in them." How we shall regret if we have then been only hearers and not doers of the Word. Lost opportunities will then rise up before the mental vision, and on how many possibilities to do God's will the door will have been shut! If we have been up and doing it will be only a blessed waiting.

> " Only waiting till the reapers
>   Have the last sheaf gathered home;
> For the summer-time has faded,
>   And the autumn winds have come.
> Quickly, reapers! gather quickly,
>   All the ripe hours of my heart;
> For the bloom of life is withered,
>   And I hasten to depart."

NOT OUR OWN.

AN Eastern allegory runs thus: A merchant, going abroad for a time, gave respectively to two of his friends two sacks of wheat each, to take care of against his return. Years passed: he came back, and applied for them again. The first took him into his storehouse and showed them to him; but they were mildewed and worthless. The other led him out into the open country, and pointed out field after field of waving corn, the produce of the two sacks given him.

How frequently striking contrasts similar to the above are presented to our view! Two who have started out with equal abilities, one content to let his talents lie idle, the other resolved to produce as large a harvest as possible; one, after years, can show over his barren talents "nothing but leaves;" the other with glowing gratitude can point to ripened grain and luscious fruit, and can look forward to the appreciative words of commendation, "Well done, thou good and faithful servant."

It is a common mistake for people who have but one talent to think that, because they only have one, they are justified in folding it in a napkin. If only one, we are required to cultivate it, and it often brings forth fruit a thousandfold. It is not the number but the use of talents that fills the world with blessing. From a single dollar actively employed princely fortunes have sprung. The feeble shout of a tiny child has saved the thundering train from wreck, and snatched a hundred souls from death. In all lands the widows' mites have filled God's treasuries. He who will do nothing until he can do a great thing will never do anything. Krummacher tells of a countryman, the owner of great estates, noted for his wisdom and prudence, who was obliged to go on a journey for several months. He called his son, and gave him charge of all till his return. The youth was dismayed at the task, but his father bade him farewell and departed. The youth undertook the work with much fear, but took courage and said, "My father hath confided it to me; therefore I must fulfil my work." So he wrought vigorously and improved greatly. After many months the father returned and found the estates, the flocks and herds all in good order; and the fame of his son spread through all the country. Then the father praised the good management of his son. The son said, "But, my father, what if I had had ill success?" The father smiled and said, "I knew your abilities, but you did not know them. I wished to give you self-reliance; therefore I demanded a great thing of you. You were a youth; but now you have become a man."

Our Father has demanded great things of us. Better than any human friend he knows our abilities, and will judge accordingly. He has given them to us to be used, and we are to remember that we are not only to enjoy our own talents but see that they are used for others.

> "Talents are seeds by heaven's good gift bestowed
> To render back their incense unto God.
> Talents are deeds to do, or duties done,
> Whate'er their number be, five, two, or one
> As is their use, so is their worth;
> As is the impulse given
> They wither here upon the earth,
> Or ripen here for heaven."

RESTRAINING GRACE.

WE know not how sinful we might be, what wicked crimes we might commit, but for the grace of God restraining us. But we sometimes seem to forget this; we look about us and see misery, oftentimes the result of wrong-doing as well as of ignorance, and read daily of crimes too horrible to be mentioned; feelings of pity sometimes mingle with the sense of justice in the punishment of the criminal; but how many of us ever realize why it is that we differ from the very worst, and who has made us to differ; or that we might be as bad as any, except for God's restraining grace?

In the earlier history of the Bible we read that the Lord himself appeared to one man, who was about to commit a great crime, and said, "I also withheld thee from sinning against me;" and we may call to mind many instances where God's people were prevented, in a remarkable manner, from doing what would have been harmful and sinful, as well as led to do that which was right.

In the New Testament our Saviour said to his impetuous, erring, wilful disciple: "Simon, Simon, behold, Satan hath desired to have you, that he may sift you as wheat;

but I have prayed for thee, that thy faith fail not." This is perhaps one of the chief arguments in favor of a special Providence, which so many in this day seem to ignore, and even pretend to disbelieve—an overruling, guiding Hand, which not only leads us in the right path, but puts hindrances in the way to prevent us from doing the wrong thing.

To the earnest reader of the Bible no other argument is needed; its pages are full of special providences, and it is a comforting thought that we may ask for, and expect not only to have grace and strength for daily duties and trials, but deliverance from evil; and even with the temptations that must assail us, there will be provided a way of escape, so that we may be kept from sinning against God. "But for all this, I will be inquired of, saith the Lord;" so let us see to it that we seek the Divine guidance and grace, and then if we are withheld from sin, and there is any good thing in us, let us give God the glory, and say with Paul: "By the grace of God I am what I am."

UNDER SEALED ORDERS.

A GOVERNMENT vessel was about to leave the dock, to sail away for some unknown port. No one knew her destination, whether it was to be near by or far away. Those who had loved ones on board felt sad and anxious. Were these loved ones to be within reach of cheering words, of letters full of love and encouragement, or were they to be sent afar to some foreign port from which no word would come in weary weeks and months? This question could be asked many and many a time, but there was no echo to the words, no answer to be had. The ship was to sail under sealed orders; orders from the Navy Department, sealed by the Government seal that could not be opened until it was far out at sea, and away from all possible communication with the land.

The Captain of our salvation sends us away on sealed instructions. Whither? You do not need to know. You might not like your destination; you might object to the buffeting waves; the billows of trouble might threaten to wreck your soul; the harbor might be hard to reach and the rocks of danger might lie between you and it. Do you care? Does it matter to you if the passage is a stormy one when you know that safety is at the end? that the Father is at the helm, and that he neither slumbers nor sleeps? Therefore take courage, and whether you find yourself in storm or sunshine, by day or by night, go forth boldly under "sealed orders." Let the peace of God that passeth understanding abide with you, and rest confidently in the full assurance that God knows and cares for his own.

WAITING ON THE LORD.

ARE you praying to-day, Christian reader, for the conversion of the world and the well-being of your own soul, and do you believe that prayer will be answered? Then you must not rest in your belief after a few feeble petitions, but follow always, day and night, the command of the Psalmist: "Wait on the Lord: be of good courage, and he shall strengthen thy heart: wait, I say, on the Lord." It will not do simply to pray occasionally, once a day or once a week, whenever you think of it. You must be waiting on the Lord with your soul full of importunate pleading, hour after hour, day after day, for weeks and months if the Lord see fit to tarry so long.

What if Jacob had put forth his strength but for a little against his unknown antagonist and then given up conquered instead of wrestling all night by the brook-side? What if, even at break of day, he had granted the petition, "Let me go," without further request? He would not have gained the blessing, would not have had power with God and prevailed. So neither will you unless you go and do likewise.

Even Jesus Christ, who at the grave of Lazarus prayed to his Father, "I know that thou hearest me always," was wont to spend whole nights alone in prayer. Is there hope of your prayer obtaining readier answer than those of the Son of God himself, who even in the agony of the garden called again and again upon a Father's sympathetic heart before the ministering angel came?

What are we that we do not need to say with David: "O my God, I cry in the day-time, and in the night season I am not silent"? And what is the testimony of those unto whom God hath granted gracious answer? Is it not that the burden of prayer was never lifted from their souls day or night until the hearer himself gave them their heart's desire? Therefore, "Wait, I say, on the Lord," for "whatsoever ye shall ask in faith, believing, that shall ye receive."

NEITHER COLD NOR HOT.

HOW many persons there are in the world who are of an undecided character—that is, without firmness or stability of purpose, vacillating here and there, blown about with every wind of doctrine, now on one side, now on another, advancing opinions one day only to correct them on the next, never knowing what they do or do not want, and bothering every one who does. The world never knows where to find them, and worse yet, the church never knows where to find them. Is any one willing that such a verdict be uttered against him?

Laodicea was a large and wealthy city of Asia Minor. It was known by another name until, having been greatly enlarged by Antiochus II., it was called after his wife, Laodice. The soil was fertile and there was much wealth among the people. The ruins of a great amphitheatre, one thousand feet in extent, with many of the seats still remaining, have been found by recent travellers; but to-day all is still as the grave, and not an inhabitant remains to tell of the once opulent city. No sound of the flocks of sheep is heard there; only traces can be found of the city walls; and the fragments of pedestals and the remains of numerous seats rising one above the other, are all that tell of luxurious theatres where the people were amused.

Yet in Laodicea was once established a Christian church, to which Paul addressed some of his letters: and it was one of the seven churches to which special messages were sent by Christ after his ascension. In Rev. iii. 15, 16 we read these fearful words: "I know thy works, that thou art neither cold nor hot: I would thou wert cold or hot. So then because thou art lukewarm, and neither cold nor hot, I will spew thee out of my mouth."

How is it with us? Are our souls burning within us as Christ talks with us by the way? Are we up and doing in the service of God? Have we taken to ourselves the "whole armor of God: with our loins girt about with truth, and having on the breastplate of righteousness, our feet shod with the preparation of the Gospel of peace: having the shield of faith, the helmet of salvation, the sword of the spirit, which is the Word of God: and praying always to make known the mystery of the Gospel"? Or are we like the Laodiceans, "neither cold nor hot," not to be depended upon, good for nothing in the work of the Lord? Let us be careful lest coming suddenly he find us sleeping at our post, with lamps untrimmed, and ourselves unprepared to go in to the marriage supper.

GOD'S LAWS INFLEXIBLE.

HARD and severe, men call them, and chafe at their restraints and seek to free themselves from their restrictions. But did you ever stop to realize that the very existence of the world itself depends upon these laws? The whole universe is under law, every particle of it is bound as by an iron fetter, and no device of man can for an instant free it from its pressure. Law is the world's existence. By blind obedience only the globe keeps its place, and is clad with such grace and beauty.

In the vegetable kingdom all transmission of life is according to God's original enactment that every herb and tree should bring forth seed after its kind; accordingly like produces like, and this law reigns supreme over all vegetation. The stupendous changes which have taken place since creation have not weakened this law one whit. The cedar and the oak of to-day are the cedar and oak of long ago; neither in form or development or color or fibre are they materially changed. The odors which greet us in spring-time are from the same flowers which perfumed the garden where man walked in innocence with his Creator. The thorns and thistles with which God cursed the land are the thorns and thistles which to-day encroach upon our gardens. Each plant produces its like seed after its kind. The law of the harvest is immutable; that which is sown is that which shall be reaped, and for this we ought to be thankful, for it is a beneficent provision of God, and implicit obedience to it is the only hope of creation. Law must close its iron hand around every seed that is planted, or all is confusion and uncertainty.

Gravitation is a law—that mysterious force by which all matter attracts and is attracted. The whole universe is under that law. Ever since chaos fled from the mighty moorings of the Eternal Spirit, every plant has swung in its ceaseless orbit, and every dew-drop has sought the bosom of the flower under the resistless rule of this law. This was the original law of formation from the plant to the drop of dew. Those majestic worlds and ours were rounded into spheres, in systems and in clusters, by this one law. The mountains rose up on their foundations, the sea fled to its level, brooks and rivers started towards the ocean, the dry land smiled in beauty after its baptism, the dew-drop assumed its tiny sphere, the man was placed upon the earth to walk upright in the image of God. Neither then nor since has any atom ceased to obey, and obedience to that law of God is our only safety; it stands between a living universe and the gulf of annihilation.

The moral law is as much God's law as any of these natural ones. If there are any degrees the argument becomes stronger in the spiritual than in the natural world. If God vindicates his natural laws, how much more shall he vindicate the laws which make up his moral administration! If God says sin shall be punished, we may be sure it will be, just as sure as that any natural law will be fulfilled. Some people say that God is too merciful to punish sin. Did the fire ever cease to burn because a saintly martyr was in its grasp? No, because it is the law of fire to burn, and it is executed on saint and fiend alike. God is merciful, but it is under immutable ordinances.

The laws which hold the universe together must be upheld, and the moral laws are equally important. In temporal things it certainly matters greatly whether men attempt to gather grapes from thorns or figs from thistles, but does it matter less in spiritual things what the harvest of men's actions shall be?

God's laws are no insignificant things to be broken with impunity. They are immutable, adamantine ordinances, set to guard all great and universal interests, lifting themselves up as impassable barriers between sin and holiness, and as long as God reigns they will never be relaxed in one tittle of their righteous requirements, nor fail one jot of their full vindication.

GRACE WILL TELL.

THERE is an old saying that "blood will tell." Put a nobleman, reared and educated to his position, into rags and a home of poverty, yet in some way the mark of rank will betray itself. And, *vice versa*, dress the rude and untaught beggar in royal purple and send him to court, and out through kingly vestment and princely surroundings will stand the unconcealed character, lacking and faulty at every turn.

A man elderly, bent, and having the appearance of one hampered by narrow means, entered the prayer-meeting one evening. He was a stranger to all present, and one of the deacons who noticed the odd figure on the back seat wondered vaguely whether his devotional attitude was induced by fatigue or due reverence for the time and place. But during a somewhat protracted pause which occurred during the service, the stranger slowly shambled to his feet and essayed to offer prayer; and before he had said "Amen," all the people in the vestry knew that the man who had just prayed in their hearing was the son of a King, the man who like Prince Abraham of old "walked with God." For the grace that dwelt in the lowly Christian's heart was unhampered and unchecked by his temporal condition, and the minister wished that the voice of the poorly dressed stranger with the bent form and napless coat could often be heard in their meetings of prayer.

Sometimes the life of the Christian seems crusted over

with worldly cares and ambitious desires. But ever so slight a touch of the Master's hand will rouse the slumbering spirit of grace yet dwelling in the heart. Only see to it that it is *there*. Make sure that grace, the religion of Christ, is implanted in the soul, and it will be sure to manifest itself. If grace dwells within us, grace perfected, even the salvation of the soul is assured us. And it will tell in some way in the life we live. That which finds lodgment in the heart must influence the words and deeds, not only our own, but of those with whom we associate. We are only blessed when the light or grace within us so shines that others, seeing our good works, will be led to glorify our Father who is in heaven.

TAKE NEAR VIEWS.

TO the Christian the first years of his life are spent in looking ahead; the last in taking nearer views. He trusts in God, puts himself under entire subjection to the Divine will, desires to know no other, prays for daily bread, to be led step by step, and never for an instant doubts that for one meal and for one step he is trusting the dear Lord to care for him. In youth he keeps an eye upon the far-away future, planning for the days that have not yet dawned, taking thought for the morrow that may never come, and although feeling that everything is in subjection to what God wills, forgetting the little French proverb, *L'homme propose, mais Dieu dispose* ("man proposes but God disposes"), he goes on drawing plans for farms and store-houses that are to hold the grain that may never be cradled, and setting up looms that may never hold warp and woof of any fabric, and casting the wheels that may never be needed to run the engine.

In the vineyard of the Lord each of his dear children has his portion of work; and according to his work so his reward shall be. "Do men gather grapes of thorns or figs of thistles? Even so every good tree bringeth forth good fruit." If you raise thorns and thistles no good reward can come to you. In this light we can all judge ourselves by ourselves; holding ourselves and our work in the light that God gives, and proving it to be of the kind that shall bring forth good fruit to the glory of the Father.

But after a while, when we grow weary of making plans that we can never carry out, we begin to take short views. We can never count with any certainty beyond the present moment; we all have a to-day, but who has a to-morrow? We do not any longer make plans far ahead, for by experience we have learned how very useless it is to do so. Even if the clouds in our horizon are dark and lowering, even if we are beset round about by an impenetrable hedge of seeming impossibilities, at God's time, if we ask for help, the clouds part and the sun shines through, a way is opened in the hedge and we rejoice.

We have learned not to carry to-day the burdens of to-morrow, to cross in imagination any bridges until we come to them, for we might be like the couple who quarrelled while walking fourteen miles as to how they were to cross a certain bridge, and when they came to it the waters were dried up and they went over on dry ground. It is good to take note of Abraham Lincoln's reply to a discouraged friend: "My rule through life has been never to cross the Great Bigmuddy Creek till I came to it."

And when we have learned to take these near views, when we can just thank the dear Lord for the care of yesterday, for the blessings of to-day, and fully trust him to show us the same goodness for to-morrow, then and then only can we cry out with the Psalmist: "Every day will I bless thee; and I will praise thy name for ever and ever."

THE BRANCH AND THE VINE.

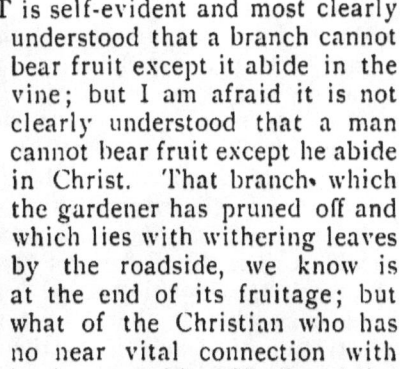

IT is self-evident and most clearly understood that a branch cannot bear fruit except it abide in the vine; but I am afraid it is not clearly understood that a man cannot bear fruit except he abide in Christ. That branch which the gardener has pruned off and which lies with withering leaves by the roadside, we know is at the end of its fruitage; but what of the Christian who has no near vital connection with Christ, who has cast himself off and lies at a distance from his Saviour? Christ says it is no worse with the vine than with the man. "As the branch cannot bear fruit of itself except it abide in the vine, no more can ye except ye abide in me."

It is the Christian's great duty to bear fruit to the glory of God. Next to the salvation of his own soul comes the fruitage. No one is translated to heaven as soon as he obtains a title-deed to the blood-bought inheritance. We are to remain here in a state of pupilage, that we may be prepared and trained for the upper kingdom; and not for that end alone, but that we may be lights to the world, that we may finish the work God has given us to do, and that we may glorify God in our bodies and spirits, which are his. Do we realize as we ought that this work only begins when our souls are saved; that we must show our faith by our works? The Epistle of James, the epistle of straw as it was at first called, which narrowly escaped being thrown out of the New Testament canon as a forgery, as a contradiction of Divine teaching, was preserved by Almighty wisdom for a high use. James says: "Thou hast faith and I have works. Show me thy faith without thy works, and I will show thee my faith by my works." It is a fair challenge, and while we have never come to place works on an equality with faith, or trust in works to save us, yet we have come to see that faith cannot be shown without works. It is dead then. It is like a vine cut off from the branch without vitality enough to put forth a single twig or fruit.

If anything can keep our modern civilization from paralysis, it is this Epistle of James, for it gives the kind of preaching which is needed. Faith will produce some kind of works; if there be none, faith is dead. The illustration of such a life is that mutilated branch separated from the parent tree.

It is as evidently then the Christian's duty as it is the vine's function to bear fruit. It is worth noting too, that the way to bear fruit is plainly implied. Fruit-bearing and abiding in Christ are inseparably connected; the exhortation to the one is the exhortation to the other; they cannot be separated. We have various duties to perform, and their faithful performance constitutes fruitfulness. Now, what is the best way of doing all these things? Shall we fix our attention upon each one separately as it devolves upon us? Shall we undertake them as so many duties that must be done at such times? That is one way to do, but there is danger in that way of being cumbered about much serving. There is danger of duty becoming a task and a bugbear, something to be dreaded, and from which we would escape if we could. There is danger of many duties making life a burden instead of a joy, for really such a spirit is an attempt to bear fruit of oneself. Now, instead of that, suppose we commence further back and further in. Suppose we reach for an inspiration which will assist in any duty, whatever it may be, and all duties, no matter how many. Assuredly that would be the better way, and that is what the Saviour wants us to do. Abiding in Christ is the secret of constant, spontaneous, increasing doing of duties which glorify God—of fruit-bearing.

The term abiding in Christ means an intimate communion with him. In a spiritual sense we are to make Christ

the abode of our souls, to identify ourselves with him. As some one has truly said, the command is not abide *with* me, abide *near* me, abide *under* me, but abide *in* me. The fruit-bearing branch is not merely in the same place with the vine, nor under its shadow simply; it is in it and abides in it. One life flows through both, the life of the vine. So when our Lord says abide in me, it is as if he said, "Think as I think, feel as I feel, will as I will, choose as I choose, and let my views of all objects and all events be yours because they are mine. Let my wisdom be your wisdom, my strength your strength." It is impossible to express in words the fulness of meaning, but there is no obscurity in the figure. The branch united, clinging to, and dependent upon the vine; the impossibility of marking where one ends and another begins, the community of life in both, marks a union inexpressible fully in words, but as intimate as it is precious.

The life thus prescribed is constant. Neither the natural nor the spiritual life of any one was ever meant to be uncertain. What is there to make us one thing to-day and another thing to-morrow, except in the way of growth and progression? We ought to be different from ourselves at one time and another only because we are better every day we live. Constancy is not, however, a characteristic of the lives of most Christians. We often see a great life shooting out hither and thither, and making great apparent growth, which yet knows nothing of patient endurance. It depends upon excitement and impulse only. When these die out it seems to die too. We look for it to accomplish great things and bring forth fruit an hundredfold, but we look in vain. When we expect to hear of the good works of the promising Christian, we find only the melancholy history written by the Apostle, "Demas hath forsaken me." Unstable as water, such a life cannot excel. It is worth while to inquire if there be not a counterfeit of true grace which exhibits even greater vitality than the real, and puts out of countenance the steady, modest, silent working of true piety, but which has none of its constancy.

The growth of the soul is little by little, but unceasing; every day finds some addition to its life. It is ever producing the fruits of the Spirit, love and joy, and

THE BRANCH AND THE VINE.

peace. The fruit is ever coming nearer and nearer to perfection, the growth of the branch is steadily approaching the symmetry and stability of the vine. The true Christian is day by day reaching forward unto the image of Christ until he arrives at the stature of a perfect man. The reality of this life may be measured by its earnestness to grow, its consciousness of present deficiency, its hungering and thirsting after more of all that belongs to the believers of God. We have no right to expect religion to be born at its maturity, for then all that remains is for it to become more infirm and less animated. But we have a right to expect progression from a weak state to a strong one. First comes the blade, then the ear, then the full corn in the ear. So does true religion grow in the heart and life. In that progress we become more pure in heart, more humble in spirit, less selfish in aim, more benevolent toward others. By faith let us enter into him as a dwelling-place of our hearts and minds. Seek that he may dwell in us, so that being rooted and grounded in him we may be branches of the true vine.

SELF-DENIAL.

SELF-DENIAL, for the sake of self-denial, does no good; self-sacrifice for its own sake is no religious act at all. If you give up a meal for the sake of showing power over self, or for the sake of self-discipline, you are not more religious than before. This is mere self-culture, which being occupied forever about self, leaves you only in that circle of self from which religion is to free you; but to give up a meal that one you love may have it, is properly a religious act—no hard and dismal duty, because made easy by affection. To bear pain for the sake of bearing it has no moral quality at all. But to bear it rather than surrender truth, or in order to save another, is positive enjoyment, as well as ennobling to the soul.

Did you ever receive even a blow meant for another in order to shield that other? Do you not know that there was actual pleasure in that keen pain far beyond the most rapturous thrill of nerve which could be gained from pleasure in the midst of painlessness? Is not the mystic yearning of love expressed in words most purely thus: Let me suffer for him? This element of love is that which makes this doctrine an intelligible and a blessed truth. Sacrifice alone, bare and unrelieved, is ghastly, unnatural, and dead; but self-sacrifice, illuminated by love, is warmth and life; it is the death of Christ, the life of God, the blessedness and only proper life of man.

AMBITION FOR GREATNESS.

WE have plenty of evidence in the Gospels that several of the Apostles possessed an ambition for personal greatness. Prominent among them were James and John, the sons of Zebedee and Salome. These young men were bright, talented, and zealous. They were full of push and pluck, and entertained high opinions of their Master and the kingdom which he came to found. Sparkling with the thought that eminent positions in the new kingdom, occupied by themselves, would afford them a wide range of influence and confer upon them the appellation of "great men," they sought, through their pleasing mother, to have Christ grant them the highest seats of distinction and honor which could be created for them. But their "application" was summarily rejected, and a very timely and wholesome lesson was imparted, which doubtless gave them a very different view of greatness from that they had entertained. Yet, it may be observed, Christ did not give a rebuke against the indulgence of a desire to become truly great. Nor did he ever say anything which can be properly construed against the exercise and cultivation of personal ambition of the right kind. There is a certain kind of ambition which is praiseworthy. It is one of the fundamental features and characteristics of true manhood and true womanhood. Strip a man of his ambition and he is robbed of one of the noblest elements of his nature. Destroy that, and the mainspring of a man's energy is broken; he lies before you little better than a wrecked machine. It would be a sad derangement of all that is promising and progressive in man. When God created man, he designed that he should be ambitious. In Pope's "Essay on Man," he asks this question:

> "Who knows but He, whose hand the lightning forms,
> Who heaves old ocean, and who wings the storms,
> Pours fierce ambition in a Cæsar's mind?"

Willis, in a poem read at Yale College over fifty years ago, gave this inspiring sentiment:

> "Press on! for it is God-like to unloose
> The spirit, and forget yourself in thought.
> Bending a pinion for the deeper sky,
> And, in the very fetters of your flesh,
> Mating with the pure essences of heaven!
> Press on!—' for in the grave there is no work
> And no device.' Press on, while yet you may!'"

But a greater man than Willis, even the ambitious Paul, said: "I press toward the mark for the prize of the high calling of God." And there never was a more ambitious man than Paul. The fires of a lofty ambition burned in his bosom, and they bore him onward with resistless energy. In one place, according to the revised version (including the marginal note), he says: "We are ambitious, whether at home or absent, to be well pleasing to him." In two other places in Paul's writings the word "ambitious" is used, showing that the Apostle was energized with a mighty and masterful ambition. And let us remember that if men were not truly ambitious, they never would become truly great. Hence it follows that there should be a healthful encouragement and cultivation of one's ambition in the right channels, that we may attain unto a greatness which is bounded by modesty, truth, and principle. God has no pleasure in an ambitionless man. He tells the sluggard to go to the ant and consider her ways. A marked feature in Christ's dealings with men was his constantly urging them to make the most of themselves. He wanted them to be something more than mere ciphers in society. There were many who did not count in the scale of social and moral influence. They were mere stumbling-blocks in the way of the world's true progress. Christ endeavored to inspire these and others with thoughts and purposes which would lead them out into various fields of noble service, and thus make them ambitious to enter the path of true greatness.

"JUST ONCE."

THE temptation to step aside "just once" from the narrow way comes not infrequently to the young Christian. If Satan can but gain our consent to one departure, he knows that succeeding steps in the wrong direction will easily follow. The following extract from the recently published life of Dr. Judson, by his son, may come as a timely word to some tempted and hesitating soul: "A native Christian woman told me that she was about to engage in something which Dr. Judson considered not conducive to her spiritual good. He sent for her and remonstrated; but she would not give up her darling project. 'Look here!' said he, eagerly, snatching a ruler from the table, and tracing out a very straight line upon the floor; 'here is where you have been walking. You have made a crooked track, to be sure; out of the path half the time; but then you have kept near it, and not taken to new roads, and you have—not so much as you might have done, mind, but still to a certain extent—grown in grace; and now, with all this growth upon your heart and head, in the maturity of your years, with ripened understanding and an every-day deepening sense of the goodness of God—here,' bringing down the ruler with emphasis to indicate a certain position, 'here you stand. You know where this path leads. You know what is before you. Some struggles, some honors, and finally eternal life and a crown of glory. But to the left branches off another very pleasant road, and along the air floats, rather temptingly, a pretty bauble. You do not mean to leave the path you have walked in fifteen years—fifteen long years—altogether; you only want to step aside and catch the bauble, and think you will come back again; but you never will. Think! Dare you deliberately leave this straight and narrow path, drawn by the Saviour's finger, and go away for one moment into that of your enemy? Will you? *Will you?* WILL YOU?' 'I have made a great many crooked tracks since,' she added, tearfully, 'but whenever I am unusually tempted I see the teacher as he looked that day, bending over in his chair, the ruler placed upon the floor to represent me, his finger pointing along the path of eternal life; his eye looking so strangely over his shoulder, and that terrible "Will you?" coming from his lips as though it was the voice of God; and I pray for help, just as Peter did of old.'"

COMMON SENSE IN RELIGION.

IF there is anything more than another that is needed to pervade our lives, our thoughts, our actions, it is common sense. It is needful in the home, the office, the shop, the factory, in fact in every grade of life, and not less in our religion. Every man and woman needs it; and while all cannot be giants in intellect, all cannot attain to the pinnacles of earthly splendor, every one can, whether in the palace or the hut, lay claim to a live necessity for *common sense*. It is a balance-wheel in every emergency.

A necessity arises, something must be brought to a definite point at once, and while some are dallying, wringing their hands, and crying out to know what is best to be done, he who is possessed of common sense is alert, seizes the opportunity to act, and danger is averted, success is achieved. How many times in every one's life are mistakes avoided, blunders shunned, and the point of vantage gained by using common sense. Try it, and see if it is not the very best possible way to get along. Do not creep behind some one else; do not shirk your own decisions, but stand up bravely upon your own ship, and with the wheel of common sense to guide the helm you will be brought to a safe harbor.

"JESUS OF NAZARETH PASSETH BY."

SINNER, know you that the time is coming when, in your great fear and anguish and bewilderment, you will hide yourself in the dens and in the rocks of the mountains, and say to the mountains and rocks, "Fall on us and hide us from the face of him that sitteth on the throne, and from the wrath of the Lamb," unless the "Great Physician," who is now passing by, stop and heal you of your malady, put a white robe upon you, and write his Father's name upon your forehead?

And who is this Great Physician? Jesus of Nazareth! And he is now passing by—it may be, never to return. He alone, of all that are in the heavens, or under the heavens, can save you from the wrath to come. Oh! call upon him, as did blind Bartimæus of old, "Jesus, thou Son of David, have mercy on me!" Heed not the world and the devil when they charge thee to hold thy peace, but "cry the more a great deal," "Jesus, thou Son of David, have mercy on me!"

And he will hear thee—will stop. With infinite condescension and love unbounded, he will notice and call to you: "What wilt thou that I should do unto thee?" Then fall at his feet, and say, "Lord, that I might be made clean;" and he will put forth his hand and say, "I will; be thou clean;" and from that moment thy sins are forgiven thee.

JESUS OF NAZARETH PASSETH BY

THE REAL SOURCE OF POWER.

IGHT from on high can light up the darkest and most rugged of places. At rare times many of us have our mounts of vision and our moments of surprising others with pictures of the glories of our spiritual landscape; but what we need to-day in our Christian experience is the equanimity of conscious and constantly indwelling power. How shall we gain this power? Tons of religious manuscript have been written, and thousands of voices have been engaged in prayer and in argument, much of it, alas! profitless, because there was not a wise recognition of the elements of spiritual power.

It is surely singular when we can have the real power that we take its semblance instead. We only half believe, and thus we never convince. What we want first is to surrender ourselves to the simple close-at-hand truths of the Gospel. Half-surrender people are without deep conviction, and therefore without power.

Paul's power came through his convictions; all of the apostles who have since the foundation of the world lifted the flaming torch of truth to light the path of bewildered wayfarers, have held the never-dying flame within their own souls.

ASK AND YE SHALL RECEIVE.

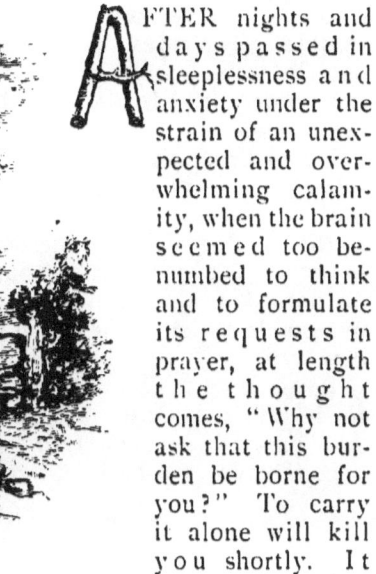

AFTER nights and days passed in sleeplessness and anxiety under the strain of an unexpected and overwhelming calamity, when the brain seemed too benumbed to think and to formulate its requests in prayer, at length the thought comes, "Why not ask that this burden be borne for you?" To carry it alone will kill you shortly. It might have been even worse than it is. Thank God that it is not, and ask him to carry it for you. And with the very uplifting of the heart, there will come relief. All things whatsoever ye shall ask in his name, believing, ye shall receive. All things. Is anything too much to ask, or is anything too great for God to give?

Asking from our fellow-men is a different matter. We may get our requests granted, and we may meet with a more or less courteous or even discourteous refusal. We have to trust much to the temper and disposition of the person from whom we ask the favor we desire. But with God it is a different matter. He needs not to be approached with caution, or even with any hesitancy. We can bring our requests timidly or boldly. He understands our desires, and will give us the proper answer to our requests. Let us therefore come boldly to the throne of grace, and look for help in every time of trouble. The cares and trials of life are many. We see not the way clearly before us. By prayer shall we get the burdens of life lifted and light shed upon the darkness around us.

Most Christians could multiply instances in which answers to prayers have been signal and significant. We may not always clearly see the way in which we are led, even in the gaining of our requests, but most certainly we are led, and that by a Father's hand. We get much that we do not ask for. We are in daily receipt of blessings innumerable which come to us like the sunlight and the dew.

But much else certainly does come to us because we pray for it. If we seek we do find. If we ask we do receive. And past experiences strengthen our faith. If we have once received we shall yet again find mercy, for

"He who hath led will lead;
He who hath fed will feed."

Yea, even unto the end of the journey the rugged places shall be made smooth unto our feet, and the bread and water upon our way shall be sure. By asking much shall we do much, for the Lord shall increase our strength if we be of willing mind, and opportunities will open on every hand to him who seeks to do good. And the difference between asking much and asking little shall make the difference in our lives, whether they be meagre or full of blessings to ourselves and others. At the Fulton Street Prayer-meeting which I attended lately, a gentleman arose and said that he always made it a habit to go to God *first*, that God might sometimes send him to others, but that he never applied to any one without first laying his case before God, who would invariably direct his footsteps. If this were always the rule of our lives, how much of suffering we might oftentimes save both ourselves and others. Ask indeed we must, but first let us ask of God. If he directs us to human help, well and good. If not, his plans and ways are devious, and in him will we trust, securely resting on his promise, "Ask and ye shall receive."

INDIVIDUAL RESPONSIBILITY.

GOD does not regard men in the mass, though there are some who seem to think that he is so great as to overlook the individual in his care for the aggregate. But there is an infinity of littleness which does more to illustrate and exalt the power of God than the infinity of greatness. Any being with an arm strong enough could chisel the mountains, any one with a hand large enough could hold the ocean; but it is not the strong arm alone nor the great hand alone which could fashion an insect or paint a flower. He who does both must combine delicacy the most wonderful with power the most mighty, and such is our God. It is as individual persons that God always has and always will regard men, not as a mass. As long as we can pluck in the wildest glades of the mountains a flower that is as perfect in all its parts as the mountain itself, we may know that God cares for individuals.

What is an individual? Very different certainly from a creation of circumstances. However powerful our environment may be, it is not omnipotent; yet we often fall into an error of judgment about this. We say we do not see how a man can help being just what he is; it is only what might have been expected under the circumstances. But why might this have been expected? Only because the person is weak, not because the circumstances are strong. There is never a sin we fall into but we might have escaped it. There is never a temptation into which we fall but we see afterward how we might have resisted it. It has been our own fault, and no plea of the power of circumstances will avail with the God who sees us as individuals. We have a will given to us, active and indomitable, which can override even the most adverse circumstances and make them stepping-stones in the heavenly race. No person is in any sense a creature of chance, but is rather the sum total of causes which he himself has set in motion, the resultant of forces which he has held in his hand all his life. We all make ourselves. Great orators, great statesmen, scholars, or poets are self-made men; but so also is a great drunkard or a great fool. We have had opportunities, we have held clues in our hands, we have made discoveries, we have had strength; whether we have used these things and profited by them or not, we are self-made. If we look into the past we can see just what amount of good or evil we have extracted from everything, and how we have thereby been making ourselves. We are individually responsible for what we make of ourselves, and God will so judge us.

DOING HEARTILY.

IT is one thing to hear, but quite another thing to do. Jesus knew how easy it was to make one thing stand for the other, and that his disciples might not make such a mistake, he charged them to be doers and not hearers only. The dear Lord calls to us, and we answer, "Speak, Lord," and then words of gracious love are told us, words of hope, and joy, and comfort. We are called children, the children of a Father who knows just what is best for each one of us; just how much discipline is necessary to fit us for the kingdom; just how many trials are needed to bring us to the foot of the cross; just how many pleasures we can bear without being led away from him; just how much praise is healthful to encourage us in the way to the heavenly home.

In former times when a race was run, the victor was crowned with a wreath of laurel, and the judge spoke words of congratulatory praise. That did not prevent him from trying to win another race, it only made him the more anxious to win; and the louder the applause that greeted him the more he agonized to deserve it. That is the way God deals with us. We are running a race; we are trying to win the prize of high calling that is before us. Better than any laurel wreath is our reward—the life with God in heaven.

Do you ask what heaven is? Who knows? The Bible does not give us any tangible idea; it is a place of rest, of happiness, of joy, but better yet, it is a place where Christ is; where we will do and enjoy whatever God wills, and from which we will go no more out forever. But we must earn it; we must not only do God's will, but we must do it heartily. How impatient we become with those who are bidden to do service for us if they lag, if they only do things in an indifferent way, as if it was only because they were obliged to do it: not with the gracious pleasure that makes us feel as if we asked a favor instead of issuing a command. Hearty service is tenfold more welcome than that which is only endurable.

Doing heartily for the Lord those things that he wills is what he desires. When so much has been done for us; when our Saviour left the joys of heaven, the presence of the Father, to die for us that we might not perish, but have everlasting life, is it too much to expect that whatsoever lies before us in the line of duty will be done with our might; that in our manner of doing it we may manifest to all men the love that we possess for our God? "Whatsoever ye do, do it heartily, as to the Lord, and not unto men, knowing that of the Lord ye shall receive the reward of the inheritance: for ye serve the Lord Christ."

PERVERTING THE TRUTH.

FOR some reason the present age seems to be one of unusual doubt and inquiry. Christians are heard asking the views of each other as to whether this or that pleasure should be participated in by church members. Then questions arise constantly as to whether the teachings and precepts of the Bible are to be taken in an entirely literal sense. To an old-fashioned, or perhaps it would be better to say, to an old-time, Christian, these doubts and queries seem out of place, for the time was when truths of Scripture were accepted as meaning just what they say. With a due regard for those parts of the Bible which are plainly intended to be allegorical and illustrative, this would seem to be no more than reasonable. The laws of business are observed and adhered to with a fidelity which shows how desirous men and women are to present only a fair and creditable rule of conduct in their transactions with one another. But when it comes to obeying the best and greatest of all known laws, the divine law of religion, sad to say, even professing Christians are prone to question and wonder and give themselves all the license conscience possibly will allow.

What every person entering the Church of Christ should do first of all, is to resolve firmly to resist evil and everything tending to evil, to obey the law and the whole law of God. And any one already professing the name of Christ who has been inclined to waver and evade the plain requirements of a religious life, ought to at once pause and determine to thrust out of his life and daily practice whatever is at variance with the revealed law of the Scriptures. What more pitiable than to see any one who has espoused an important and sacred cause, placing himself in an attitude to invite the thief of irresolution and unbelief to enter his mind and heart, stealing away his best and most valued interests in life! What dutiful child would ever think of questioning with other children as to how far he could go in acts of infidelity and disobedience without fear of detection or punishment from his parents? And then such questionings as have been hinted at on the part of Christians are mostly a mere pretence. In every human breast God has implanted a conscience which is faithful in its promptings, and rarely fails to dictate with unerring fidelity the best course to be pursued at all times and under all circumstances.

The truth is, it is often too hard to obey the strict yet simple command of the Master, to come out and be separated from the world, or from worldlings, as the text implies. What Christians need most in our day is the firm, resolute will to shut and bolt the door of indecision, forcibly resist the devil, and cause him to flee. The pleasures of the world are too shallow to be trusted, too fleeting to be at all relied upon. Religion is abiding. No period of time, no course of events, can weaken its mighty power. Embrace it, cling to it, adhere with indomitable resolution to its requirements as set forth in the Gospel; its teachings will never betray those who trust it, but it will yield a thousand dear delights even before, through its saving agency, "we reach the heavenly shore, and walk the golden streets."

A RAINBOW IN THE CLOUDS.

WE all know what a rainbow is; that it is the refraction of the beams of the sun in passing the drops of falling rain; the rays being separated into the prismatic colors are then reflected from the cloud opposite to the sun and the spectator. The rainbow is the token of the covenant which God made with Noah when he came forth from the Ark, that the waters should no more become a flood to destroy all flesh.

Of the colors noticed in the Bible only white, black, red, yellow, and green are mentioned; only three of these are prismatic (white and black being the absence of color). Blue, indigo, violet, and orange are omitted. Yellow is very seldom noticed, and is apparently regarded as a shade of green. This latter color is frequently referred to, and conveys the idea of something vigorous and flourishing. Newly plucked boughs are said to be green; and a different meaning is that of sprouting, or putting forth of leaves.

The only fundamental color of which the Hebrews appear to have had any clear conception is red; and even that they do not often use. Some writers have attempted to explain certain passages in Revelations by telling us that by emerald, green is meant; that for jasper we should read yellow, etc., etc.; but for ordinary minds it is safer and better to believe that the picture given to us conveys the idea of pure, brilliant, transparent light. White was the symbol of innocence; the raiment of angels, the robes of glorified saints, and whatsoever is pure and good, and pertains to the kingdom of Christ.

Sorrow causes the blackness of night to hover about us, and our hearts grow weak in the darkness, for there is no light, no hope, no God for us to see. Despair seizes upon us, and in our agony we cry aloud for help. We hear the mutterings of the thunder, we see the flash of the lightning, and we lose all hope; discouragement reigns, and we feel very sure that God is not in the tempest. But it is only through spiritual warfare that we become strong. When the storm has passed away, when the angry clouds have gone over, although the effects of nature's disturbance have not disappeared, the sun comes out and there appears overhead the rainbow of promise.

The Captain of our salvation tells us to take to ourselves the whole armor of God, that in the great day we may be able to stand; but if we do not know how to use them, of how little service are the helmet of salvation, the sword of the spirit, the shield of faith, and the preparation of the Gospel of peace with which our feet are shod. We must fight and learn to use our own armor, that with our loins girt about we may take to us the breastplate of righteousness.

There is a bow of promise in every dark cloud; behind the blackness the sun is ever shining; and back of the cloud, the darkness, and the rainbow, we always have the King on his throne, and nearer to us the dear Jesus, who says, "Fear not, little flock; it is your Father's good pleasure to give you the kingdom."

> "Why then not walk beside him,
>   Holding his blessèd hand,
> Patiently walking onward
>   All through the weary land?
>
> "Dwelling beneath his shadow
>   In the burden and heat of the day,
> Looking for his appearing
>   As the hours wear fast away."

"WORDS FITLY SPOKEN."

'T was a lovely morning late in winter. Although the air was crisp and cold, and the newly fallen snow swept down in showers from the branches of the grand old maples, which gave to the exterior of our home its chief charm, there was that in the sunbeam and in the air, as well as in the lights and shadows here and there upon the snow, which suggested thoughts of the beautiful spring-time, with its warm sunshine, its wealth of flowers, and luscious fruits to come. It was a luxury to breathe the morning air, and to enjoy these foreshadowings of spring, after a long, dreary winter.

But the sunshine was all without, for within a beloved friend had long been ill; and such was the nature of the malady which had prostrated him, and such the circumstances attending his illness, that all cheerfulness had forsaken him.

I spoke to him of the beauty of the morning, and brought from among the plants and vines which luxuriated in a sunny window, one which had been a special favorite of our loved one, a beautiful fuchsia, laden with flowers and a profusion of buds in various stages. "Not now, I cannot see it now," were the words, faintly said, in response to my efforts.

A few hours passed, during which the watcher sought, under an aspect of cheerfulness, to conceal the feelings of hopelessness which for some time past had been gradually becoming stronger, even to a settled conviction.

A friend who, until then, had not fully realized the condition of the invalid, called to see him. Entering with a smiling face, and avoiding all allusion to the appearance of the sufferer, he spoke of the lovely morning and the speedy advent of spring; then, in bright, happy tones, of the pleasure in store for all, when the invalid, restored to health, would be able to mingle with friends who were anxious to see him again among them. The dull eye brightened as the pleasing picture was sketched, and then the idea dawned upon him that perhaps he might still be spared to his family and friends.

Other words of cheer and deeds of kindness followed. The look of hopelessness and suffering little by little passed away. The heart so long heavy because of financial losses consequent upon the long illness, became lighter as it opened to the friend whose attentions were unwearied. Other visits followed, and tempting delicacies often came, which were enjoyed the more because the invalid knew that in other homes he was thought of, and that these were the overflowings of the sympathy felt for him in those homes and hearts. Kind messages and tokens of remembrance, many of them of great intrinsic value, and all priceless to him to whom they were sent, because expressions of regard and sympathy, all came, and often borne by the same faithful friend.

At length, after many weary months, we felt that our loved one was saved.

Those were truly "words fitly spoken," and the deeds of love which accompanied the words attested the sincerity of the regard to which the words gave utterance.

As we see the evidences of returning health upon the face so recently very pale and haggard, our hearts are filled with gratitude to the Great Giver of all good for putting those precious words of cheer into the heart of our friend.

May it not be that the progress of disease could sometimes be checked if only cheerful words were spoken in the sick-room? If "little words of kindness, little deeds of love," are sweet to those in the vigor of health, how much more so to those who are shut out from participation in the enjoyments of active life, and deprived of the privilege of labor and the profits resulting therefrom!

With how little sacrifice either of time or of strength might those who are well bear to the sick some message so full of encouragement as to turn the scale, and call back to life one who might otherwise go down to the "narrow house."

Are there no sick and sorrowing ones to whom we may go with cheering words and loving deeds, in the spirit of him who went about doing good?

With such a high and holy example, let us "go and do likewise."

RECOGNITION IN HEAVEN.

WE here know but little about heaven. And yet we know all that in our present state we need to know. We know the way there, and it should be our great endeavor to walk in that way, and to get there. And we know that it is a perfectly holy and happy place; that all of its employments are such as holy beings most delight in; that there the great Father more immediately dwells, and reveals his glory; that there we shall see the blessed Saviour face to face, and be like him, and that we shall have for our associates the holy angels and the spirits of just men made perfect. "There shall we see, and hear, and know all that we desired or wished below."

As regards the extent of our acquaintance in heaven we

are not informed. It has been a question of interest with some, whether we shall there recognize the friends that have been dear to us here. I think that there can be but little doubt in this regard. It may be that they will be among the first to meet and to greet us on our arrival there. I certainly and confidently expect to meet there all those friends in Christ to whom I have here sustained endearing relations, and to hold pleasant converse with them. I anticipate this as one of the pleasures of that blessed world.

I expect also to become acquainted with all those eminent saints of whom I have read, both of the Old and the New dispensation. I expect to behold, at a distance it may be, the faces of Abraham, of Moses, of David, of Peter, and John, and Paul, and other worthies of whom the time would fail one to speak. And although there will be there a great multitude, which no man can number, of every kindred, and tongue, and people, and nation, it is probable that I shall become acquainted with them all, and with all the important facts of their history. How long it will take I cannot say, but there will be ample time; nor will knowledge be gained by the slow process by which it is here acquired. We may need no introduction there. All will be of one family, and bear the image of their common Saviour, and there will be among them all most friendly and familiar intercourse. There will be no reserve and no concealments. The great Father will be known to all, so far as they shall be capable of comprehending him. And most intimately shall we know our Saviour and our fellow-saints; and to know will be to love, to trust, and to enjoy. And so shall there be "fulness of joy, and pleasures forevermore."

POWER IN RIGHT MUSIC.

WHEN we say, "right music," we do not mean the "first-class music" of which nowadays there is such rich provision, where skill, execution and sound are *all* that the people can carry away with them. The music of God's house should do a deeper work than that. It should be adoration, and bring solace to many a pained and penitent spirit.

Works of art are good in themselves, but oftentimes they are far above the masses, and even the average church-goer. The organ may be grand, and the most elaborate music may be given by a trained quartette, but it never has touched and never will touch the deep spirit of the people. The angels who sang above the manger, and now sing around the throne, can give us a true idea of its magnificence. When all the people sing, the preacher is more eloquent. There is a great deal of truth in the old statement, "Fill the church with Gospel music and his Satanic majesty will freeze on the top of the steeple." Of course if there is no congregation, you cannot have good congregational singing, but if you do have a large assembly and a good leader, it is grand singing, because timid people and people with poor voices all sing, and the discord is drowned. There are times when the voice of a multitude is truly wonderful, and there are other times when a single sweet voice leads to repentance and the Saviour.

No money or renown can reward a great composer who gives to the world such hymns as "Am I a soldier of the cross?" "Rock of Ages," or "Jesus, lover of my soul." The hymn, if not written with the soul of the author in it, is not worth singing in church or anywhere else. Of what use are heartless hymns? Did they ever do any good? The beginning of every line should start at the heart of the Master, and end with our own.

The Bible has two great hearts—the praying heart and the singing heart. The praying heart sways before the mercy seat like the golden censer before the Tabernacle, and the singing heart warbles forth its praises for mercies given, and tells always of the works of God. The grandest song-book ever written is the Bible. When David kissed the marble lips of his boy he sang, "I shall go to him," and among the tombs Jesus sang, "I am the resurrection and the life." So the songs of David thundered through Jerusalem when the Ark of God was being brought from Obed-edom.

There was evidently a large place given to music in the ancient Church. There were songs of mourning, but there were days of singing. The ancients loved music greatly. Among the Hebrews, Egyptians, Greeks, and Romans, there were many stringed instruments, and marvellous were the tunes and the hymns associated with them.

You read in various places where singers were appointed to sing. Nehemiah put singers, joyous men, over the house of God. David's songs, too, were sung by the human voice and accompanied by instruments. Upon the news of victory, you hear an outburst of song, and when the tribes came up to the Temple you remember their service of song.

What was prophecy but a song in anticipation of the coming Redeemer; or the Gospel, but the advent song of redeeming love? So in a less fervent spirit, perhaps, song accompanied the birth of Jesus, and was the worship of the Primitive Church. Hear David's songs of deliverance in the prayer-meeting at Jerusalem, and from the sorrowful hearts at the "Last Supper."

A CHARACTERISTIC ORIENTAL SCENE.

The Lord's people do not as a general thing realize the immense power there is in right music and song. The people's own singing should attract them to the house of God. And no one can appreciate the power of Christian song in the prayer-meeting and church worship upon the morals of a people.

Many and many a conversion has been brought about by the singing of a Christian song, the tender, earnest singing that tells of Calvary and the victory of the resurrection; for a hymn without a heart is like a heartless sermon; God cares nothing for either.

Beethoven's affections were great, his reverence for God profound. This accounts for the pathos in every strain of the great composer's music. Take those old hymns, "All hail the power of Jesus' name" and "Rock of Ages;" immortal words, living water is always gushing out of them, and can the effect be anything but gracious? Surely thirsty souls can drink and rejoice.

It is said that John Newton led more souls to Christ by his hymns than his preaching, and Paul recommends "singing and making melody in our hearts unto the Lord." How many broken strings may be mended in human hearts, and trained perhaps for the great orchestra of heaven by the singing of some touching hymn. Somehow or some way everybody can do this, and though the singer may in time be forgotten, the words of the song will long be remembered, and may work out an "exceeding weight of glory" to them who are exercised thereby.

LIGHT AND LOVE.

"GOD is love." "I am the Light of the world." Two wonderful propositions! God is love and Jesus is light; so as God and his only begotten Son are one God, love and light are one. Let us consider how love is light. God so loved the world that he sent his Son to be the light of the world. Thus the love sends the light and is the light. Think how the love of God prompts the ministers of the Gospel to carry light into dark places, to bring light to darkened intellects. Think how love inspires to deeds of heroism and self-denial, as light causes the seeds to swell and burst in their efforts to obtain more light by means of branch and leaves.

To love and light let us add liberty, the glorious liberty wherewith Christ doth make us free, free from sin. Light, love, and liberty! Three priceless gifts granted to every disciple; light to guide us on our way, love to encompass and shield us from danger, liberty to forsake sin and accept salvation. May we have grace to walk in the light, and love the liberty with which Christ has made us free.

ALONE WITH GOD.

IN every instance the man who prevails in prayer is alone in his communion with God. Abraham leaves Sarah behind him when he pleads for Sodom; and if he fails it is because he ceases to ask before God ceases to grant. Moses is by himself beside the bush in the wilderness. Joshua is alone when Christ comes to him as an armed man. Gideon and Jephtha are by themselves when commissioned to save Israel. Once does Elijah raise a child from the dead, and Elisha does the same, and in each case not even the mothers come in while the prophet, alone with God, asks and receives. So of Ezekiel, so of Daniel.

Although others are present, Saul journeying to Damascus is alone with Christ after the light breaks upon him. Cornelius is praying by himself when the angel flashes upon his solitude, nor is any one with Peter upon the housetop when he is prepared to go to the Gentiles for the first time. One John is alone in the wilderness; another John is by himself in Patmos, when nearest God. It is when alone under his fig-tree in prayer that Jesus sees Nathaniel. All religious biography, our own closest communion and success with God, show what Christ means, when, as if it were the only way to pray, he says: "And thou, when thou prayest, enter into thy closet, and when thou hast shut thy door, pray to thy Father which is in secret, and thy Father, which seeth in secret, shall reward thee openly."

EUROCLYDON.

A CURIOUS wind is the Euroclydon. The name was given to a gale that at the present time is called a Levanter. It is described as a whirlwind or typhoon, accompanied by terrific gusts from the high mountains. And before we speak of the celebrated voyage mentioned in the history of Paul, let us notice that he had been tried as to his faith in Jesus of Nazareth before Festus Porcius, the Procurator of Judea, and in the presence of Herod, Agrippa, and Bernice, his sister, who had come to him in great pomp. It was to entertain them that Paul was brought forth into the judgment-hall of the palace.

No fault was found with his manly defence of his faith, and he would have been set at liberty if, as a Roman, he had not appealed unto Cæsar (Nero the Emperor). Therefore Julius, a centurion of Augustus' band, received Paul and certain other prisoners, and set sail with them for Italy. Julius was very kind to Paul, and when, the next day after they had sailed, the ship touched at Sidon, the apostle was granted liberty to go ashore and see his friends. Many days thereafter they sailed slowly on account of adverse winds, and they kept close to the islands, for their sailing was dangerous, and they began to look about for a safe harbor.

The south wind blew softly, and supposing the danger passed, they drew up their anchors and sailed close by Crete. But just as they thought themselves safe, a tempestuous wind arose, called Euroclydon, and the ship was so caught that they had to let her drive. This trying north-easterly gale had continued fourteen days and nights, neither sun nor star coming into view in the dull, leaden sky, and the heavy rain falling over them made them look forward to certain shipwreck, and they lost all hope of safety.

There was great danger that they should be driven into the Syrtes, on the North African coast. The Syrtes or quicksands (the word being derived from Sert, an Arabic word for desert) were an object of peculiar dread to sailors. The drifting sands, the intense heat along the shore, the shallow water, and the rocks that were hidden under the current, added to the north-easterly gale, were enough to alarm all those in the ship.

But the dear Lord had them in keeping, and although they were doomed to lose the ship, to teach them a lesson for not hearkening to his message through his servant, Paul, yet they were saved, and the two hundred three score and sixteen souls escaped safely to land, some on boards and some on broken pieces of the ship.

Do we need to go to the Mediterranean to find an Euroclydon? God often speaks to us, but we do not listen because our ears are occupied with the south wind that blows softly, lulling our senses and luring us to destruction, and then to save us, even if by the shipwreck of all that we care for and possess, there arises an Euroclydon. For days and nights, winds blow and toss us about, not a star by night, not a ray of sun by day comes into our sight, and we grope about in the gloom, agonizing to find a place to cast anchor; quicksands so treacherous that their shifting particles threaten to draw us upon the rocks that will shipwreck us are before us; and while we grope, Jesus says, "Peace, be still," and immediately there is a great calm. Did we think he was asleep, deaf to our danger while the wind beat the ship, so that it was likely to sink? Why are we so fearful—why is our faith so small? Ah! even the wind and the sea obey him.

Through fourteen days and nights of storm, Paul, who loved God, and who had been told that he would be brought safely to land, never lost courage. Is it any harder for us to trust God to bring us through an Euroclydon?

> "Learn to wait! Life's hardest lesson,
>   Conned perhaps through blinding tears,
> While the heart-throbs sadly echo
>   To the tread of passing years.
>
> "Constant sunshine, fondly welcomed,
>   Doth not ripen fruit or flower;
> Giant oaks owe strength and greatness
>   To the tempest's scathing power.
>
> "Thus the soul untouched by sorrow
>   Aims not at a brighter state:
> Joy seeks not a brighter morrow;
>   Only sad hearts learn to wait.
>
> "Human strength and human greatness
>   Spring not from life's sunny side;
> Heroes must be more than driftwood
>   Floating on a waveless tide."

THE PRINCE OF PEACE.

"His name shall be called the Prince of Peace."—Isa. ix. 6.

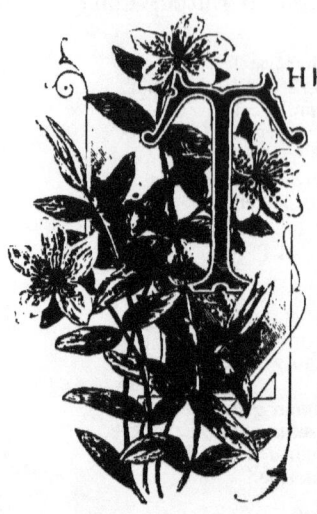

THE rest of the Prince of Peace comes only to the soul that treads the path of obedience. That path may be full of thorns, it may lead us into thickest darkness, to bear mental and physical suffering daily, to take up the innumerable duties of the household or of the workshop, to go forth like Abraham, not knowing whither. Be it so! As with him, every step of the way will be sweet, holiest rest to our souls. That rest is "the rest of faith." The sun shall no more go down for such a traveller. Pillowed upon the bosom of Jesus, yet mounting still higher with unfaltering footsteps—up, up the steeps of life to the final goal—we shall enter at the last upon that rest which "remaineth for the people of God." But even this shall not be inactivity, nor selfish enjoyment, nor consummated revelations. Onward! upward! in the songs of those who "rest not day nor night," in the ceaseless disclosures of infinite love, in the ever-increasing glory of the "beatific vision." Oh, bright land, so restful even in anticipation, thou art not very far away! When our weary feet shall press thy sacred soil, when our eyes shall feast upon thy ever-widening landscape, one voice shall rise above the acclaim of the innumerable company of the redeemed—the voice of the Lamb before the throne. That voice, "I will give you rest," ofttimes has stilled the tempest of our earthly grief. Now, evermore, it shall be the full, increasing melody of our celestial home.

THE PRINCE OF PEACE.

GIVING UP OLD HOPES.

MANY years ago I prepared a sermon, in which it was my endeavor to persuade all who might listen to it to give up any hope that they might cherish. I took the ground that many hopes are worthless; that they must be given up soon or late, and that it would be wiser to give them up now, than when too late to get something better. And I also went farther, and said that even were a person's hope a good one, it would do him no harm to relinquish it and to hope anew.

But I postponed preaching the sermon from time to time, until I finally destroyed it and it was never preached. I felt that while the preaching of it might be beneficial to some, it might be harmful to others. I feared its effect upon some of God's dear, trembling children; I would not break the bruised reed, nor quench the smoking flax, and so I hesitated and finally gave the sermon to the flames, which I have never seen cause to regret.

But there is many a long-cherished hope that must fail when God shall have taken away the soul, if not before; and the sooner it is relinquished the better. It is a hope that was taken up without any good reason, and it has never been attended with any appropriate fruits. Its possessor does not live essentially different from what he did before, nor from the mass of men around him. He gives no satisfactory evidence that he has ever been born again. He is controlled by worldly principles. His affections are supremely on earthly things; and for these he lives supremely, making it his great aim to get worldly goods. Better, a thousand times better, were it for such a man had he no hope. So long as he clings to the one that he already has, he will not seek a better, and there is great danger that he will die sheltered in a refuge of lies which the first view of eternal realities will forever sweep away.

ADVANTAGES OF CONFESSING CHRIST.

DISTINCTLY from our Saviour's lips comes the declaration, "He that is not with me is against me," and the words are plain and unequivocal. They have a serious meaning for all who are not distinctively with Christ on the Lord's side, for they contain a declaration of war. There are only two parties in religious matters; there are only two camps, only two sides. Are we with Christ and working in his cause? If not we are doing harm. There are many persons who need to have this truth pressed upon them. They endeavor to steer a middle course in religion; they are not as bad as many sinners, but still they are not saints. They feel the truth of Christ's gospel when it is brought before them, but they are afraid to confess this feeling. Because they have these feelings they flatter themselves that they are not as bad as some others, and yet they shrink from the standard of faith and practice which Jesus sets up. They are not boldly on Christ's side, yet they are not openly against it. But this sentence of our Lord's cuts the ground from beneath the feet of those who hesitate about standing openly on the Lord's side. People say that this entering into fellowship with the church is a very serious matter; it must not be decided hastily; and so on the ground of its seriousness it is postponed, and postponed indefinitely. It is really too serious a matter to be put off from time to time. The one thing that we should dread is this, that when the voice of the Master is heard saying, "Take my yoke upon you," we should stop for a moment and listen, and then pass on and give him no answer. That is indeed a very grave and serious responsibility to take, and when he invites us to the feast of his love, to turn away in indifferent silence is truly a serious matter—a responsibility to be dreaded.

There is ever a separation existing between the followers of the Lord and the world, and it must needs be a wall of separation, for Christians, while they are in the world, are not of it.

The Lord justly asks some mark of distinction from them, not that he may know them, but that the world may, and the brethren may. Surely it is not possible to be a secret Christian. We cannot surrender ourselves wholly to the Master, and yet refuse the public acknowledgment of his authority.

In the kingdoms of this world no one is admitted to the privileges of citizenship without a profession of allegiance, and surely it is not unreasonable that as much should be expected from those who desire to enter God's kingdom. "I cannot decide to be a Christian," is the answer of many upon whom the claims of Christ are urged, but they forget that they do decide whenever the subject is brought before them. To say, "I cannot decide for Christ to-day," is another way of saying, "I can and do decide to refuse the service of Christ to-day." A choice is made one way or the other, for it only requires a negative position to be in direct opposition.

We must allow, at least, enough to God's wisdom to believe that he instituted the Church and its sacraments for some purpose which could not otherwise be accomplished. That purpose evidently was to make palpable the difference between his people and the world. How, then, can a man keep the fact of his being a Christian secret, when Christianity has been made to assume a visible, organized form by its author? A Christian is one, moreover, who obeys Christ, and desires to follow all his commands. How can one be a Christian who leaves out of account the tenderest and almost the last of his Saviour's commands, "This do in remembrance of me?" This simple, touching service, so full of tender associations, commemorates the Saviour's dying love. Can any one hope that he is a Christian whose lips have never touched the sacramental cup, and thus obeyed Christ's dying command?

One of the reasons for public confession is the usefulness of the act. How much more one's zeal is drawn out when he has declared himself for any cause, and he partakes of the spirit of the party! That which is kept concealed within is apt to lose much of its hold upon us; it is by speaking of it and acting upon it that we feel most of its impression and influence. There is no feeling more strengthening to any one than the feeling that he is not standing alone. So it is a joy to feel that one is part of a great system working for one end, to feel that he is a fellow-laborer with apostles, martyrs, prophets, saints, even with Christ himself. . We can never be fully aware of the usefulness of the ordained means of grace. The public worship of God is of inestimable value to mankind. In the midst of the cares and toils of life God is known in his palaces for a refuge. There the tempted are succored, the weak are strengthened, the wandering directed, and the oppressed relieved. The sanctuary opens a door for the weary and heavy laden to enter and refresh themselves. According to his promise Jesus is with his Church to the end of days; there he is most often found of his people, and draws most graciously near to them, supplying all their needs with the riches of his grace. It is a source of strength to feel, therefore, that we have a place there as well as a secure retreat.

Merely joining the Church is not a source of safety, simply to profess faith in Christ is not to possess it; and without faith we cannot be saved. All who are enrolled upon the records of the Church have not their names written in the Lamb's book of life, so by the safety of a public declaration is meant merely that it fortifies individuals against temptations and evil influences. It puts the longest possible distance between the old life and the new. It cuts us off forever from the old life of sin, and henceforth we are bound to serve the Lord.

But far above both of these considerations is the greater one that by declaring ourselves upon the Lord's side, we gain the consciousness of having obeyed Christ. Not in the sense of a recommendation would this reason be urged, but because our consciences rest freer from the charge of ingratitude, when we remember all that Christ has done for us and can look up into the face of our Saviour, and say, "Touched by thy love I give myself to thee, O Christ."

There is, of necessity, something which precedes public confession—the work of grace on the heart. If we do not believe on Christ, and determine to take him as our Saviour, of course there will be no profession to make, save a false profession; but if we purpose to give ourselves to Christ, and take him for our portion, then it should be done openly; for this is the standard by which we are judged, "He that is not with me is against me."

OUR RESPONSIBILITY.

ID each professing Christian in the world to-day realize the tremendous responsibility that rests upon all believers to make their faith known to those who are yet in darkness, to spread the Gospel of glad tidings to their perishing fellow-men, and act as men would do under a sense of such responsibility, we should not have to wait long for the complete regeneration of mankind. If we believe in our hearts, as we profess to do, that those who do not make their peace with God in this life have no opportunity for repentance hereafter and are doomed to eternal despair, a doctrine which the Bible plainly teaches, how can we do less than manifest the utmost concern for the conversion of our fellow-men and especially those who are dear to us by ties of blood or friendship? If we saw one whom our hearts held dear carelessly drifting down a rapid stream towards a plunging cataract and inevitable destruction, how quickly we would sound the note of warning; with what frantic energy we would hasten to rescue him from the fatal flood. We would not give him up in despair because of his indifference to his own fate, or his repeated rejection of proffered assistance. No; we would follow him with increasing energy of appeal, and in an agony of soul that words cannot express, to the verge of the cataract, if haply we might reach him even there. How can we show less solicitude for the safety of those who are slowly but surely drifting down the river of life to a fate far worse than that encountered in the foam of a material cataract?

In this respect our demeanor towards those who are out

of Christ, our feeble efforts in dissuading friends from evil courses, our apparent unconcern respecting even those who are very near to us by ties of blood, practically belies our profession of belief in the awful fate which awaits those who die unrepentant. It is one of the most incomprehensible things to the sceptical mind that men who assert their belief in the eternal punishment of the wicked should put forth so little effort to save others from such a terrible end. And it is not strange that this should be looked upon as a practical denial of the assertion itself. Men are too frequently disposed to shift the responsibility of this work of evangelism upon the shoulders of the few—upon the ministry, upon the teacher of the Sabbath-school, upon the more devout brethren of the church. They act as though, having made their own profession of faith, they have fulfilled all the duties which God requires of them. Seemingly assured of their own salvation, they wrap their cloaks of righteousness about them and pass on unmindful of the fate of those who are perishing in their sins. Such are selfish Christian lives—very little of Christ and very much of self. If a man has found a goodly treasure, a boundless and inexhaustible supply of sweet and precious things, he will not be so ungenerous as to keep his discovery to himself, since there is enough to supply all who can come—all the world if need be. Neither will he who has once tasted of the riches of redeeming love, who has drunk at the fountain of the water of life, desire to keep that knowledge to himself. Rather will he cry aloud in the fervor of his soul to all his fellowmen, "O come, and taste and see that the Lord is good."

HOW ARE WE BUILDING?

We are building a structure, not as an ornament, not for time only, but a building of far more importance and of far greater duration.

"Our to-days and yesterdays
Are the blocks with which we build."

Slowly and silently the work is being carried on, so silently that those who stand nearest to us cannot see our work. They hear no sound; yet in the solemn silence we are building—building for *eternity!*

Every word, good or bad; every deed that is noticed by the all-searching eye of God; every thought, pure as those of the angels or smirched with sin; every impulse born of a God-given spirit, or every sin-laden action of which we need to feel ashamed, one and all are the material with which our structure will be raised.

Shall the temple that we raise be strong in the Lord, fitted for the Master's use, worthy to be commended at the last day? Or, shall our building, which we have raised during the years of our life, be only fit to be cast down and trodden, as unfit for a part of that city where "there shall be no more death, neither sorrow nor crying, neither shall there be any more pain. The city has no need of the sun, neither of the moon, to shine in it, for the Lamb is the light thereof"?

Are we in God's sight building for our own salvation, for our own comfort and peace here and hereafter? How are we building for *eternity?*

"We shape ourselves the joy or fear
Of which the coming life is made,
And fill our future's atmosphere
With sunshine or with shade."

THE MASTER IMPULSE.

IN this, it seems to me, we have the secret of a Christian life. A man is a Christian when the master-motive of his life is love of Christ, when that is the germ which assimilates and co-ordinates all its forces. Jesus Christ is the central form of Christianity, and he who loves him supremely is adopted into the family of the redeemed. Sometimes in reading the New Testament we wonder at the absolute self-assertion of Christ. He claims a place in the heart above that given to the most sacred of human relationships. "He that loveth father or mother more than me is not worthy of me: and he that loveth son or daughter more than me is not worthy of me." (Matt. x. 37.) The reason is that for the man to belong to Christ at all, the love of Christ must be the desire which crystallizes his life; the co-ordinating germ which determines what he shall be. Wheat and tares may grow together in the field; but if the tares are assimilating to themselves the forces of the earth, and leaving to the wheat only a starving and sickly growth, you cannot properly call that "a wheat field." *One* must be first; "No man can serve two masters." The stream cannot flow both ways at once. One must be first in the Christian heart. God will put up with a great many things in the human heart, but there is one thing he will not put up with—a second place.

LIGHT IS SOWN FOR THE RIGHTEOUS.

IN their pilgrimage through this world, the people of God often walk in darkness. The light does not always shine upon their path. Sometimes they are in the dark as to their being the people of God. They are exercised with doubts and fears in this regard. Sometimes the face of their Father is hidden from them. They do not always walk in the light of his countenance. And not infrequently his providences concerning them are veiled in darkness. "Gloomy clouds his ways surround." So it was with respect to

Job and Jacob and David. And so always has been and still is with respect to large numbers of God's dear people.

But let them take courage. Light is sown for them; sown by the hand of their Father; and it will spring up in an abundant and joyful harvest. Sooner or later light will arise unto them, and gladness will cheer their hearts. So it is oftentimes here in this present world. Here not infrequently the clouds break, and the shadows flee away. So it was in the case of Jacob, who so sadly grieved for the loss of his beloved Joseph. Instead of going down into the grave unto his son mourning, as in his sore bereavement he said he would, the cheering news at length came to him that Joseph was yet alive, and that he was governor over all the land of Egypt. The captivity of Job, too, was ere long turned, and the Lord blessed his latter end more than his beginning. And David was permitted to sing: "Thou hast turned for me my mourning into dancing; thou hast put off my sackcloth, and girded me with gladness." Nor have similar experiences been uncommon with the people of God in all ages. If not sooner, it has often been their experience that at even-time it has been light.

But it is more especially in another world that the harvest of light and gladness shall be reaped. More or less of darkness may attend the people of God all along their pilgrimage here to the end. But they will bid a final farewell to it all at death. Then they will be introduced to a world of which it is said: "There shall be no night there; and they need no candle, neither light of the sun, for the Lord God giveth them light, and they shall reign forever and ever." No more shall they be troubled with perplexing doubts as to their spiritual state. No more shall their Father's face be hid. No more shall dark providences frown upon them. "The Lord shall be their everlasting life, and the days of their mourning shall be ended."

> " Immortal light and joys unknown
> Are for the saints in darkness sown ;
> There glorious seeds shall spring and rise,
> And the bright harvest fill our eyes."

THE DEVICES OF THE TEMPTER.

THE devices of the tempter to win men away from God are manifold and contrived with the greatest cunning. He does not tempt all men in the same way; he is as various in his devices as the chameleon in his colors. What a difference, for instance, between the tempter of Judas to the dark deed of betrayal, and the tempter who came to Christ with words of Scripture upon his lips. Judas needed no perversion of Scripture to tempt him—the greed of his soul was sufficient; but on the other hand the one possible chance of tempting the Son of God was through the Scriptures

Every one is tempted according to his nature and circumstances, and where one form of evil fails another is tried. The great fact confronts us all, whether we are Christians or not, that we have a great enemy who is continually devising mischief against us. In the case of those who are out of Christ, the one object of the tempter is to keep them away from him, and if he succeeds in this purpose his object is gained. His device with them is to blind their eyes to the truth, to lull them into security and keep them in fancied peace, and if the conscience can be quieted and the higher faculties benumbed, then the soul is his.

Christ was tempted immediately after his baptism, so

we need not be surprised if the enemy makes his fiercest onslaughts upon us just after some high spiritual privilege. His malevolence and jealousy cannot endure the sight of our communion with God. He sees our happy state of mind, and how joyful our hearts are, and then he comes and tries to change our joy into levity, our relation into presumption. It is no unusual thing for a young Christian to descend from the top of the delectable mountains into the valley of humiliation; even in the hour of the first love there has been more than one who has fallen directly into sin.

Then comes a sudden revulsion of feeling, a loss of all joy and peace. We feel as if we were greater sinners than ever, and had never found Christ at all, and this is one of the devices of the tempter to bring men to despair. Oftener he has a subtler device than that, one that takes more time to develop, but is more likely to have lasting results, and, strange to say, that device is not to tempt the young Christian at all. We deal with one who is an adept in cunning arts and wily snares, so we must expect strange things. He will not put an obstacle in the young Christian's path; he will give him a free path and let him go singing on his way; but there is the deepest philosophy in this. Oftentimes there is not much to be gained by tempting one who has just found Christ; the heart is too much taken up with his love to have room for anything else, and so our enemy leaves the soul unmolested to enjoy its happiness. But we can foresee the effects. Days, weeks, and even months go by—the longer time the more danger—and all is well. We begin to think that the Christian life is the easiest thing in the world, and it is no trouble to do right, while we wonder how the enemy ever gained the ascendancy over us. Finding no temptations in our path, we begin to relax our watchfulness, to call in the sentinels as unnecessary, and cease to pray for the strength we never feel the need of, and so the device of the tempter succeeds. All these months of quiet have had that one end in view, to catch the soul off its guard and keep it so much at ease that it will cease to be watchful. Such a period of calm, when muscles are relaxed and the soul at ease, is the enemy's grand opportunity. Then, if ever, there is need of increased watchfulness and a determined effort against the carelessness that does not seem sinful. For the enemy will come with subtlety; he will take care not to alarm us with too open a temptation; his approach will be with the serpent's guile, and his motto, "Little things lead to great things."

He will persuade us to see how near we can come to danger and not be hurt; how much we can associate with ungodly companions; how much vice we can see without becoming vicious; how much unholy conversation we can hear without losing our spirituality. But there is danger there. If we go nearer and nearer to the edge of a precipice we will come within the actual reach of gravitation, which compromises with no one. The Christian who runs no risk willingly is the one to be relied upon. Many fall through being too remiss, but none through being too scrupulous. If we avoid that which is evil and keep close to Christ we are safe. Sometimes the enemy's device will be to lead us into little sins first, persuading us to do or leave undone something so minute, so near the boundary of good and evil, that it can hardly be called a sin. They used to bridge chasms by shooting an arrow across to the other side, carrying a thread as fine as a film, but that thread drew after it a small string, and that string carried a rope, and the rope a cable, so that soon the impassable gulf crossed by a thread was spanned by a bridge. Our arch-enemy is wise enough to profit by this device and use it for his own purposes.

It is only a thought that he shoots into the mind, but the thought brings desire, and desire is father to the act, and the act strengthens into habit—strong and hard to break. Let us remember, when tempted to despair of fighting this cunning enemy, that we have a great High Priest wearing our own nature, who by being tempted himself is able to sympathize with and succor all who put their trust in him.

THEIR EYES WERE HOLDEN.

TWO of the disciples (one named Cleopas, the other, some conjecture, Luke) were going from Jerusalem to Emmaus, a village that lay some sixty furlongs, or seven and a half miles, from the city, probably to enjoy the warm baths that were for public use. As they journeyed along the steep road up the mountain they talked no doubt of Jesus of Nazareth. Along came another traveller, as it seemed to them a stranger in Jerusalem; and he asked of what they were conversing that they looked so sad. With astonishment they told him that, even if he were a stranger, he ought to have heard of Jesus, a prophet, a mighty man who had been doing such wonderful things, and whom the chief priests and rulers had crucified; and this to their disappointment, for they had hoped that he was their coming Messiah, who was to redeem Israel. He chided them for believing that Christ was not to suffer death in order to enter into glory—quoting many predictions from the writings of Moses and the prophets concerning the Christ.

They did not know that he was talking of himself, for "their eyes were holden that they should not know him." And so they reached the little village and the house of Cleophas, and although the stranger seemed to desire to go farther, they persuaded him to tarry and sup with them before returning to the city of Jerusalem to hold the sacred meeting, with the doors closed for fear of the Jews; at the same time Jesus lifted up his hands to bless them, and said, "Peace be unto you." And while they broke bread after he had blessed it, their eyes were opened and they knew him.

Do you live in the great city of Jerusalem? do you enjoy its cares and its pleasures, day by day? Do you walk in a valley of shadows, or up the steep hill to the sunlight? Are you alone, are you tired and foot-sore, is the climbing hard? As you get up two steps do you fall back two? Can you see afar off the streets paved with gold, the gates of pearl, and the light of the city, which is the Lamb? Do you carry a heavy cross that would be lighter if you looked up to the Saviour who bore a heavier cross out to the place called Golgotha, beyond the gates of the city? Do you fret because you can never lay the cross down? Do you forget that

> "Thy weary path shall lead in light,
> And hope e'en now makes sorrow bright"?

Have you not entered into the rest that remaineth for you, not after death, not beyond the grave, but here, to-day, this moment? Can you not just take it? Are you walking alone? Your eyes are holden that you cannot know that at your side, talking with you, is the dear Saviour whom you seek. So near that your gentlest whisper comes to the ear that is ever open to the cry of his children. Are your eyes holden wilfully? Do you not see Jesus with white robes washed in his own blood beside you? Do you have to walk many furlongs with him without seeing him? Is the village to which you are going to enjoy your own pleasure the only object to which you look with such longing eyes that they are holden so that you cannot know him?

Open your eyes and see Jesus at your side, able and willing to do far more for you than you can ask or think. Live with the certain knowledge that Jesus is walking beside you, quite near, talking with you as friend with friend—your Elder Brother.

> " Live! though life hath deepest sadness,
>   Still it fits thee for the end,
> And with grief is mingled gladness,
>   Blossoms o'er the thorn bush bend.
>
> " Hark! from out the shining portals
>   Comes a gush of spirit-song:
> List, ye pale and sorrowing mortals,
>   Learn to suffer and be strong."

THE DAILY TASK.

> "Awake, my soul, and with the sun
> Thy daily stage of duty run;
> Shake off dull sloth, and joyful rise
> To pay thy morning sacrifice."

THE inspiring words of this grand old morning hymn are full of power to call us cheerfully to the routine of life, to help us to contentment with our lot, and to beget within us a joyful and peaceful submission to the will of Providence and the call of duty. It is very true that the contemplation of our day's work is dreary enough; we have pursued the same monotonous round perhaps for many days or years, and each succeeding day brings with it only the promise that its predecessors have brought — a round of well-known and oft-performed duties.

Yet to those who are called upon thus to pass their days upon earth, there is very much in such a life that is calculated to instruct us in those weighty matters and eternal things which go to make up that perfected nature becoming to those who entertain the hope of an immortal state of existence. "Let patience have her perfect work," says the Apostle. Truly patience is a wonderfully perfecting principle, and when incorporated fully into the Christian life leaves little to be desired; yet let all the other moral virtues be present, if patience be lacking we come sadly short of even that degree of perfection which will satisfy the demands of an unbelieving and exacting world. Patience is more than mere endurance. Many have learned to endure who have not learned to be truly patient.

It is not until we realize, by having the truth constantly forced upon us, that we are among that large number who have been called by God to perform tedious and perhaps for the most part apparently trivial duties—not until then, we being faithful, does the peace of a contented life reign within us. And that peace brings with it, too, in most cases, the best opportunity to rise to higher and more useful things. It is rarely indeed that truly great or good lives have not grown in a most natural way out of the faithfully performed routine of average life; and if those of us who are discontented with our daily tasks have not learned this truth, and are impatient because we imagine we might more profitably employ our time for ourselves and others, we leave unlearned a most useful lesson.

The faithful performance of our daily task—be that task a great or an humble one—discharges our responsibility in the sight of God as effectually in the one case as in the other. Great minds are called to do great things, and if the possessors of great talents do not ultimately bring them into use, the reason will almost invariably be that they have not patiently performed those humble duties which would, like stepping-stones, have led them to the haven of their desires. There is too much ambition among Christians to do something important and striking. Such an ambition is evil, since it begets a spirit of proud impatience and entails the great loss of a peaceful and contented mind. The truth is often lost sight of that, even if the ambitious should, by dint of hard work, attain the object of their hopes, and be talked about as having done something of importance, the risk is exceedingly great, and they will forfeit the blessing promised to the poor in spirit. If we are destined to fill a striking position in life, the sooner we learn faithfully and patiently to perform our daily tasks—however humble and mean they appear to be—the sooner shall we fulfil our destiny.

SUNLIGHT IN AUTUMNAL DAYS.

DREARY November is usually associated with the thought of chilling winds, the falling of rustling leaves, sombre skies, and days that are " the saddest of the year." Yet how often in walking abroad on a November day the air is found to be bracing, clear, and delightful. True, the mellow light of the earlier fall no longer lies athwart the pathway, and no song of birds greets the ear, but there are yet gleams of bright sunlight, and cheery sounds are in the air. There is very much to be enjoyed in November days. What if the breezes are somewhat crisp as they whisk to and fro, there is health in the ruddy glow they send to the cheek, and the walk or drive can be a brisk one with no fear of suffering either from heat or cold. It is time for sunlight to grow pale, for leaves to fall from the trees, for puss to seek the cosey chimney-corner rather than the breezy roof, and for the canary to enjoy the shelter of the warm sitting-room rather than the broad, free outlook from the piazza beam. Seldom, and yet more seldom, do the older members of the family care to venture out, for the uncertain sunlight is too suggestive of the caprices of the weather-vane, which may fly around from westward to eastward point so suddenly that one of those trying colds might be the result which elderly people especially dread to have "settle in the fall," too often to "stay by" all winter. Never is the pleasant shelter of the snug home more enjoyable than when the winds begin to whistle, the leaves to go scurrying by, and everything outside of the house indicates the change that is creeping over the great world of nature. But over all the glad sun yet shines, and despite the bare hedges and leafless trees, the cold ground and hurrying feet, the blessed sunlight smiles and dances. And if its beams rise late and depart early, it is only because in obedience to Nature's laws it must be so. Old age is fittingly likened to the declining sunlight of autumnal days. Many and many a weary toiler longs for the fervid heat of summer to be past, and the cooling breezes of autumn to come and refresh the overworked brain and feverish brow. There is something restful in the hush of nature when the season of growth and of harvest is past. It would seem that the tired earth is resting after having brought forth bread for the eater.

When the autumn of life comes on there has usually been quite enough of labor and anxiety experienced to make the quiet, restful days full of welcome. Nor need they be at all devoid of sunlight—the rare, sweet sunlight of God's loving grace, and the calm, clear shining of a peaceful, contented existence. This is presuming, of course, that the life is a religious one, that God and Christ dwell in the heart and make sunlight there. It would be hard to imagine anything much sadder or more desolate than an old person with no love for God or relig-

SUNLIGHT IN AUTUMNAL DAYS.

ion in the soul. It seems as though a long life spent without God or the fruits of the Spirit must prove an empty and utterly sunless existence at the last. Seneca says: "There is nothing more disgraceful than that an old man should have nothing to produce as a proof that he has lived long except his years." A wasted life! What more deplorable picture could be contemplated? The sun never looks upon the world through autumnal skies, but everywhere it views its fructifying influences; the corn it has helped to ripen, the flowers it has brightened, the hearts it has gladdened with its glorious rays. But for an old person to look back over a life unillumined by rays from the Sun of Righteousness, unhallowed by Christly deeds, unblessed by the sweet influence of religion, is sad indeed.

We venture to hope, however, that there are few if any such lives among the readers of "The Christian Life." The very cares against which human nature cries out, the afflictions, the adversity, the pain, in short, the general discipline of life, is blessed in making religion a necessity as well as a comfort and support for nearly all, long before old age brings some relief from constant toil and care. And in like manner as the welcome sunlight comes creeping in at the closed window, shining along the floor and resting on every object it can reach, the same genial, cheerful sunlight in autumnal as in summer days, even so let our dear old friends remember that the sunlight of God's love is ever about them. And unlike the sunlight which warms the earth, the diviner light never grows distant, nor its rays pale and uncertain, but like goodness in the soul, and like the path of the just, it grows brighter and brighter, and "shineth more and more unto the perfect day."

THE WILL OF GOD.

DOING the will of God is paramount to every other consideration. Those of us accustomed in years gone by to the study of the Assemblies' Shorter Catechism have been taught that "man's chief end is to glorify God and enjoy him forever." From this it would seem naturally to follow that the end of life should be, not only to secure one's own salvation but also the salvation of as many others as possible. If Christians believe that the wicked shall go away into everlasting punishment and the righteous into life eternal, it would seem that the winning of souls must be paramount to every other consideration whatever.

Christ came to save souls, but what says he concerning the terms of salvation? "Not every one that saith unto me, Lord, Lord, shall enter into the kingdom of heaven; but he that doeth the will of my Father which is in heaven." And what says the Saviour of his own mission on the earth? "Lo! I come to do thy will, O God." It will in deed and in truth be the maximum achievement of any life after it is over, to have done the will of God. And this means so much, so very much more than merely having actively done good in a general way, or even having won souls to Christ. It involves cross-bearing, the patient endurance of manifold temptations, a willingness to forgive that almost limitless number of offences— the "seventy times seven." It means a fearless facing of every event sent into our lives, with no cowardly attempts to creep under or to soar above, or in any way to elude meeting and accepting the will of God.

A strict performance of a Christian's duty will almost inevitably call for deeds involving the "doing good" and the "winning souls" which attach so strongly to every truly consecrated life. Yet the lonely sentinel, the bed-ridden professor, the deaf mute—all, in every state and station of life, can learn to do the will of God. Very often it requires great faith, great strength, many prayers, to do and meet what we know or feel to be the will of God, but it is an achievement when at last this can be done with calmness and serenity. There is little danger that any one truly desiring to do the will of the Father will be left in the dark as to what duty requires. David's prayer is one that all can offer, that should often be on the lips of all Christ's followers: "Teach me to do thy will; for thou art my God."

CONQUER AS YOU GO.

DOES a skilful general, as he advances into an enemy's country, leave cities behind him half subdued, fortresses half dismantled, armies half subjugated to rise in his rear and attack him unexpectedly? We must adopt the same tactics in the Christian warfare: Conquer as you go; keep your enemies in front of you. Have you an evil habit? Don't try to get around it; don't overlook it or leave it partially subdued, but attack it bravely, manfully; conquer it wholly, and then march on. Have you done an injury to a fellow-man? Have you been unjust or dishonest or false? Make reparation now; repent now. Don't try to cover up your sin; don't try to forget it, to ignore it; repent of it, overcome it, and then pass on your way.

You will find enough sins to overcome in your pathway every day of your life, without having to suffer annoyance from the unrepented follies of the past. The memory of a wicked deed committed years ago, a wrong for which you have never made reparation, may come down upon you when you least expect it, to drive you with its keen lashes into abject despair. It is better not to "let the sun go down upon your wrath," upon sins unatoned, wrongs unrequited; and better still, as far as possible to avoid the necessity for making such reparations. You need all the grace in your heart to withstand present trials and temptations, and to conquer the foes of to-day.

STRENGTH FOR TO-DAY.

Strength for to-day is all that we need,
   As there never will be a to-morrow;
For to-morrow will prove but another to-day,
   With its measure of joy and sorrow.

Then why forecast the trials of life
   With such sad and grave persistence,
And watch and wait for a crowd of ills
   That as yet has no existence?

Strength for to-day—what a precious boon
   For the earnest souls who labor!
For the willing hands that minister
   To the needy friend or neighbor!

Strength for to-day, that the weary hearts
   In the battle for right may quail not,
And the eyes bedimmed with bitter tears
   In their search for truth may fail not.

Strength for to-day, on the down-hill track,
   For the travellers near the valley;
That up, far up on the other side
   Ere long they may safely rally.

Strength for to-day, that our precious youth
   May happily shun temptation,
And build from the rise to the set of the sun
   On a strong and sure foundation.

Strength for to-day, in house and home,
   To practise forbearance sweetly;
To scatter kind words and loving deeds
   Still trusting in God completely.

Strength for to-day is all that we need,
   As there never will be a to-morrow;
For to-morrow will prove but another to-day,
   With its measure of joy and sorrow.

ST. PETER'S AND CASTLE OF ST. ANGELO.

THIRTY-AND-EIGHT YEARS.

THERE have been very few of the children of men who at one time or another have not known the wearing of illness, not only by observing others, but by a personal experience of greater or less degree. How many weary days and nights have they passed, how often have they wished for the darkness to hide the glaring sun from their aching eyes; and as often have they pined for the shadows of night to gather, that its dews might cool the fevered nerves. Twenty-four hours seem an eternity of time in which to suffer, yet they count for but one day. What would you think of thirty-and-eight years? Or, to realize more fully the time that is held within that period, let it be reduced to days, and you have 13,880. If one day's agony is unendurable, "if your heart faints within you ere its close," could you endure fourteen thousand days of suffering?

Close by the temple in Jerusalem there was, by the sheep-market, a pool or reservoir for water, that was between three and four hundred feet long and seventy-five feet deep. Attached to the market was an open building, supported by colonnades; thither went a "great multitude of impotent folk, of blind, halt, withered, waiting for the moving of the water." Jesus had gone up to keep the feast of the Passover, in the month Abib; and he went, as he always did, in order to help the sick and the suffering, to the pool of Bethesda.

The pool was fed from ancient reservoirs under the temple. An old writer describes it as two pools, one fed by periodical rains, the other (according to tradition) being of a reddish color, from the fact that the flesh of the sacrifices was washed in it before being offered. But, according to a tradition that held until 1102 A.D., it was the largest one, close by St. Stephen's gate, that answers to the Bethesda of the time of Christ.

John tells us that at a certain season an angel troubled or stirred the waters of the pool, and that whosoever stepped into it after the coming of the angel, was cured of his disease. What anxiety must have been in the hearts of the weary, waiting ones! How the poor, the lame, and the blind must have waited in suspense for the troubling of the water! and what agony it must have been when the moment came and no one was there to help the sufferer down into the water! There were two flights of steps, one of thirteen and one of sixteen steps, with a platform of twelve feet between them; that was a long journey for the helpless to traverse before the pool was reached. Jesus saw a man lying there who had been sick during thirty-and-eight years, and he said unto him "Wilt thou be made whole?" How eagerly the man must have looked up from his bed on the porch, as he told Jesus that there was no one to help him! And *immediately* the man was made whole.

Are you lying beside a pool of Bethesda waiting for human help? Have you been blind, lame, helpless, weary of sin, often discouraged—one of a multitude waiting for an angel to perform a miracle? Have you been waiting for the "certain season" for twenty, thirty, fifty years? Can you not look up and see Jesus standing by your Bethesda? Do you not know that he was "compassed with infirmity," "tempted in all points like as we are, yet without sin," our Saviour, who knew sorrow and suffered from grief? Would you be made immediately whole? It is so easy to say "Lord, help me," and when you do say it, the angels in heaven will rejoice over your praises; and your songs, once begun, will never cease until one day in the many mansions you should know the Beloved, even as you are known.

BUT ONE PETITION.

WERE it your privilege to present one petition, and but one, at the mercy-seat, and that in the words of Scripture, what would that petition be? Such a privilege was allowed Solomon, and he chose what, in the circumstances, was a wise thing for him to ask. As for myself, I think that mine would be that of David, in the tenth verse of the fifty-first Psalm: "Create in me a clean heart, O God: and renew a right spirit within me." I can think of nothing that I so much need for time, or for eternity, as this. Were I to possess all other things, and to be destitute of this, I should be poor indeed. The treasures of this world would be unsatisfying, even while they lasted, and that would be but for a brief time. I must soon and forever leave them all, and enter on eternity; and

then, without a clean heart and a right spirit, I must be wretched wherever my abode may be. Without such a heart, I could not enter the abode of the blessed, for nothing shall enter there that defileth. Only the pure in heart shall see God. Even though I were allowed to enter that holy place with my sinful heart, I could not be happy. I could have no fellowship with God, nor with the holy angels, nor with the blood-washed saints; nor could I take any satisfaction in their holy pleasures and employments. I should be miserable, even in heaven. Holiness is an indispensable qualification for that holy place.

My petition, therefore, would be. "Create in me a clean heart, O God, and renew a right spirit within me." With such a spirit I shall be more happy in this present world than I should otherwise be, and with such a spirit I shall be prepared to dwell in the presence of God, where there is fulness of joy, and at his right hand, where there are pleasures forevermore.

"HE WILL BRING IT TO PASS."

BRING what to pass? All the desires of our foolish, ignorant hearts? No! Thank God that his love and mercy spare us any such lifelong misery as that gift would bring upon us.

When we pray God to grant our petitions according to his own wisdom and knowledge of what would be best for us, because "we know not what to ask for as we ought," we place ourselves in God's hands to do for us as he sees best. In no other way can we claim answer to prayer. Christ, our Saviour, while here upon earth, said that "Whatsoever ye ask in my name, believing, ye shall receive." Yet furthermore he himself taught us to pray, "Thy will, not mine, be done."

Have we any claim to the promise of answer to prayer if we approach him in a spirit contrary to that which his professed followers are expected to possess?

Submission to his will we must have, but our father has given us the blessed privilege of coming to him and telling him our wants, asking of him "whatsoever things we desire." Not some things, not a particular class of things, not great things, but everything.

Have we any right to suppose our father in heaven so different from Christ? And was there anything too small or insignificant to escape his notice? Can we find one single instance of a single individual, however humble or wicked, who failed to secure his attention? Is the world too large? Is there any danger of an omnipotent, omnipresent God overlooking one of his creatures? Our chiefest joy and blessing come from the fact that God has a plan in life for each one of us. And our answers to prayer depend entirely upon the help or hindrance the answer might be to that line of living. Why cannot we overcome that perverseness of heart which chafes at restraint, and grows sick and faint over deferred hopes? Remember, God knows just exactly when that petition, so earnestly asked, can be granted so as not to retard our Christian growth; or if the prayer were for another, just the moment to render him the best possible good.

Cannot we trust it to him? "He will bring it to pass." Or cannot we trust our Creator to change or improve upon our poor human plans? The Apostle James tells us that the "trying of our faith worketh patience," and to let "patience have her perfect work." He clearly states that this waiting on the Lord is essential to the perfect man in Christ Jesus. It is a distinct and important part in our Christian education, without which we are found wanting. "Cast not away, therefore, your confidence, which hath great recompense of reward." Oh, let us all who bear his name cast from us all these miserable doubts and fears so unworthy of him, and in whole-hearted service, truly and entirely, commit our way unto the Lord, not hoping but knowing in his own good time "he will bring it to pass."

TREASURE IN EARTHEN VESSELS.

PAUL was writing one of his letters to the Church at Corinth; he was encouraging them to do the things which were right, to shun those that were evil. Factions had arisen in the Church, using the name of certain that had preached to them, and even of Christ, in their bitter contentions.

The news of their condition was conveyed to him by members of the household of Chloe. It is not known whether this woman was a member at Corinth, or whether she merely had friends there; but she seemed to have the good of the Church at heart.

Corinth was a great place for commercial and manufacturing enterprise. Its wealth was so celebrated as to be proverbial; but so also were the vice and profligacy of its inhabitants. Venus was worshipped, and evil reigned.

The epistles to the Corinthians are supposed to have been written about A.D. 57; the first from Ephesus, the second from Macedonia, shortly before Paul's second visit to Corinth, which, we are told in Acts, lasted three months. We may conclude that there were many Jewish converts in the Corinthian Church, though it would appear that the Gentiles predominated. Stephanas, Crispus, Caius, and Erastus were among the eminent Christians who lived in Corinth.

The city has lost its grandeur; it is no longer the home of wealth and learning, but is shrunk into a wretched village, which is on the old site, and bears the same name, which, however, is often corrupted into Gortho.

There were formerly to be found the baths erected by Hadrian, now a crumbling heap of bricks; the remains of an amphitheatre, with subterranean arrangements for gladiators; the ruins of the ancient Greek temple; the old columns, which have looked upon the rise, prosperity, and desolation of three successive Corinths.

To such a city, and to the Church that had been gathered there, Paul wrote his epistle. In it he tells them that they had renounced the hidden things of dishonesty, and as the love of God had shined into their hearts, they should remember that the treasure was held in earthen vessels, and that although death worked in them, it was only a death into life; the death of the body, the earthen vessel, and the resurrection of the same. For although the earthly house for which we are caring so much must perish in the grave, yet God had prepared a body that should be raised incorruptible; that through Christ, who knew no sin, yet was made to pay the penalty of sin for us, we might be made the righteousness of God through him.

We are the earthen vessels of which Paul speaks; what treasure have we hidden in us? What is a treasure? It is something that we prize; something that we would not sell, nor give away, nor lose; we are so fearful of loss that we have hidden it. Where?

Is it like the leaven that a woman hid in three measures of meal? Have we sowed it in a field? Or, have we hid it in the field, so that when a man finds it he counts it such a rare thing that he is willing to sell all that he has to buy it? What is our treasure? Is it unto eternal life, or is it unto eternal death? Is it treasure of corn, of oil, of wine, of honey? Or, is it gold, silver, or brass?

Let us lay up treasures in heaven, where they can neither be hurt nor destroyed. The good treasures of the heart are holy thoughts and affections, the keeping of our God's commandments, loving the dear Saviour who died for us, and being always prepared for the marriage feast, so that when our Lord cometh he will say, "Well done, good and faithful servants, enter into the joy of your Lord."

WORK THAT ENDURES.

IN one sense a large proportion of the world's toilers do not choose their own work. Circumstances largely beyond personal control seem to shape out the particular calling it becomes their destiny to follow. Deplorable as it is, yet men and women are continually saying, "Could I but begin life over again, I should never choose my present occupation," or, "Could I only begin again a business career, my present employment would be the last one in which I would engage." To our thinking, some of the most expressive words used to describe human life are contained in the familiar lines:

> "In devious way
> The hurrying stream of life may run."

Life is in very truth a restless, hurrying stream, winding its tortuous, devious way, pushing us often sorely against our will, with its strong, resistless current, into the paths our unwilling feet must tread. The first occupation of which we have historical record is that of our great forefather Adam; nor was he allowed to choose in the matter. "Therefore the Lord God sent him forth from the garden of Eden to till the ground from whence he was taken." No choice for Adam. In the sweat of his brow he was to earn his bread and find sustenance for himself and his family. This has been the inheritance and lot of man ever since. And even as Cain followed the employment of his father, so thousands of men since his time have followed a father's trade, business, or profession. But whether the work which becomes our own is a voluntary choice, or seems thrust upon us, it can be ennobled by the manner of doing it, always supposing it to be of an honorable kind. Canon Farrar says: "A life spent in brushing clothes and washing crockery and sweeping floors—a life which the proud of the earth would have treated as the dust under their feet; a life spent at the clerk's desk; a life spent in the narrow shop; a life spent in the laborer's hut, may yet be a life so ennobled by God's loving mercy, that for the sake of it a king might gladly yield his crown." In these sentiments are embodied a fact too frequently overlooked, and that is—any employment may be made to serve a double purpose. Not only may bread be earned by means of the daily occupation, whether humble or of a more exalted nature, but the kingdom of God may be advanced in human hearts by the manner in which the work is done. Right along in the line of a daily duty, a life may become a sermon, a psalm, an active exponent of Christian principle and godly living. And influence is a very abiding power. Dean Stanley rightly says: "Each of us may have fixed in his mind the thought that out of a single household may flow influences that shall stimulate the whole commonwealth and the whole civilized world." But it will take a long time for any influence or power to affect the civilized world, and this shows how important it is that anything so far-reaching should be of the right kind. It is so generally the rule of the world that everything shall quickly pass away, that it is matter for special satisfaction when anything that is said or done in the right direction can be made to endure. In this connection no grander utterances than those of Daniel Webster are at our command at this moment, at least no utterances of man: "If we work upon marble, it will perish; if we work upon brass, time will efface it; if we rear temples, they will crumble into dust; but if we work on immortal minds—if we imbue them with principles, with the just fear of God and our fellow-men—we engrave on those tablets something that will brighten all eternity." No one can live or work to himself alone. Contact and influence are inevitable as the breath we draw. Neither are they generally inconsequent, because, either for good or for ill, we affect the lives of those about us. As the great statesman has intimated, it is our privilege to work on immortal

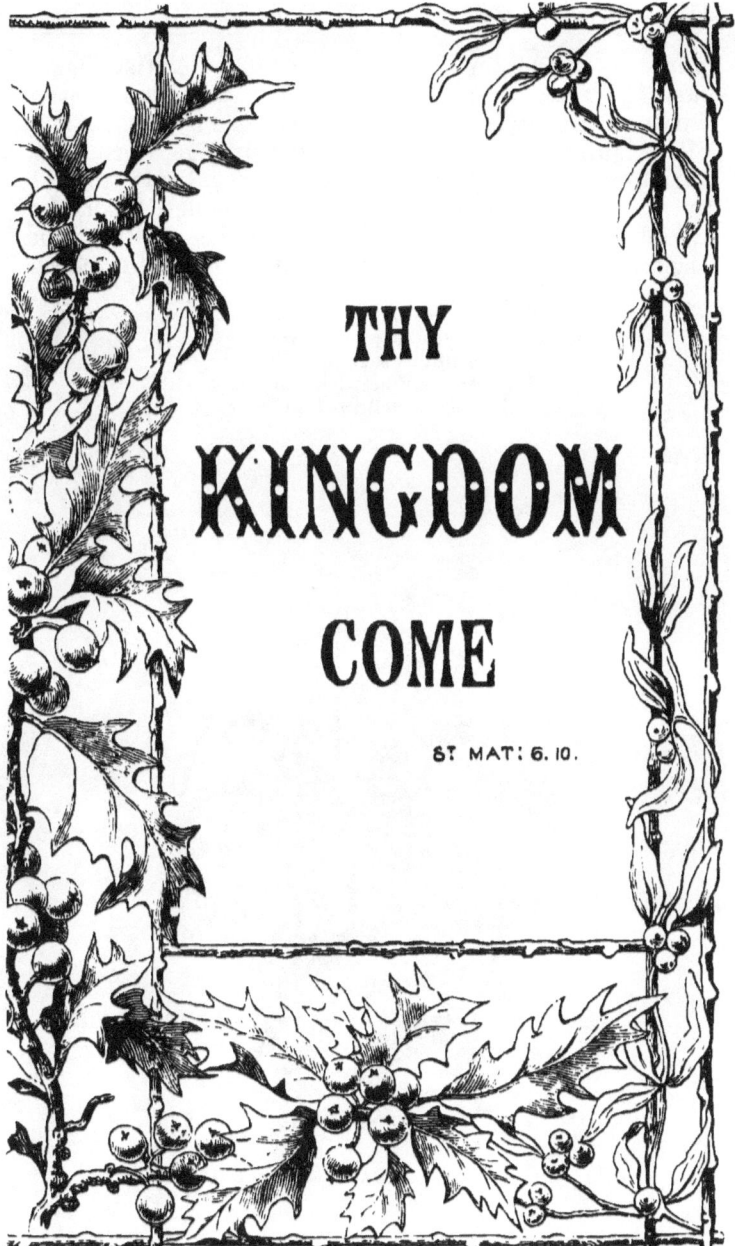

minds; is there, then, but one course for Christians to pursue? Time is short, but yet long enough for each Christian to realize that work may be done by each, which will brighten all eternity. Blessed privilege, open alike to rich and poor, to the high and to the lowly, that of living a life so full of Christ that the simplest labor, the arduous tasks, the every-day work, may be a witness for Christ! A kind of life for which a king might indeed "gladly yield his crown."

> "On! let all the soul within you,
> For the truth's sake, go abroad!
> Strike! let every nerve and sinew
> Tell on ages—tell for God!"

PERSONAL OBLIGATION.

I RECENTLY heard a very intelligent lady say that she would not unite with the Church because she would not dare to take solemn vows upon herself for fear she might break them. She failed to realize apparently that her own personal obligation to serve her Lord remained the same even though she "were out of the Church." Obligation was born long before the Church was. The Lord was "King," and all people his subjects, before church organization was thought of. Right is right, and wrong is wrong to all people under the sun. It is a deplorable mistake to think that "belonging to a church" makes our obligations to God, but it is a happy fact, nevertheless, that it is a most delightful and satisfying help in performing them.

It was Henry Ward Beecher, I think, who said, "Sink the Bible to the bottom of the ocean, and man's obligation to God would be unchanged. He would have the same path to tread, only his lamp and his guide would be gone; he would have the same voyage to make, only his compass and chart would be overboard."

In 1st Cor. iv. 1, it reads, "Let a man so account of us as of the ministers of Christ, and stewards of the mysteries of God. Moreover, it is required in stewards that a man be found faithful." In Matt. xxiii. 8, we have this verse, "But be not ye called Rabbi, for one is your Master, even Christ; and all ye are brethren." In 1st Peter iv. 10, we find this rule: "As every man hath received the gift, even so minister the same one to another, as good stewards of the manifold grace of God."

Dr. Cumming, in speaking of personal obligation, says: "It is by each soldier feeling his obligation in doing his part that the army conquers; it is by each bee doing its work that the hive is stored with honey; it is by each insect putting forth all its might that the coral reef becomes an island and cities rise upon the bosom of the main."

Personal obligation has its source back of consciousness. Whether Christians or not, we are the Lord's, for we have been bought with a price. Therefore our personal obligation demands that we serve our Saviour, that we surrender ourselves to him soul and body.

Spencer relates a story of a beggar who asked something of a lady. She gave him sixpence, saying: "This is more than ever God gave me." "Oh, madam!" said the beggar, "you have abundance, and God hath given all that you have; say not so, good madam." "Well," said she, "I speak the truth, for God hath not given but *lent* unto me what I have, that I may bestow it upon such as thou art."

There are few sights so lovely in this world as a person who deeply feels his or her obligation to the Lord (and the world, which, of course, is necessarily included), and resolutely, earnestly and unswervingly performs it, no matter what discouragements are in his way.

CHILDHOOD OF JESUS.

JUST as the plant does not open to the sun till it has cast its roots into the soil to a depth not measured by the eye, so Jesus, by secret and intense prayer, drew the sap and life of his soul from the bosom of God. Some favoring circumstance was all that was needed to strike from him, before the eyes of all, the spark divine. This was afforded by the journey to Jerusalem to celebrate the Passover feast, at the age when the young Jews began to take part publicly in the religious life of their people. This solemn visit to the Temple filled the soul of Jesus with emotion not to be described; under the symbols he beheld the divine realities. He felt himself truly in the house of God, and perhaps for the first time became fully conscious of the greatness of his mission; he comprehended that he would be called to fulfil those solemn types. When his mother, grieved at his tarrying behind, addressed him in words of tender reproach, he gave that deep and mysterious reply, "How was it that ye sought me? Wist ye not that I must be about my father's business?"

His precocious wisdom had been already revealed in an interview with the doctors in the Temple; his questions showed such richness of thought and feeling, that the illustrious masters were themselves confounded. The questions of a child are often more embarrassing, by their artless depth, than the arguments of the most consummate dialectician. They go straight to the truth by the royal road of simplicity. There was not a white-headed rabbi in the schools of the law who could meet the questions of this child of Nazareth. This scene in the Temple was of great moment in the development of Jesus, by revealing him to himself. The next eighteen years he passed in the most complete obscurity. We may not seek to penetrate their mystery; it is enough for us to know that they prepared him in solitude for his great mission. He spent them in prayer and a holy life.

HIS WAYS ARE NOT AS OUR WAYS.

ALTHOUGH the Scriptures tell us plainly that the ways of God are "past finding out," yet human nature is constantly dissatisfied that so little knowledge is granted concerning God and his mysterious ways. And it puzzles poor humanity to a pitiable degree that things so often seem merely to "happen" anyway. What has been most earnestly and eagerly sought after is the very prize which repeatedly eludes the grasp. The fond dream continually lacks realization; the dreaded calamity is the one permitted to fall. Valued possessions slip away and the hand is powerless to stay them. Adverse and trying events overtake the bravest and most hopeful, and they are not to be warded off. Great pity arises in the heart of a Christian that any one can be so blinded to the only true and reliable comfort to be found in life as to shut the heart to a belief in the providences of God. It becomes clear, in view of the resistless power and control which manifestly dwell in God and his sovereign will, that the best his children can do is simply to trust submissively to his will and try in every possible way to further its divine workings. If only men and women would strive to conform to what is felt to be the will of God, the discontent and misery which often haunt and spoil a life would be banished to a very comforting degree. When rebellion and insubordination are utterly fruitless, what folly to beat and bruise the wings against the fetters of restraint. George MacDonald says: "I find the doing of the will of God leaves me no time for disputing about his plans." The great trouble is, mankind is so

short-sighted that there is no due recognition of the fact
that a Supreme Ruler must follow his own plans and
manage affairs in his own way in order to bring about his
own purpose. We cry for help, then we often wonder at a
state of increased perplexity; but there is lacking that
nobility of patience in the human soul which admits of
waiting, uncomplainingly, the ripening and perfecting
of the purposes of God. Says Flavel: "When God intends
to fill a soul, he first makes it poor; when he intends to
exalt a soul, he first makes it humble; when he intends
to save a soul, he first makes it sensible of its own miseries and nothingness." And should any one ask how these
things can be affirmed by any man, we think the reply
should be: Experience and the lives of those who have
gone before us prove each assertion to be true. Over
and over again men have testified to such facts, and have
found that out of a sense of emptiness has come the fulness of the blessing of God. Out of a consciousness of
spiritual poverty has come a sense of possessing all things;
out of self-abasement has come the exaltation of a renewed
spirit; and out of a sense of sinfulness and nothingness
has come an assurance of the salvation which is through
Christ. This is often the way in which God sees fit to
move upon the heart, producing one extreme state to bring
about another; and what seems strange and ill-appointed
to finite vision and understanding is often the wisdom and
power of God evincing themselves through his unerring
methods and plans. Trust and obedience are virtues which
must help a soul Christward and heavenward. Trust and
obedience will naturally beget love. A lady who was
placed in a responsible position in a charitable institution
said that at first it was her main desire and effort to make
the children love her; obedience, she thought, would
naturally follow if only she could first secure the affection
of the children placed under her charge. But the fallacy
of this belief speedily manifested itself, and the first and
main power in securing either love or respect revealed
itself to be that of insisting on prompt and invariable
obedience. To the untaught and almost unreasoning
children the lady's ways and requirements often seemed
needless and the restrictions unnecessary, but her testimony
was, that obedience and subjection soon convinced the

THE ASCENSION OF OUR LORD.

little ones that each rule was a just one; and she added, that once the children learned to obey her, there was no trouble in securing the love she had so desired. In the great school of life we soon learn that our will and wishes must be subordinate to a mightier will than our own, and our wishes controlled by One whose ways are not as our ways, but are as much higher than our ways as the heavens are higher than the earth. A noble nature will not yield obedience to a superior will simply because perforce it must. Who would wish to be "like dumb, driven cattle" because God rules supreme over the objects of his own creation? Willing obedience is sure to bring peace. David, in a song of thanksgiving, says: "As for God, his way is perfect;" and two verses further on he says, "And he maketh my way perfect;" but previous to either of these declarations, he says: "For I have kept the ways of the Lord . . . and as to his statutes, I did not depart from them." Could the lesson be taught more plainly that keeping the ways and statutes of the Lord tends to the perfection of our own ways?

THE HUMAN SIDE.

AT no season of the year do we more fully appreciate the humanity of Christ than during the Advent and at the Christmas-tide. He came among us the child of Bethlehem, and, as a little child, the little children of each succeeding generation learn to love him. The story of his birth in the manger, because there was no room for him in the inn, is ever new, and children never tire of it. And no teacher or parent who seeks to train the children up to Christian life should omit the opportunity which Christmas time gives of pressing home to the understanding of the children the beautiful thought of the real human boyhood of Christ. The manger may be forgotten and overlooked in the thought of the miraculous which accompanied it—the glorious song of the angels and the visits of the shepherds and magi, with their costly gifts to lay at his feet. Yet although these anthems have their place, the human nature of our Lord ought not to be set aside and forgotten. As an elder brother, his life will appeal more nearly to the homely every-day lives of the children about us than if we think of him as only Divine. And all this human sympathy is greatly needed in forming a character to fight this world's battles. What would Christ have done had he been in my place? is an every-day matter-of-fact reasoning, while Christ, the Almighty and all-powerful, is much more likely to be forgotten. So at this Christmas season, when glad and joyous ring out the bells, and the anthems are chanted, and merriment rules the day, the babe in the manger should be shown as a real human babe. He came among us, not in power, but in weakness. Not as a king, with all the pomp of power, but as a little, unattended child. Not with any outward pomp, or even so very much to distinguish him from ordinary children. Yet we find him growing up with a moral nature which needed no checking and reproof; for although he was oftentimes tempted, just as children nowadays are tempted, to do wrong, he did no wrong. So that he was human, but of a strongly-marked, perfect human character. So when we sing the Christmas carols, let much of their burden be that Christ, our king in glory, was once a child who lived with us; and then shall we more easily remember that God, through Christ, will hear us when we call upon him; and the experience of each child so trained shall be like that of the late Dr. Charles Hodge, who used to say:

"As far back as I can remember, I had the habit of thanking God for everything I received, and of asking him for everything I wanted. If I lost a book or any one of my playthings, I prayed that I might find it. I prayed walking along the streets, in school or out of school, whether playing or studying. I did not do this in obedience to any prescribed rule—it seemed natural. I thought of God as an everywhere-present being, full of kindness and love, who would not be offended if children talked to him."

THE LIVING BREAD.

BREAD, in the Bible, signifies any manner of food that is necessary for the sustenance of life. The manna sent from God to feed the Israelites in the wilderness was called *bread;* but the usually accepted meaning is food made from wheat. One of the earliest undoubted instances of its use is when the angels visited Abraham in the plains of Mamre; and he bid Sarah make a cake for them.

The ancient Hebrews had several ways of making their bread after they had ground the wheat in different kinds of stone mills. Occasionally the grains were mixed with other ingredients, such as beans, lentils, and millet, a little water or milk was put to it, and if they were not in haste leaven was added. It was kneaded by the hands or the feet, and left to rise. One of the lesser prophets tells us that their "baker sleepeth all the night." The dough was then divided into round cakes not unlike flat stones in shape and appearance, about a span in diameter, and a finger's breadth in thickness. Three of these were required for a meal for a single person; these cakes were sometimes punctured, and mixed with oil, and sometimes were only coated with oil. Sometimes the dough was kneaded a second time, and probably some stimulating seeds were added before it was baked.

The shew bread of the priests that was put every Sabbath upon the golden table which was in the sanctuary before the Lord, was made into twelve cakes or loaves, to represent the twelve tribes of Israel. They were large in size, as they used two-tenth deals of flour, or about six pints for each one. They were served hot on each Sabbath, and then the stale ones that had been exposed for seven days were taken away; these could be eaten by the priests alone. It was the proper business of the women of the family, the mistress of the house or one of the daughters, to bake the bread. Baking, however, as a profession, was carried on by men; and Nehemiah speaks of the town of the ovens or furnaces.

As the bread was made in thin cakes, it dried quickly, and being then unpalatable, it was usual to bake daily. Unleavened bread was ordered to be eaten at the Passover, to commemorate the hurriedness of the departure of the Israelites from Egypt. This bread was composed of flour and water, and the thin paste was then spread over a portable oven or urn in which a fire had been made; when cooked, it was broken off in pieces.

Bread was also baked in cavities sunk in the ground, and lined with cement. In the oven a fire was built, and it was thus prepared for baking. The portable oven or jar, which was about three feet high, and was heated by wood, or flowers and grass (our Saviour tells his disciples when he reproves them for the want of faith, "Wherefore if God so clothe the grass of the field, which to-day is, and to-morrow is cast into the oven," etc.), is still common among the Bedouins. When an oven was not to be had, the pastoral Jews spread their bread either over or under hot stones; or, lastly, they roasted it by placing it between two fires made of dried cow-dung, which burns slowly, and therefore answered their purpose.

The Hebrews did not cut their bread, but they broke it, as did our Saviour when he instituted the Supper. "And Jesus took bread, and gave thanks, and *broke* it and gave unto them."

The *living bread* is he which, having come down from heaven, giveth life unto the world. He says: "I am the bread of life: he that cometh unto me shall never hunger; and he that believeth on me shall never thirst. Your

THE TABLE OF SHEW BREAD.

fathers did eat manna in the wilderness, and are dead. I am the living bread which came down from heaven; if any man eat of this bread, he shall live for ever."

> "He who hath led, will lead
>   All through the wilderness;
> He who hath fed, will feed;
>   He who hath blessed, will bless;
> He who hath heard thy cry,
>   Will never close his ear;
> He who hath marked thy faintest sigh,
>   Will not forget thy tear.
> He loveth always, faileth never;
>   So rest on him to-day, for ever."

ELIJAH FED BY THE RAVENS.

AN OLIVE-TREE.

ONE of the very earliest trees mentioned in the Bible is the olive, a leaf of which the dove that was sent out of the Ark by Noah had in her mouth when she returned to him, because the waters had not yet dried off the earth.

Palestine numbered it among her most valuable trees, and the land is said to be full of oil, olives, and honey. It is often mentioned in the classics, was dedicated to Minerva, and employed in the crowning of some of the gods.

It thrives best in the warm sun; it grows slowly, and lives to a great age; some writers think that some olive-trees are two thousand years old. It is said to be neither large nor beautiful as a tree; its color is of an ashen hue; the bark is smooth, but the trunk is knotty and gnarled. Travellers tell us that its leaves are dark green upon the upper surface, but of a silvery hue beneath. Solomon used these trees in building the Temple, because the wood was hard, and very close in grain. It blossoms profusely, and bears fruit every other year.

The flower is at first yellow, but it becomes white as it progresses, and at last loses all the yellow except the centre.

The fruit resembles a plum, in shape and color, first green, at last almost black. It is gathered by shaking the trees, beating them with poles, and by plucking. A full-sized tree, in good bearing condition, is said to produce fifty pounds of oil.

Shoots come up from the roots, and as the parent tree dies they are ready to take its place. The oil was used in lamps, to anoint the body and hair, to anoint the sick, to pour upon wounds, to use in the bath, to consecrate kings, to assist in sacrifices. Even in the wilderness the Israelites were directed to have " pure olive oil beaten for the light, to cause the lamp to burn always."

The fruit was first shaken off, or plucked, and then

trodden; so one of the lesser prophets speaks of the "oil vats." High winds were greatly dreaded by those who cultivated the olive-tree, for even by the ruffling of the breeze the flowers were apt to fall. Job says, "He shall cast off his flower like the olive." The locust also was a great destroyer of the trees, making the "labor of the olive to fail."

We are told that "the sites of many of the deserted towns of Judah bear witness to the former abundance of the olive where it no longer exists, by the oil-presses, with their gutters, troughs, and cisterns hewn out of the solid rock."

In St. Paul's arguments concerning the Jews and Gentiles the olive-tree gives to him a very forcible illustration; and in Romans he gives an allegory of the grafting, growth, and bearing of the fruit of the olive-tree. And he advises his hearers not to have "that blindness in part that happened to Israel, until the fulness of the Gentiles be come in."

A FEW DAYS.

THE Lord had spoken to Moses from Sinai in the beginning of the second year after he had led the Israelites out of the land of Egypt, to command again the keeping of the feast of the Passover.

Many days of discouragement had come to them, and oftentimes they wished that they had been left to die in the land of bondage. Sometimes they would be led to the very borders of the wilderness, just at the edge of the promised land, and when they expected to be led into it to find the milk and honey of which they had heard, they were forced to turn back.

Because of their sins, God had sworn that not one of the people who had come up out of the land of Egypt, except Caleb and Joshua, should be permitted to enter into Canaan. So they travelled around and around in almost a circle for forty years.

But all this time they were keeping the feasts that were appointed for them. And God led them by a cloud by day and a pillar of fire by night. When the tabernacle was reared a cloud covered it; and at even there was upon it in place of the cloud the appearance of fire. When they were to continue their journey the cloud was taken up, and when the cloud tarried for a few days they tarried in their tents, and journeyed not.

So God led them on from day to day, from night to night, until they entered into the rest of the land of promise.

The world is only a great wilderness through which we are journeying to the land of promise beyond all of our weariness, fightings without and fears within. If we attain to a state which we call almost perfection, and then we sin, we have to begin all over again; and we go over and over the same ground until we often get discouraged, just as the Israelites did in the wilderness.

As God led them so he leads us. Are we discouraged because he keeps us quiet for a *few days?* Moses said, "Stand still, and I will hear what the Lord will command." Cannot we *stand still* until we hear the still, small voice, until upon our ears falls the whisper, "Be *still* and know?"

Is our life more than a *few days* of care, of anxiety? We build houses and barns, we sit down to take our ease, forgetting that the *few days* will soon pass.

DOES JESUS CARE?

THE Sea of Gennesaret, or as it was called in the Old Testament, "the Sea of Chinnereth," received its name from a fertile plain on its northwest shore. It is thirty-five miles south of Mount Hermon, twenty-seven east of the Mediterranean, and sixty-four from the Dead Sea. It is said to measure thirteen miles in length, four to seven wide, and is one hundred and sixty feet deep. It is of volcanic origin, and surrounded by rocks that rise from its sides to a great height, the top of some of them being seventeen hundred feet above its narrow pebbly beach. Naturally, as its depression is so great, extreme heat is occasioned, and in the summer is very trying to the traveller; in winter, snow never lies upon its border, although the neighboring mountains are often whitened by it.

In the time of our Saviour some considerable towns studded its shores, and the plain of Gennesaret was a marvel of fruitfulness and beauty. But now only two of them remain; the surrounding hills are usually bare and desolate, and though capable of producing figs, olives, and wheat, the country is so much neglected that thorns abound, and while the thorny tote-tree and palms grow luxuriantly, and indigo is cultivated in the fields, ruin is everywhere to be seen.

Upon the shores of the beautiful lake our Saviour did much teaching; its quiet beauty was hallowed by a voice such as no other man ever possessed. Then, as now, although brackish springs flowed into it, notwithstanding the waters of the Jordan rushed into the lake in a turbid torrent, its water is sweet, cool, and transparent. As then, the lake abounds in fish, but even that seems to be ignored, and no longer do numerous boats let down their nets into the sea. Fish are now taken either by being caught in a hand-net by a man who walks in shallow water, or else they are fed crumbs of bread that are mixed with a preparation of mercury, and when dead they are easily gathered from the surface of the water.

On the lake Peter essayed to walk to Christ, but becoming frightened, he cried out, "Lord, save me, or I perish." Jesus, walking by this sea, saw Andrew and Peter casting their net into it, but at his call they left all to follow him. There was given the parable of the sower who went forth to sow. In one of the towns by its borders, Jesus being moved with compassion because the day was far spent, fed the five thousand with five loaves and two fishes. Crossing the sea, he met the man with an unclean spirit, and healed him. On its western shore, about five miles from where the Jordan enters it, near the city of Capernaum, Christ asked, "Children, have ye any meat?" They had not, but at his command they cast their net, and were not able to draw it in for the multitude of fishes.

And on the same sea when Jesus with his disciples took ship to go over unto the other side, and a tempest arose; Jesus, wearied with his labors, was in the stern of the vessel, asleep. The narrative tells us that, but it would be very difficult to believe that our Lord did not know of their danger, for his eye is never closed when his children need care. And when the disciples called, he rebuked the tempest, and there was a great calm.

Were those disciples any dearer to him than are we? When waves of anxiety and care far harder to endure than those of the Sea of Gennesaret are beating upon us, do we feel that our Saviour is sleeping? Could the ear of the One who died for us ever be closed even to our faintest cry? We are not to go to our eternal home on " flowery beds of ease." We must not expect Apollyon to be conquered without a fight: the wicket-gate is before us, and although, like Christain, we may have to "knock more than once or twice," the gate will be opened at our will.

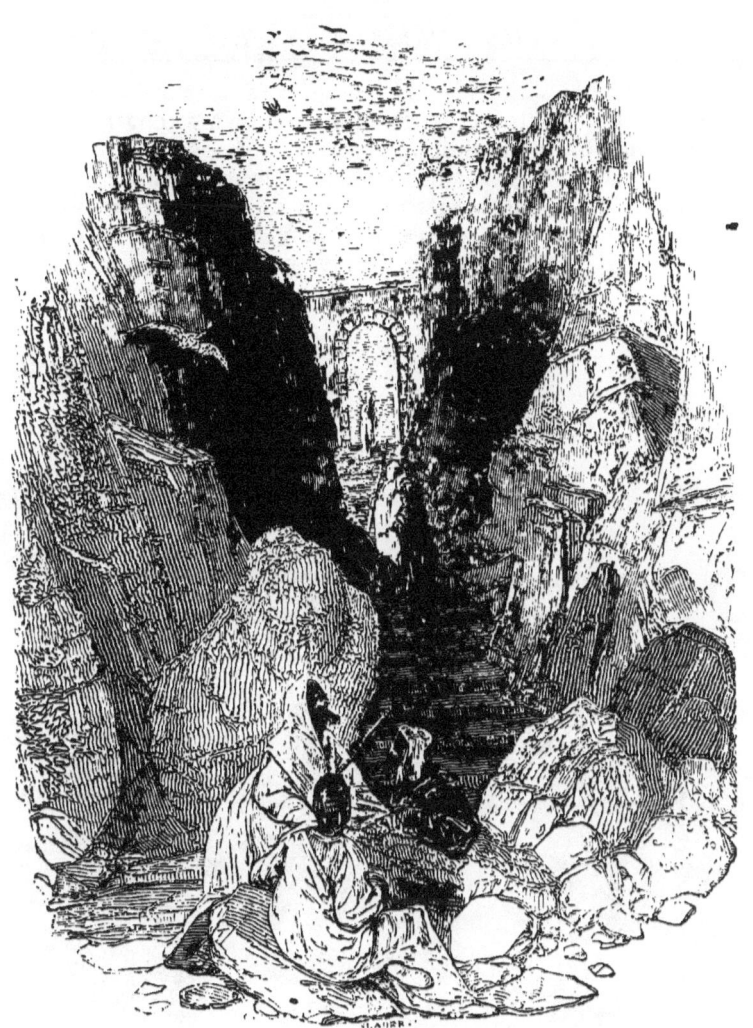
STEPS IN THE ROCKS LEADING TO MT. SINAI.

The trouble with us is, that we grow faint in well-doing; our hearts are altogether fixed on our own strength, and not upon what we can obtain from above.

Our Jesus is ever beside us, near us; so near that he can put out his hand and quiet the waves that threaten to overwhelm us; and when we feel our danger we have only to say, "Lord, carest thou not that we perish?" And almost before we have uttered the words there will be a great calm.

THE CHURCH AT LAODICEA.

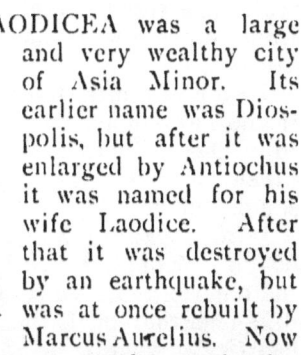

LAODICEA was a large and very wealthy city of Asia Minor. Its earlier name was Diospolis, but after it was enlarged by Antiochus it was named for his wife Laodice. After that it was destroyed by an earthquake, but was at once rebuilt by Marcus Aurelius. Now it is nothing but a scene of utter desolation, but so extensive are the ruins that it is said fully to justify the vivid descriptions that are given of it by Greek and Roman writers.

A Christian church was early gathered in the city, but not, presumably, by St. Paul. When he wrote from Rome to the Christians at Colosse, and sent a greeting to the church at Laodicea, it is thought that he had never yet visited it.

In subsequent times it became a Christian city of eminence, the See of a bishop and a meeting-place of councils. It was destroyed by the Mohammedan invaders; and it is now a scene of utter desolation. It is thought by some writers that Paul's letter to Philemon is the letter to the Laodiceans.

The church at Laodicea did not consist of people who were firm in the right, but of those who were wavering. St. John writes that they were neither cold nor hot, but lukewarm; and he counsels them to buy only gold that had been tried in the fire.

We all know how very uncomfortable a thing the uncertain friend is. Just at the moment when we expect decided words, deeds, actions, there is nothing but a wavering spirit, neither cold nor hot, just a lukewarm love that really amounts to nothing, and in despair we turn aside from him, and wish that we might know just where to find him.

If you are in trouble; if sorrows are thick about you; if the "grasshopper has become a burden," and you need love, cheer, comfort, can you endure to be met by such a lukewarm love that your heart aches more than before you sought the help?

If you look into the eyes of your little child, and instead of the look of glad surprise that you have a right to expect the tones of your voice will call up, you see only an indifference that chills the love that is welling up from your heart, and sending to your words the deep, full echoes that love alone can give to them, can you endure to see only flitting shadows of appreciation in the eyes of the child? Would our God endure in the children whom his Son died to redeem luke-warmness? When he says to us, "My son, give me thy heart," when he reaches out an arm to save, sets his eyes to watch, and bends a listening ear, when he holds out to us the Everlasting Arms to keep us from falling, could we receive the gifts, help, blessings indifferently?

God loves happy Christians just as earthly parents love happy children. If you love him, hold up your head, and let all the world see that you have learned to love Jesus. Why do you want to be always looking at the ground at your feet, intently watching for rough places, for rocks of offence, for pitfalls, for miry depths? Surely you have forgotten that the Everlasting Arms are about you, and that the angels who are sent forth to minister to the loved ones do bear you up that you may not stumble.

> "And Thy guiding hand still held me,
>   Though my feet would turn and slide,
> Held me while I wandered blindly,
>   That I might not turn aside.
>
> "Now I know Thou hast been with me,
>   And Thy face again I see,
> And I feel Thy hands upholding,
>   Helping and directing me."

LAODICEA.

Paul knew that the wealth and sins of the Laodicean Church had distracted the Christians there, and to him who so emphatically preached to them to stand up and fight like men, it must have been very discouraging to know that their piety was only lukewarm, that they were neither cold nor hot. Let us ever bear in mind that the dear Lord wants, will only have and own, real love, real work, real faith, real decision of character, not lukewarmness, but a Christianity that, in the face of discouragements, be they never so great, will cause us to look up and say, "Lord, I love thee!"

WAITING FOR FEELING.

SOME one has remarked that "He who looks upon Christ through frames and feelings is like one who sees the sun in water, which quivers and moves as the water moves; but he that looks upon him in the glass of his Word, by faith, sees him ever the same." Newton says: "Our union with Christ is the union of the covenant, and therefore not dependent upon frames and feelings."

Bate writes: "To depend upon feeling in religion is unsafe and dangerous. A man may as well think of holding fast to the clouds, building upon running sand, or relying on the wind. The clouds, the sand, the wind, are no more changeable and uncertain than our feelings. A change in circumstances, or a change in health, or a change in friends, will often produce an equal change in feeling. Our religion should be like the sun, which, cloud or no cloud, goes on in its shining course; like the earth which, wind or no wind, rolls on its orbit. We should 'stand by faith,' 'live by faith,' and 'hold fast the profession of our faith.'"

It is a fatal mistake—made by many otherwise beautiful lives—this waiting for feeling; this refusal to anchor themselves on the Rock, Christ Jesus, because they experience no strong emotion. It is resolution such souls need, resolution to pay the debt they owe to Christ, who gave his life for them. It is sad to believe the terrible fact that men and women whom we respect and love, who are honest and true as far as any and all debts and friendships of this world are concerned, fail in payment of the great debt to the Saviour of the world, fail to acknowledge the Friend above all others. What a blessing would come to such souls if, instead of waiting for feeling, they would turn about and look for Christ for the purpose of discharging the debt they owe. President Tuttle told a good story illustrating this personal obligation to the Lord of all. He said:

"I asked a young man, 'Do you have any anxiety about yourself as a sinner against God?'

"The reply was, 'I know I am a sinner, but I feel very little on the subject.'

" 'Are you trying to do what God tells you to do as well as you are able and with such light as you have?' I asked.

" 'Oh, no, sir! for it would seem to be mockery for one who feels so little as I do to attempt to perform any religious duty.'

" 'You admit that God does require of you repentance and faith and worship and a holy life, do you not?'

" 'Yes, sir; I must admit all this, but I do not *feel* it.'

" 'What would you advise a customer to do who had contracted a debt at this store, who admits the debt, and that he ought to pay it, but says he knows all this, but has so little feeling about it?'

"In an instant he said, 'I would advise him to pay it, feeling or no feeling.'

" 'That is just what I want you to do,' I said.

" 'What shall I do?' he asked.

" 'Come to the inquiry meeting to-night, and meanwhile do you search your Bible and ask God for help.'

" 'I will do the best I can,' was his reply.

"That evening he admitted no progress, only he saw his guilt more clearly; but he would do all God required as well as he could. I never saw him shed a tear, or betray a tithe of the emotion the young man does who has just left my room, but as fast as light came he obeyed it. In a little time he was hoping he had passed from death unto life, and for years he has lived a faithful, beautiful Christian life."

The *feeling* will come when one has taken up one's duty. No one ought to question that. The Holy Spirit will touch any and every soul that is willing to obey. Spurgeon says, "It is astonishing how whimsical people are about the way they will be saved." There is only one way. Christ says, "Come unto me." Obey him.

THE POOL OF SILOAM.

SADNESS AND SOLACE.

IT cannot be denied that the general tendency of the human heart as age advances is toward sadness and depression. It might also be said it is the natural tendency. This is not always the case, as there are many pleasing exceptions, but the general tendency is in a serious, sombre direction. It is not to be wondered at that this should be so. The world is a stern disciplinarian; cares press, trials wear, and sorrows give anxiety; and it is a constant struggle to overcome and rise superior to first one, then another, besetting ill. True, natures differ widely, and where one will brood and mourn, another may, through buoyancy of disposition, successfully cry, "Away with melancholy!" There can be no real pleasure, it would seem, in that which is mournful and sad, and yet there is that in the soul of man which makes many a pathetic story far more fascinating and attractive than the loveliest, wittiest matter could possibly prove. There is a mournful sweetness to some of the saddest of poetry which rivets the eye and chains the attention until the weirdly attractive lines have lodged in the memory, ready to be recalled in serious moods with dreamy satisfaction. And it is often from the most gifted, able, and best-trained minds the saddest sentiments find expression. It seems as though the very extreme of sadness were reached in a definition of the word "pleasure" which appeared some years ago. Here it is: "Pleasure, the comma with which we divide our griefs." Was it not going too far? We have always thought so, and yet a companion definition of "sleep," from the pen of Matthew Henry, is hardly less impressively sad: "Sleep gives some intermission to the cares and pains and griefs that afflict us; it is the parenthesis of our sorrows." Conclusions like these are not often reached by the young. It is well they are not; and yet the young, as well as the middle-aged and the old, need to be fortified against the depressing influences sure to overtake them in the strange, mixed journey of life. Gay surroundings never relieve, but only pall on a stricken heart. The old adage, that "misery likes company," is true to a certain extent, and yet misery likes to choose its company quite as decidedly as does happiness. But all the accumulating events of life, especially its sorrows, its disappointments, its depressing losses, force the inquiry which frequently finds forcible utterance—how *can* people live in the world and endure to live without the religion of Jesus Christ and belief in the promises of the Bible? How, indeed! Of all the pitiable objects on earth, the most pitiable to our mind is an *old* sceptic. While some of the glamour of youth remains—while life still holds forth promises of bright days and joyous scenes, of merry re-

ANCIENT GETHSEMANE: INTERIOR VIEW.

unions and glad holidays, full of mirth and pleasure—it
is piteous, even then, to see the affections entirely set on
things of the earth. But after the moth of care and the
corroding rust of sorrow have torn all the glamour of youth-
ful promise and allurement away, when the great thief—
time—has broken into the life and stolen most of its
treasure away, if the support of religious faith be wanting,
what but a lamentable wreck and ruin would remain! But,
turning from so melancholy a picture, it is delightful to
consider how many bright, happy, hopeful Christians feel
themselves comforted and their lives enriched, from year
to year and from youth to age, by the sweet solace of religious belief and a childlike trust in the unfailing promises
of the Bible. And there is not a sad phase in life, not a
depressing picture of memory, not a disappointment or
sorrow, for which solace cannot be found, if the heart will
only receive it. The world has been called a disciplinarian; it is such, but discipline either hardens or softens
the nature. When the divine voice told Saul of Tarsus it
was hard to kick against the pricks, a very stern, abiding
lesson was given to man for all time. And when Jesus
Christ said, "Come unto me, all ye that are weary and
heavy-laden, and I will give you rest," both invitation and
promise were for all time also. If only men would "taste
and see that the Lord is good" there would be small need
to urge that the sweet solace of religion be tried as an
antidote for all the sadness of mortal experiences. Yet it
is true, sublimely true, that

" Earth has no sorrow that Heaven cannot heal."

MISSIONARY WORK.

BE willing to work for others, and be zealous in every good work. In this our day of missionary endeavor, when the subject is so constantly brought before us, one need not wait, nor be idle for want of work. Be active and busy. You know the need of missionary zeal, of missionary money, and the need of willing, working hands and ready hearts. You and I each bear our own responsibility in this matter. Can not each one of us do much more, if we have already done a little in our own way, to help this cause? The steady progress of the work abroad and the added interest awakened each year at home, go far to make up much that is hopeful and encouraging for our own individual effort. What others have done, you can do. It is your own part that is needed in the great whole. If you do it not, some one part is left out, or filled by another whose zeal exceeds your own.

Do you doubt your ability to do a great thing? Then just do a little thing in your own way for the Master. He will look not at the greatness of the gift given, or the deed done, but at the spirit back of it. The widow's mite, in the estimation of our Lord, outweighed all the more costly gifts of the rich. "She hath done more than they all" was the comment of the Master.

You are just where you should be; the soil of endeavor is about you, and the seed lies within your hand. None is denied this. It is not the quantity you hold, but the way in which you sow it, that will tell. Prayer breaks up the soil of doubt and fear, patience sows it, perseverance tends it, and, at last, will not faith reap it?

The implement of labor a woman wields is commonly her needle. That is rather an insignificant instrument in one's hand, is it not? But that needle of hers has wrought wonders in the sight of God. He knows how many poor and needy have been clothed and fed—unmarked save by him—with its cunning craft. It has often cost personal toil and sacrifice to do missionary work for the Master. It costs self, and its mean satisfaction. But in the end it pays. It has been truly said that, even in the heart of the most disinterested person, there is a secret sense of satisfaction, because of some good done to others. A good deed brings its own reward. How much more when done for his glory. That we are not always willing grows out of the fact that we are still unused to self-denial. We have not tasted the full measure of delight in loving service for him and his.

We can all do something to bring others to Christ. We can at least bear testimony. John stood and looked at Jesus, then pointed out the way to others. "We are his witnesses," now and here. Do you mean to do something for him sometime? Do it now! Don't put it off! You cannot serve him by the things you mean to do. Doubting work or dreaming work is no work. It is the hidden force within you that is waiting your pleasure. There lies your chance. If you have not money, give your work. Only give something. The right means will make itself felt. Half-willing disciples are not those who follow closest. Give willingly if you give at all. The rest will follow.

There is your personal influence. Somebody looks to you for example, and will do very much as you do. Then, a quiet word, a seed sown where none fell before, a good deed done where none else have wrought, will bear fruit;

or, if nothing else follow, you have for the time done your duty best where duty led. Take, then, that which you have, and use it for the Master's sake, never doubting but that he will be mindful of it. Will you do less than the flowers, whose fragrance is all for others, and none for self? A beautiful ministry theirs. Ours should be like it.

> "Who gives to whom hath naught been given,
> His gift in need, though small indeed,
> As is the grass blade's wind-blown seed,
> Is large as earth and rich as heaven."

IN EVERYTHING GIVE THANKS.

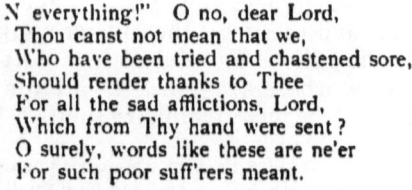

"IN everything!" O no, dear Lord,
Thou canst not mean that we,
Who have been tried and chastened sore,
Should render thanks to Thee
For all the sad afflictions, Lord,
Which from Thy hand were sent?
O surely, words like these are ne'er
For such poor suff'rers meant.

"In everything!" The good, the ill,
The poverty, the pain,
The deep distress which sin hath wrought
And hope and trust has slain?
O no! 'twere mockery, indeed,
To offer thanks for these,
More meet and fit it were to bow
In tears, on bended knees.

"In everything!" O Father, yes,
How easy it were then
To render thanks, if only joy
And happiness had been
Our portion, and our guests alone
Throughout the year just gone,
O surely, then, our lips and hearts
Would overflow with song.

"In everything!" O must we kiss
The rod Thy hand extends,
Until in deep humility
Our stricken spirit bends?
Oh! then, dear Lord, we ask of Thee,
Give patience, faith, and grace,
And help us see behind the clouds
The shining of Thy face.

"In everything!" Ah, yes! for then
Our hearts can give Thee praise,
Our lips give thanks, that Thou in love
Hath ordered all our ways.
Whatever is, is right and best,
Forgive if we rebel,
For whether joy or grief, we know
Thou doest all things well.

GIVING THANKS.

ANY one accustomed to reading the Scriptures cannot fail to have noticed how continually all through the books of the Old and New Testament the giving of thanks is enjoined upon all tribes and people. It is easy to count in a very short time more than a score of instances in which the Psalmist speaks of giving thanks, and the expression is generally added, "To the Lord." Among the strongest of these expressions are: "It is a good thing to give thanks unto the Lord;" "O Lord, my God, I will give thanks unto thee forever;" "At midnight I will rise to give thanks unto thee;" also in repeated instances he exhorts the people to come before the Lord "with thanksgiving." Paul, in writing his various epistles, repeatedly reminds the people to be thankful; to the Colossians he says, "And be ye thankful;" to the Phillippians, "With thanksgiving let your requests be made known unto God;" to the Ephesians, "Giving thanks unto God and the Father in the name of our Lord Jesus Christ;" to the Hebrews, "By

him, therefore, let us offer the sacrifices of praise to God continually . . . giving thanks to his name." And in the solemn Revelation we find, "Blessing and glory, and wisdom, and thanksgiving, and honor, and power, and might, be unto our God forever and ever." These are a few of the passages where the giving of thanks is enjoined in the Bible. In the same chapter of Colossians in which Paul writes, "And be ye thankful," a little farther on he says, "And whatever ye do, do it heartily, as to the Lord, and not unto men." The chapter concludes with the words, "And there is no respect of persons." So here we have three distinct and important reminders. And first, it is seen to be a simple and sacred duty to be thankful; then thankfulness should be rendered in a hearty, sincere manner, very different from the lax, indifferent way in which we often acknowledge obligation to our earthly friends; and again, none are exempt from this required duty of expressing gratitude to God for mercies received. The king on his throne, the rich man in his stately mansion, the cottager, the inmate of the almshouse, all alike are commanded to be thankful, and each and all have much to be thankful for. Every year we live increases our cause for gratitude that we live at the present time, and in our day and generation. The dreadful day of martyrdom, of the inquisition, the dungeon, of persecution, banishment, and other terrors from which Christians have suffered, and over which they have triumphed, has long since passed away. Never was liberty to serve God and to obey the dictates of conscience more entirely to be enjoyed than in this blessed country and at the present day. The accumulated knowledge and experience of all the known past are largely within our reach, with the immense profit and instruction to be derived from their useful teachings. But causes for thanksgiving to Almighty God are too abounding to be enumerated. The question arises, How best can return be made for some of these, the great blessings of a wise Creator? Adequate return we can scarcely approach, because finite gratitude cannot adequately compare with infinite bounteousness. True, we can say, in prayer, our hearts are thankful for all the goodness and mercies which crown our lives, but although this is requisite, it still is not nearly enough. Gratitude, like faith, should show itself in works, and in generous, gracious works. It is not enough, as the Bible warns us, that we say to our destitute brother or sister—and especially at this season of lavish provision and feasting in our homes: "Depart in peace; be ye warmed and filled; notwithstanding ye give them not those things needful to the body." One word in the verse embodies the best manifestation which can be used to express gratitude to God—"Give!" and none so poor but they have something of value to give to others. The very poor, those who are objects of charity themselves, can give their prayers, and of them only such things as they have to give will be required. Nor need it be said that prayers and good wishes cost nothing. We take it, it often costs considerable in a certain way for the poor to pray for the rich. Said a very poor woman a little while ago, "I used often to watch with the sick before I was sick myself." Did it cost her nothing to watch all night beside the couch of pain? In a thousand ways we can minister to each other's needs and necessities. And let each professing Christian especially remember another Bible assertion, "For unto whomsoever much is given, of him shall much be required." Conscience will easily decide what should be the proportion given back to the Lord as a thank-offering at this time of thanksgiving and prayer. Above all, let life be consecrated to his service, and then from it will naturally flow the good deeds acceptable in his sight.

> "Be ours the bliss of holy living
> With love divine enthroned within,
> Our life a psalm of glad thanksgiving
> Till heavenly songs our lips begin."

NEW YEAR THOUGHTS.

BEFORE us lies the new year, pure and unsullied yet as the untrodden snow. If we could lift the veil which hangs over the future, what would we meet of joy or sorrow, of greatness or distinction in this coming cycle of months?

The probabilities are that this year will be an ordinary, commonplace year, for most of us must expect to live ordinary lives and attract no attention or admiration from the great world. The duties which will press upon us will for the most part be those which spring out of our natural relations, family, social, business, and religious. Life's necessities will keep us from turning aside from its usual path. Whatever our life has been, directs to a greater or less extent what it will be; we take up the burden of living with the new year if it has been a burden, and we take up the joy of living if it has been a joy. Whatever service we do for God or man will probably be done along the line of daily avocations, and the routine of life will go on as usual, daily worries and cares, daily joys and happiness, daily work and prayer for daily bread.

Shall we turn away from this life, and call it monotonous and uneventful? It takes years and years of such things to make up an ordinary life, and those who despise or complain about the prosiness and humdrum or the quiet routine are sadly out of tune with life.

Some people are always pining for something higher than this daily life affords, and have such a high ideal that the real seems of no earthly value. They think they could shine in some lofty place, and because they are not there, they do not try to shine in their own place.

There never were truer words spoken than our Lord

uttered, "He that is faithful in that which is least, is faithful in that which is great." If you hide your candle under a bushel in an humble position you will do the same when you are put in a high position. One's place in life is never at a distance from where he is, one's vocation is always the simple round of duties that the passing hour brings. With these probabilities before us, what attitude shall we assume toward the new year? Shall we make the vital mistake of thinking that there is no opportunity for ordinary lives to be beautiful and useful?

One who has endeared himself to many by his writings, says: "In the common relations of life there is room not only for duty, but for heroism. No ministry is more pleasing to the Master than that of cheerful and hearty faithfulness to lowly duty, where there is no pen to write its history, and no voice to proclaim its praise. To live well in one's place in the world, doing one's most prosaic work diligently and honestly, is to live grandly. One who fights well the battle with his own lusts and tempers, in the midst of the countless temptations and provocations of every-day life, is a Christian hero." But there are possibilities also awaiting us in this new, untried year. How do we know but that the years that are past are all the years God means to give us on this earth, that we have not now seen the light of our last New Year's day?

This year may find us companions of the dead. There is that in the air, in the sky, in the earth, in ourselves which may bring the end at any moment. Are we prepared for that great change, and if not, is it not the part of wisdom to prepare at once?

Perhaps some people find themselves to-day face to face with new and difficult duties. In view of the comparative uselessness of their past lives, they may feel called upon to engage in more active work for the Master, to speak to this friend or that about his soul's salvation. Peculiar difficulties and trials may lie in the path of others, and the future may seem to hold responsibilities that they dare not assume alone, lest they make a mistake. There is but one thing to do. Ask the Lord's guidance first of all, then go steadily forward, leaving him to deter you if you are not in the right road, and he will do it. He will direct the paths of all who commit their ways unto him.

THE HOPES OF EASTER-TIDE.

THE "sweetly solemn" season of Easter comes to the Christian Church when everything in nature seems in sympathy with the sacred observance. Nature is waking from her long sleep of the winter, and is slowly, yet surely, gathering up all her regenerative forces, preparing to clothe the patient earth with new life and verdure everywhere. The brave crocus and hardy snow-drop are peeping up from the yielding soil, giving unfailing promise of other blooms soon to come forth and gladden the spirits with bright colors and fragrant scents. The lengthening days and longer twilights succeed the brief, dark days of the rigorous season just passed. Each spring-time presents a strong suggestion of the resurrection of the body. That which so lately seemed so cold and dead is instinct with new life and beauty. And no matter how long the winter may have been, how cold its nights, how fleeting its days, or how severe its storms, there is a set time, and that not so very far away, when the warmth and brightness of spring will chase away the clouds, the coldness, and the darkness of the season of frost and snow. And this because the Bible has said that while the world endures, seed-time and harvest, cold and heat, summer and winter shall return each in due season. And even as life succeeds death in the world of nature, so in like manner the Scriptures teach that after death of the body comes a new and spiritual life; and as Christ rose from death and from the grave, so the dead in Christ shall rise. Alas! for the modern school of unbelievers, scientists, so-called, who dare to raise their voices in opposition to sacred revelation, and attempt to teach that science only deals with true revelation, that many assurances of the Bible deal with the supernatural and unfounded theories which in the light of science shrink away, becoming null and void. Yet the true believer sings on, "Begone, unbelief, my Saviour is near," and his reply to the seemingly learned, yet shallow arguments of the scientist is simply, "I know in whom I have believed." It was refreshing and inspiring to recently have come across these words in reading: "The Christian verb is 'we *know*,' not 'we hope, we calculate, we infer, we think,' but 'we *know*.' And it becomes us to apprehend for ourselves the full blessedness and power of the certitude which Christ has given to us by the certainties which he has brought us." The ring of conviction is in the sturdy assertions, and yet it is but the echo of the language of Scripture, which gives out no uncertain sound in declaring its truths. Spurgeon says: "By passing through the death our Lord has made a thoroughfare for us. We take death and the grave in transit now; they do not hinder our advance to glory and immortality and eternal life." No Christian need fear to follow where his Lord has led. The lessons of Easter are plain and full of encouragement. What is most needed in this age of doubt and scepticism is a firm adherence to the literal teachings of Holy Writ. It is a thousand pities that Christians will concern themselves about the questions continually rising and being thrust upon the world by those who, having made shipwreck of their own faith, would seek to weaken and, if possible, to overthrow the faith of others. Cling fast to the promises of Almighty God, to the assurances of the Saviour. Where shall the mourner go for comfort if ever the story of the resurrection loses its power? On what scientific revelation in all the broad world shall the dying man base his hopes of a bright resurrection morn if once he lets go of a staunch belief in, and reliance on, the fact of the resurrection of Jesus Christ as taught in the Bible? As age increases and faith strengthens or weakens according as the Christian trusts the promises of the Saviour, let every Christian recognize the importance of holding fast to the Word of God, trusting its every lesson and clinging to its teachings, which will surely prove in return as an anchor to the soul both sure and steadfast. And of Easter, who can think but with gratitude and rejoicing!—the most hopeful, blessed anniversary in all the Christian's calendar of days.

> "Hail! day of light and life and love,
> Of Heaven's triumph o'er the grave,
> When Christ, who left his throne above
> Man's soul from sin and death to save,
> Arose again! Hail! glorious morn,
> That breakest on the sinner's night,
> When we again, through Christ, are born,
> And with him rise into the light!"

SWEETNESS OF SPIRIT.

SOME Christian men carry the charm of an attractive atmosphere with them. It is a pleasure just to look at them. Even when one differs in judgment from them as far as the poles are asunder, one is none the less drawn toward and fascinated by them. There is such sweetness in their spirit, such gracious gentleness in their manner, such kind catholicity, such manly frankness, such thorough self-respect on the one hand, and on the other hand such perfect regard for the judgment of others, that one cannot help loving them, however conscience may compel conclusions, on matters of mutual consequence, unlike those which they have reached.

These are not weak men, either. What people like in them is not that, with the everlasting unvaryingness of a mirror, they reflect back the thought which is presented to them, and so are always at an agreement with others; sometimes one is even more drawn to them when they are in opposition, because they are so true and just that their aspect carries with it all the refreshment of variety with none of the friction of hostility.

Natural temper has something to do with this. God gives a great gift to a man when he gives him a sunny disposition, a candid spirit, and the instinct of fairness in a controversy. It is exceedingly hard for some men to be just. They are jealous, suspicious, and morose in their natural bent. It is hard for them to believe good of others. It is easy for them always to put the worst construction upon their conduct. It sometimes seems as if it were almost more than grace itself can do to transform their tempers so that they will be just toward any man against whom they have been led to have a prejudice.

IF THEY COULD COME BACK.

SUPPOSE God should hear the prayer which we may all have uttered in our first dumb despair, and uttered again as the weary days go on, to send back to us those whose going has taken away from us the joy of living. Suppose, for the sake of our High Priest, who *can* be touched with the feeling of our infirmities, and through whom we can come boldly to the Throne of Grace, he should forgive the prayer and grant our request: would we ourselves be willing for them to come back? Oh, we are so selfish that few of us could have the strength to say no; we are so unwilling to let our beloved sleep while we are ourselves waking and in the battle. We cannot even realize what their coming back would be. We cannot understand from what they are freed. We are so used to being bowed down by burdens that we don't know what it is for them to be unburdened, with a heart filled with happiness unalloyed. We are so used to sickness, pain, and guarding against hurt that never to say "I am sick" is incomprehensible. We have groped so long darkly, the unknown future often a dread, we forget that in that land they see no longer "through a glass darkly," but face to face, all that seemed strange to them here understood and known.

Yes, we forget just the little we know about the other

world and the joy they have entered into, when we cry for them to come again to us. We forget everything sometimes, except how hard it is to live without them.

But think what it would be to them to come back; to take up the burdens they dropped, and bear them again when they know what it is to be unburdened; the fret and anxious care for the morrow, when they have been where no morrow ever comes; to mingle again with the envious, hateful, and malicious, when they have mingled with those who know nothing of slander, malice, or lies, but only love; to come from where love reigns supreme back to where envy and hatred are known; to live with the sinful when they have dwelt among the sinless; to bear pain when they have tested what it is never to say " I am sick;" to face the piercing storms of the earth when their abode has been where skies are always serene and storms cannot beat upon them, where cold and heat are unknown; to battle once more with temptations, when they have once overcome and have been " clad in white raiment;" to fight again with sin and death when they, through him who died for us, have conquered even the last enemy; to suffer disappointment when they have been dwelling where every wish is gratified, their will subjected perfectly to the Father's; to strive with the multitude, unsatisfied and longing, when they have known what it is never to hunger or thirst for anything; to struggle in life, growing discouraged again, longing for rest as we do—not the "gain" which it is to be with Christ, but for rest, almost the rest of forgetfulness—when they have once " obtained joy and gladness" and "for them sorrow and sighing have flown away;" to be weary, to suffer the grievousness of sinning, the conflict with temptation, the bitter yielding to it, when they had before " come out of great tribulations, and had washed their robes and made them white in the blood of the Lamb;" to weep when all tears had once been " wiped from their eyes;" to come back to turmoil and wrangling when they have known peace—the peace which floweth as a river, abiding in " Jerusalem, a quiet habitation;" to know here no resting-place when they have dwelt in a mansion prepared for them from eternity for eternity, "a tabernacle which shall never be taken down, not one of the stakes thereof shall ever be moved;" to gaze only upon the poor beauties of earth when they have seen "the King in his beauty and beheld the land which is very far off;" to have only our faces in which to joy when they have looked upon the face of the Lamb; to walk and talk with us when they have walked and talked with the redeemed and the Redeemer; to knit the brow with anxious care when his name has been upon their foreheads; to leave Heaven for earth; the Lord himself for us!

And what have we to offer them if they could come back? A share in our sorrows, a part of our cares, and our love—a love poor, weak, and selfish beside the perfect love they have known. That is all.

Better, then, that for them " there shall be no more death, neither sorrow nor crying, neither shall there be any more pain; for the former things are passed away."

OLD-FASHIONED CHRISTIANS.

IT is matter for which to thank God that there is a considerable number of them yet living on the earth. And if the question should arise: In what do they differ from Christians of more modern times? the answer would come promptly something in this wise: They are Bible Christians; Christians who have obeyed the Scripture requirement, and have come out from the world, and are separate, and try to touch not the forbidden things of the world. They do not take the Sunday newspaper nor allow the dust to collect on the family Bible while they toil through the almost exhaustless columns of the unhallowed sheet. They do not claim a right to exercise all freedom, not to say license of action, as to how and where they shall spend their time, even as professed worldlings would do. They attempt no defiance of the Divine affirmation, "Ye cannot serve God and mammon." The theatre is not a favorite resort, the progressive-euchre party and "german," with their late hours, do not form a part of their regular engagements. The house of God is a place of great attraction for them; they stand by the minister, and are his unfailing friends as long as he needs their stanch support. The meeting of prayer witnesses to the duty and privilege they esteem it to stand up and proclaim themselves on the Lord's side, and even when it involves cross-bearing or sacrifice, they will try boldly to speak words of good cheer and encouragement to others who like themselves are striving to walk in the narrow way.

When the ruler of the nation or governor of the State appoints a thanksgiving or fast day, and recommends that in the morning the people should assemble in their customary places of worship to thank God for his manifold blessings, or to humbly sue for forgiveness of sin and grace to walk more worthily of their profession, they make an effort to show respect for the just and reasonable requirement, and duly present themselves on such occasions before the Lord in his house. On the Sabbath they observe the rules of the service, joining in song, responsive reading and prayer, and with proper reverence refrain from conversation or other behavior inappropriate to the sacred hour of worship.

Ofttimes, to the disgust and disapproval of younger and more "liberal" Christians, they stoutly and conscientiously oppose certain entertainments, including humorous recitations and exhibitions of buffoonery, being given from the pulpit platform. Remembering that the place has been solemnly dedicated to the worship of Almighty God, they cannot so far ignore all that that implies, as to consent to such glaring infringement of the sanctity of the sacred spot as would be involved in converting it into a secular rostrum, permitting of light, frivolous, and fantastic shows. They neither attend themselves nor allow their children to attend the popular Sunday-evening concert, nor do they visit, ride, or receive visitors on the day of rest. They accept the truths and doctrines of the Bible, just as they stand. Recognizing no safe reason why they should forsake the old-time beliefs of sincere and scholarly Christians who have gone before them, they believe that when the Bible says: "It is appointed unto men once to die, but after that the judgment," the law was made once for all, and that no convincing proof can all at once be discovered for supposing that, after all, judgment will be deferred until there has been further opportunity for repentance beyond the grave.

In the world they have tribulation. Many who would naturally be supposed to support their views and uphold their doctrines are the ones to call them old-fashioned, and behind the times. What times, pray? The times when the Scriptures were supposed to mean what they say? Not that exactly, but these times, these days of "broad views" and "advanced thought." But when they die— ay, when they die! It must be acknowledged then, if never before, that it is beautiful to have been an old-fashioned Christian! There are no doubts concerning the future, no dread shrinking from "a leap in the dark," but only untroubled confidence in him in whom they have believed, and of his abundant ability to keep that which they have committed unto him against that day. They know that their Redeemer liveth, and that a crown of righteousness is laid up for them, which the Lord, the righteous Judge, will give them at that day. Yes, it is glorious at the last to have been an old-fashioned Christian! They have fought a good fight, they have kept the faith, and as they approach the river of death they are soothed and sustained by the old-time promise: "When thou passeth through the waters, I will be with thee; and through the rivers, they shall not overflow thee." And they are not afraid, because of another old-time song of victory: "Yea, though I walk through the valley of the shadow of death, I will fear no evil; for thou art with me; thy rod and thy staff they comfort me."

ON CHRISTMAS DAY.

IT would sometimes seem matter for wonder that the birthday of the Saviour should be celebrated at this season of the year. But after much discussion and study it has, we believe, been generally agreed that Christ came to earth about this time. We associate all that is pleasantest in nature with summer skies, fresh foliage and springing flowers, and had the coming of this life been heralded by singing of birds and bursting of buds and blossoms, by warm breezes and sunny skies, it would to many minds have seemed in keeping with the glad event of the Saviour's birth. But others among our best thinkers go far beyond the first superficial "seeming" as to the fitness of times and events. Washington Irving, in his delightful "Sketch-Book," says: "There is something in the very season of the year that gives a charm to the festivity of Christmas. At other times we derive a great portion of our pleasures from the mere beauties of nature. . . . As the hollow blast of wintry wind rushes through the hall, claps distant doors, whistles about the casement, and rumbles down the chimney, what can be more grateful than that feeling of sober and sheltered security with which we look round upon the comfortable chamber and the scene of domestic hilarity? . . . It seemed to throw open every door and unlock every heart, and . . . even the poorest cottage welcomed the festive season with green decorations of bay and holly, the cheerful fire gleamed its rays through the lattice, inviting the passengers to raise the latch and join the gossip-knot huddled round the hearth, beguiling the long evening with legendary jokes and oft-told Christmas tales." What more cheerful picture could be drawn of the merry-making in Old England in by-gone years? But the writer goes on to deplore that "modern refinement" has given society a more smooth and polished, but less characteristic, surface than when these simple joys were pictured. The disappearance of the games and ceremonies formerly common to the day is subject for regret. In this connection he adds: "The world has become more worldly. There is more of dissipation and less of enjoyment." In these two sentences lurks much of truth which Christians would do well to ponder. With all the smoothness and gloss of "modern refinement," is there not too much that is merely fanciful and shallow creeping into our religious lives and beliefs? Even as the simple games and ceremonies of bygone Christmas-tides are fading from the recollection of the present age, are not many of the old and once-cherished forms of belief and trust fading out of the hearts of Christian people? Verily, the world is continually growing more worldly. Yet there is no faith like the old faith. Jesus Christ was born a simple, humble child. No dross of worldly sentiment or insincerity ever crept into his plain teachings or unsullied life. What he taught his disciples nearly nineteen hundred years ago remains unchanged in spirit and doctrine to-day. The strait gate and narrow way by which his followers were told they must go to find eternal life, are the same which must be taken to-day in order to reach the eternal city of God. The life of the Saviour while on earth was made up of hard, sterile experiences from the very beginning. Like the season in which he was born, there was coldness rather than warmth, darkness rather than sunlight, while fierce storms of temptations and peril beset his lonely way. No "cheerful fire glanced its rays through the lattice" of his earthly home, for he had not where to lay his head. Although the wise men of the East brought gifts and laid them at the Divine infant's feet, yet he through whom we enjoy light, gladness, freedom from sin and condemnation through belief in his teachings, was a man of sorrows and acquainted with grief.

Oh, let us who profess a belief in his dear name really believe in him! Let us bring the offering of true, sincere hearts on this his natal day. With the simple, earnest faith of olden times, let us cling to the old beliefs, cling to the precepts and promises of Christ just as they are written, and bring to his feet this day as a love-token the offering, always acceptable in his sight, our sincere, grateful love; a willingness to sacrifice for others, and a determination to follow in the footsteps of our Lord, the blessed Christ.

FIDELITY.

THOUGH many of the followers of Ulysses were dragged to torture by Polyphemus, and had their heads dashed against the ground, they would not confess a word concerning their lord and master, Ulysses, nor discover the long piece of wood that was put in the fire, prepared to put out the Cyclop's eye; but rather suffered themselves to be devoured raw than to disclose any one of their master's secrets. This was an example of fidelity and reservedness not to be paralleled. An instance of military fidelity occurred in the town of Bardosek. It shows the discipline of the Russian army. A sentinel on duty, having been forgotten, remained at his post during a conflagration. His sentry-box was consumed, and his clothes were on fire, when a corporal arrived to relieve him. The emperor, hearing of the circumstances, sent the man fifty roubles, decorated him with the order of St. Anne, and gave instructions for him to be made a non-commissioned officer.

Anastasius, a zealous Christian, greatly coveted and often prayed for the martyr's crown. In Cesarea he openly rebuked a company of magicians. He confessed that he had once been one himself, but renounced the practice, and became a follower of Christ. Upon this he was thrown into a dungeon. After three days he was brought out, chained by the foot to another prisoner. His neck and one foot were drawn and fastened near together by a chain, and in this way he was compelled to carry stones. He was upbraided, his beard was plucked out, he was kicked and beaten. Called again before the governor and urged to pronounce the magian incantation, he would only reply: "I am a Christian." He was then disrobed, and beaten with knotty clubs, without being bound, which he endured without moving or flinching. After this he was offered a choice of office in the king's service if he would only privately renounce Christ in words; if he would only do this little thing he might adhere to him in his heart. Anastasius replied that he would never even seem to dissemble. He was then sent to King Chosroes, of Persia, by whom liberal offers were repeated, and when rejected were followed by threats and reproaches. The martyr said to the king's messenger, "Do not give yourself so much trouble about me; by the grace of Christ I am not to be moved." He was inhumanly beaten day after day, and loaded with bitter reproaches for having rejected the honors and bounties of the king. Heavy weights were laid upon his limbs, cutting to the bone. His endurance, patience, and tranquillity were so great that they were reported to the king. One more attempt was made to overcome him. He was hung up by one hand for two hours, with heavy weights attached to his feet. Seeing that his will could not be overcome, preparations were made to strangle him. He rejoiced, and thanked God for so happy a conclusion to his life. He was strangled A. D. 628.

Henry IV., on the evening of Agincourt, found the chivalric David Gam, though lying mortally wounded, still grasping the banner which, through the fight, his strength had borne and his right arm defended. Often had the monarch noticed that pennon waving in the foremost van of the men of England, who that day pierced, broke, and routed the proud ranks of France. The king knighted him as he lay. The hero died, but dying was ennobled.

The noble General Rice, expiring on the field of Spottsylvania Court-house, desired to be turned over. "Which way?" asked a lieutenant. "Toward the enemy," was his indistinct reply. He was turned so as to face in death the foe he fought in life. He was asked, "How does Christ seem to you now?" "Near by," was his answer. The hero died as he had lived, true to his country and to his God.

A story of remarkable fidelity is told by Percy. When Lord Rawdon was in South Carolina, during the American war, he had to send an express of great importance through a country filled with the enemy, which a corporal of the Seventeenth Dragoons, of known courage and intelligence, was selected to escort. They had not proceeded far when they were fired upon, the expressman killed, and the corporal wounded in the side. Careless of his wounds he thought but of his duty. He snatched the despatch from the dying man and rode on till, from the loss of blood, he fell, when, fearing that the despatch would be taken by the enemy, he thrust it into the wound until it closed upon it. He was found next day by a British patrol, with a smile of conscious virtue on his countenance, with only life sufficient remaining to point to the fatal depository of his secret. In searching the wound they found the cause of his death; for the surgeon declared that it was not itself mortal, but rendered so by the insertion of the paper.

Dr. Robinson writes thus of Christian fidelity: "There have been men on this earth of God's, of whom it was simply true that it was easier to turn the sun from its course than these from the paths of honor. There have been men, like John the Baptist, who could speak the truth which had made their own spirits free, with the axe above their neck. There have been men redeemed in their inmost being by Christ, on whom tyrants and mobs have done their worst, and when, like Stephen, the stones crashed in upon their brain, or when their flesh hissed or crackled in the flames, were calmly superior to it all."

THE PRECIOUSNESS OF CHRIST.

PRECIOUSNESS is relative; the value of stones, gold, or merchandise of any variety is changeable. Political economists distinguish value as intrinsic and exchangeable, and by intrinsic value they mean utility, adaptation to the wants and desires of men. But wants and desires vary; even in the means of subsistence there is varying demand for varying kinds of food, so that while the whole amount needed may be the same, different kinds vary in their utility, and consequently in their value.

Nothing earthly is absolute in value; a greater supply than demand renders things comparatively valueless. Rarity increases value. If diamonds should become as plentiful as pebbles, their preciousness would be lost.

Location, too, has much to do with relative value. Even the most valuable things are valuable only in the place where they are wanted. A castaway upon a desert island would care more for a crust of bread than the most precious gem in a king's diadem. It is impossible to name anything that is absolutely valuable in itself; everything must bear some relation to another, and meet some desire or want to acquire value. Earth contains no absolutely precious thing.

But not so in the other world; there we may find possessions that are intrinsically precious, and above all else is Christ precious to believers. He meets all the wants of man, and to each one's experience and capacity he appears in a different way, speaking words suited to each need, and each soul alone can tell how precious Jesus is to it.

In the hour of conviction of sin there can be none so precious as he who says, "Thy sins, which are many, are forgiven thee." In the hour of sickness none so precious as he who says, "I will make all thy bed in thy sickness." Who can be more precious in the day of trial than he who says, "All things work together for good to them that love God;" and in the hushed chamber of death, "I will be with thee, my rod and my staff shall comfort thee"? When at last we shall see him as he is, who shall estimate the preciousness of his approbation, "Well done, good and faithful servant, enter thou into the joy of thy Lord"?

Most believers have come to the rock on which we stand through great trouble and darkness. It is not natural for us to trust another for our greatest blessing, and it seems incredible that we need do nothing for the priceless boon of salvation. Almost all of us can look backward to the time when, thinking that we knew better than God, we would try every other saviour except Jesus Christ. We tried by our good works to become worthy of eternal life, and what a hard road we travelled; uphill work, and rough and thorny to our feet. Duty was our only inspiration. We do far better now with less difficulty, when love is our inspiration and duty is pleasure, because God's will is ours. We can afford to forego the pleasures of the world, because we have found something far more precious. There is but one name given under heaven whereby we must be saved, and having discovered the wretchedness of every other refuge we have learned to prize the one only Saviour because he is the only one. Besides him there is no other, and because we were sinners and needed pardon, because we were pilgrims and needed guidance, because we were lost and needed redemption, because we are mortal and long for eternal life, and believe that Christ can and will confer it, therefore he is precious as the only Saviour of mankind.

The smallest amount of Christian experience brings to the heart the consciousness of Christ's preciousness, and what is true at first is true in an increasing degree afterward. The glow and thrill of the first love may not always remain, but there never comes a time when the believer will not be able to say that Christ is precious.

And this becomes a practical matter, when preciousness

produces love and love seeks an outlet. We can find this outlet in benevolence, self-sacrifice, forbearance. Having obtained such a precious treasure, count no possession too precious to be given up for him.

Out of an abounding love, let our gifts to Christ and for Christ abound in word and deed and possessions. Let us acknowledge our indebtedness to him by generosity and fervent zeal for his cause. There are still many who know nothing of this precious Saviour by experience, and our hearts should yearn after those who are without this precious boon, and we ought to entreat them to share our joy.

Is it not strange, in view of its value, that any one needs to be urged to accept the salvation purchased with Christ's precious blood? Surely there can be nothing of equal loveliness and preciousness in this sinful world. The united testimony of the millions in heaven and earth who have believed on the Lord Jesus Christ is that he is precious, the only infinitely precious one in the universe. To all who believe, he is precious. Do you believe?

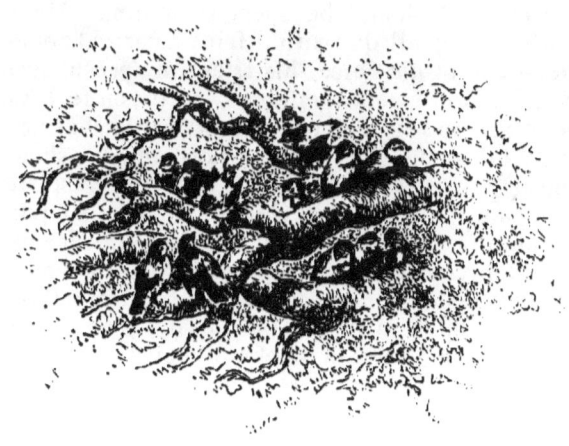

YOUR SUNDAY READING.

WE so often hear it said that "what is good enough to read on a week-day is good enough to read on Sunday." As a general rule, those who make this remark do not read anything particularly good on a week-day. So the reading which they continue on a day which God has set apart as a day of holiness is often very light and all of this world, if not directly irreligious, certainly nothing which will help the reader on in the narrow path. "But Sabbath was made for man," you quote, "not man for the Sabbath." Yes, but it was made to give you refreshment for soul as well as body, and for you to rest from worldly books and thoughts as well as occupations. It was made, too, for a day when you should draw nearer to God, and everything you do on that day should be done to draw you nearer to him. All should be done with that purpose. It is his time and should be spent with him. Have you never, after being all day with a friend, carried home with you the sound of his voice, his tricks of speech, even, his gestures, his words and opinions, until you feel that he will be so real to you that you cannot realize that he is far away? Well, such a day with the Lord Sunday should be. This one day in seven was made for you to dwell spiritually with him, and your reading should be for that purpose. You should draw so near to him that his presence is felt. He should become a living presence beside you. On Sunday, he should be the guest in your heart and thoughts. Study his life upon earth, not only in his Word, but in the writings of others, and in books of devotional reading.

so that when eventide comes you can indeed say, "I have walked with God to-day." You will be stronger for what the week will bring you. You will arise on the morrow with a feeling of nearness to him you never had when you spent the day in light reading. The memories of this kind of reading will stay by you all the week, calling you to it again, and so calling you to him.

If this sacred day is devoted to his worship, and when away from his house, to the study of the example we are bidden to follow, your growth in grace will be certain. Your aim is to grow more like the Master and to be nearer to him; then why neglect this great aid? Why, because some think it no actual sin, indulge in light reading on Sunday and continue it, when it certainly makes you no better?

There is nothing negative in religion or growth in grace. Whatever you do you know helps or hinders. Sundays even are helps or hindrances according as they are employed. What is read on that day is a help or hindrance. Can you say that your indifferent reading will help you to grow to his full stature, knowing you feel no nearer to him when the book is finished and laid aside, and your thoughts, which should have been his, were very far off? Then you have been hindered; the day has brought your soul no refreshment even if you have rested your mind and body. You are farther away from him, and the day which was made for you has been lost. Lost! one day! when your days on earth are so "few and evil." You have become weaker in grace instead of growing in it, and the time which should have been redeemed is thrown away.

WHAT WILL YE GIVE ME?

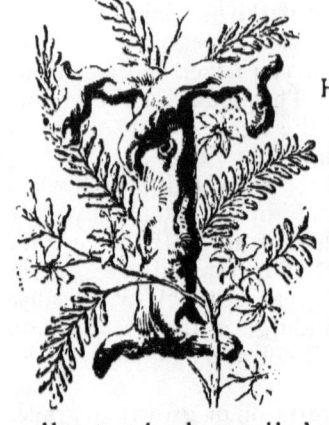

THIS is the question which Judas Iscariot put to the high priests when he was about to prove himself the traitor that he was, and to give over into their power the Master whom he had pretended to serve. "What will ye give me and I will deliver him unto you?" asking that a price might be put on the head of the Saviour and Redeemer of mankind. Men naturally start back appalled at the enormity of the treachery involved in such an underhanded transaction. And the question has come down through all the ages, with its stigma of shame and infamy attached: "Who betrayed his Lord and Master?" It was so base, so paltry, a thing, actually trading away the precious life of Jesus for the mere pittance of a few pieces of silver. It is, however, one of the sad, deplorable phases of human nature, that what shocks and repels us in others is often repeated in our own lives and almost without our consciousness of the fact. Were many professors of religion told that they practically repeated the question put to the high priests in their own experience, the accusation would be met with scornful and indignant denial. And yet the query is doubtless repeated in various forms and with unsuspected frequency by professed followers of Jesus Christ and believers in the doctrines which he taught. It may be that for a certain length of time and up to a certain point, a man will conscientiously serve the Master, then perhaps it is the pleasures of the world which come in and tempt him to try a little unlawful license, and mix more freely with those who find delight and satisfaction in a gay and thoughtless life. And the man looks the tempter in the face and asks: "What will ye give me?" Then it may follow that hours bright with laughter and dissipation hold out inducements he does not care to withstand, and the old faith is sold out that he may enjoy the pleasures of sin for a season. Another is tempted by greed. Eager assurances that a life of prosperity and self-indulgence is the only one worth living, are sounded in his ears. So the whirlpool of speculation is faced with the desire for sudden riches, and the question leaps forth: "What will ye give me?" For others, ambition and worldly honors hold out a tempting bait for the soul, and of them it is asked, "What will ye give me and I will deliver him unto you?" Alas, the piteous weakness of it all! Yielding up the Christ within the heart for something quite as shallow and profitless as the betrayer's thirty pieces of silver. Wrecking all true happiness, defrauding the life of all true gain and advancement, and surrendering the highest and most worthy honors while betraying the best of friends. As often as a professing Christian dallies with temptation, or bargains with sin in any form, just so often he says to the tempter: "What will ye give me and I will deliver him unto you?" There is no greater meanness in the eyes of a noble, chivalrous man, than the treachery which will admit of betraying a friend. Alas! that the language of the hymn we sing concerning Christ is so true:

> "You treat no other friend so ill."

The Bible teaches wisely and counsels with divine sagacity when it exhorts believers to watch and pray lest they enter into temptation. Watchfulness and prayer are the two unconquerable forces which will effectually prevent disloyalty to the Saviour, and render the Christian panoply of faith impervious to all the wiles and debasing suggestions of the archtraitor of the soul.

> "O Lord, the pilot's part perform
> And guard and guide me through the storm,
> Defend me from each threatening ill,
> Control the waves, say 'Peace, be still.'"

THE WORLD.

HAT an almost inexhaustible subject is the world. To attempt a description of it at large would fill a sufficient number of books to form quite a library of itself. Yet it may briefly be described as the dwelling-place of mankind. As long as man lives he is in the world; when he dies, all that really constituted the life takes flight to another sphere. The Scriptures in one place warn man against loving the world or the things that are in the world, thereby indicating that it contains much to captivate and enchain the affections. Again, we read that Jesus Christ assures men that in the world they shall have tribulation, but goes on to add comfort by saying he has overcome the world, showing that they, too, *can be* overcome by his strength. In another place men are exhorted to keep themselves unspotted from the world, and still again the Scriptures affirm that the world passeth away. Now here is a strange place! Plainly a place which is beautiful, attractive, doubtless full of joys and lively things to please the eye and gratify the senses. True enough, the world possesses beauty, is attractive and lovely. And yet, it contains also the opposite of all these charms, for tribulation is a long, hard word, very full of trouble, and the victorious assertion of the Saviour that he has overcome the world implies a need of strength, as there must be conflict, struggle, and endurance brought to bear, in order to overcome so strong a force as the world. And the caution to keep unspotted from the world, must mean that there is much of taint and

contagion to be dreaded and avoided in this seemingly fair world. And then " the world passeth away." It must be a perishable place, destined at last to be destroyed, so nothing in it can be abiding. It is just as described: beautiful, alluring, full of tribulation, something to be overcome and to avoid pernicious contact with, and something perishable itself at last. Yet there is need to exercise care that the teachings and injunctions of the Bible be not misunderstood.

The command not to love the world nor the things that are in it by no means teaches that the beautiful works of God as seen in the world are to be despised or unappreciated. Who that looks abroad and sees the budding spring ripen into summer's bloom could help experiencing a happy glow, responsive to nature's renewing. And not only the beautiful world of nature, but all the wonderful achievements of art are things to admire and enjoy. One of our commentators says: " To love the world and the things that are in the world, is to make them our treasure, and put our trust in them, instead of in God." And in Matthew the counsel is given to lay up treasure in heaven because where the treasure is, there will the heart be also. Nor does the injunction not to love the world include advice to keep away from other men and make a recluse of one's self in hope to keep pure and unspotted. No ordinarily intelligent person need fail to understand the plain, direct meaning of Scripture with reference to the love of the world and the things that are in it; the world is not our rest, and nothing in it will endure permanently. Not even the love of friends is strong enough to resist the inexorable law of the universe, which demands that everything earthly must be fleeting and transitory.

It makes no difference how much wealth may have been amassed, how many friends there may be to love, once the fiat goes forth that man shall return to the dust as he was, and the spirit to God who gave it, everything must be left at the solemn bidding, and the soul, stripped of every earthly belonging, must go forth to meet its God. The love of men and women is very sweet, but all must pass away; and what will you do if you have no wealth but the wealth that fadeth, no love but the love which dies, when death shall come? What will you do, indeed!

To such as have made no preparation for this inevitable "passing away" from time into eternity, how like a hopeless echo the query repeats itself, for if no love for God and the things of his kingdom dwell in the soul, how shorn and helpless must it stand before its Maker at last! But there is a wealth that never fades, and a love that never dies. Death admits the soul of the believer in Christ and his most precious promises, to a kingdom whose beauty and riches far transcend all the poor wealth of the world. The love of heaven never passes away, but endures forever and forever. What provident, worldly-wise man would build a house on a foundation so insecure, that he knows the first rough storm would overthrow the entire structure? How far more foolish and short-sighted the man who loves the world better than he loves the things of the kingdom of God, whose love and whose hopes are centred only on things which are sure to pass away.

BEGINNING AT JERUSALEM.

CHRIST'S directions to the apostles as to their work seemed at first like a commission so insuperably great that it could never be executed. He bade them "go into all the world and preach the Gospel to every creature." The world was not as large then as it is now, as far as population and extent of inhabited country were concerned, but its conversion was a great undertaking for eleven men to set about. We have heard of people having so much to do that they hardly knew where to commence; no doubt most of us have often experienced the feeling ourselves, and so we can appreciate the value of method. If the apostles had received nothing more specific than this general direction, they would probably have given up in despair at the vast proportions of their task, and done nothing because they had so much to do. But they were not left in doubt as to their starting-point; they were to begin at Jerusalem, and make that a radiating centre of usefulness.

There were two great facts concerning Jerusalem, its ancient sacredness and its later sinfulness, either of which would have been sufficient reason for the Saviour's command to begin evangelization there. But there was a deeper, wider reason than either of these for beginning at Jerusalem; perhaps some of these fishermen among the apostles understood. Perhaps Peter, for instance, at some time when he lay becalmed on the motionless bosom of the Lake of Galilee, had, in the hour of idleness, tossed a pebble or a float on the still waters, and watched the wavelets start and move in ever-increasing circles from the centre until lost to sight. He may then have thought, when Christ bade them begin at Jerusalem, that that city was the centre where they were to drop the Gospel, and the waves of influence should spread around and widen and extend farther than they could see. That would have been a very perfect illustration of Christ's design. It was not for Jerusalem's sake alone, that they were to begin preaching there; but that was the centre of influence, a national centre around which the events of Christ's life clustered, where the crucifixion and resurrection, which were to be the great themes of their preaching, took place; and from that centre in every direction were to ripple out the waves of life.

They commenced, therefore, at Jerusalem; there they prayed, there they labored, and there they preached. There they formed the nucleus of the Christian Church, and thus the radiating centre of influence was formed. The streams that should go forth from this centre were providentially right there—men who had come up to worship at the feast, or to buy and sell in the prosecution of their business. All were alike attracted by the great miracle of Pentecost. There were Parthians, Medes, Elamites, and the dwellers in Mesopotamia and Cappadocia, in Pontus and Asia, in Egypt and parts of Africa, and strangers from Rome.

These were converted, and by-and-by they went home—not leaving the Gospel behind them, but carrying it with them. They departed by every gate of the city; they went north and south, east and west; their roads diverged, and as they left Jerusalem further behind, their distance from each other increased. Thus the Gospel was spread abroad, and these converts were the waves which extended from the central Jerusalem and bore on their crest the knowledge of salvation.

But the apostles had only half learned the lesson of the pebble thrown upon the lake, and only half understood the command to begin at Jerusalem. That was to be nothing but a beginning; the Master never said that they must stay there. Yet the apostles acted as if they had thus understood the message. They showed no disposition to leave the city, and, having sent out their waves of influence, they ceased to watch them and follow them up. Like the ripples in the lake, those travellers would lose their power in proportion as they separated more and more, and met with increased opposition, until, when

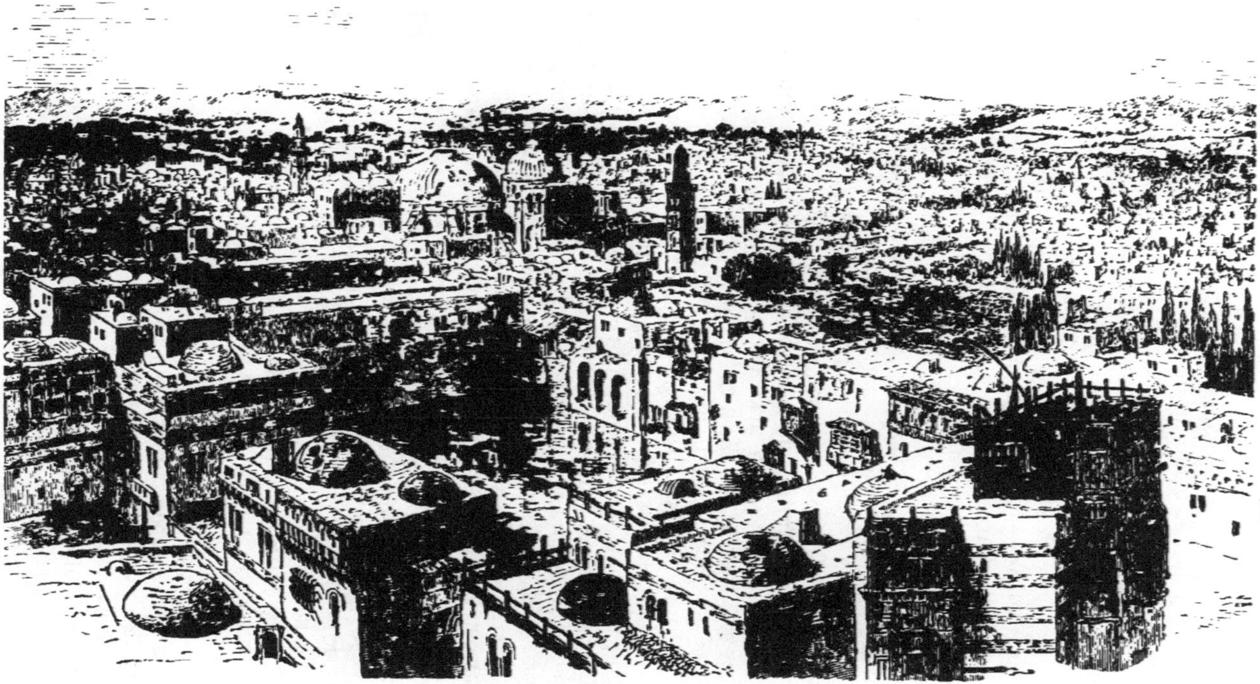

BIRD'S-EYE VIEW OF JERUSALEM. 85

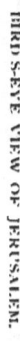

they reached their destination, their distant homes, they had not the power to make themselves felt. What was needed was, that each point where a convert had carried the Gospel should itself be made a new centre of influence to send reflex waves back to Jerusalem and onward to the regions beyond.

This the apostles failed to see, and they had to be taught by a sharp lesson. Since they would not willingly leave Jerusalem, they were made to leave it. Persecution came three times, and they were all scattered abroad—forced by providence into the world for the spread of the Gospel.

The divine method for the accomplishment of this purpose was the gradual establishment of radiating centres, or sources of influence, at important points, beginning at Jerusalem and ending at Rome. Those radiating centres were the secret of the vast progress in apostolic times, and it is the divine method for all success and progress.

We are to begin at Jerusalem, which means at home; there are plenty of heathen here. Let us look after them! Assuredly, we should by all means begin in our own family, our own community; but we must also remember the early church was persecuted because it stayed at Jerusalem, which is only one centre, the first of many. Training for missions begins in the family, but it does not stop there. We should establish centres of power in our churches; there are families and individuals who, some in one way and some in another, can exert great power for good; make them radiating centres.

Above all, let us see to it that our own lives shall send out ever-widening circles of influence. Old Augustine lives to-day in the rich discourses inspired by his teachings; Calvin sleeps at Geneva, and no man knows his sepulchre, but his vindication of God's sovereignty will live forever; Bunyan lies in Bunhill Fields, but his bright spirit walks the earth in "Pilgrim's Progress." Isaac Watts is dead, but, in the chariot of his hymns, thousands of spirits ascend to-day in devotion. For a hundred years, Robert Raikes has gathered his Sunday schools all over Christendom. So we all live in the lives of others, perhaps even more than we do in our own; and we may set in motion waves that will widen until they reach the shores of eternity.

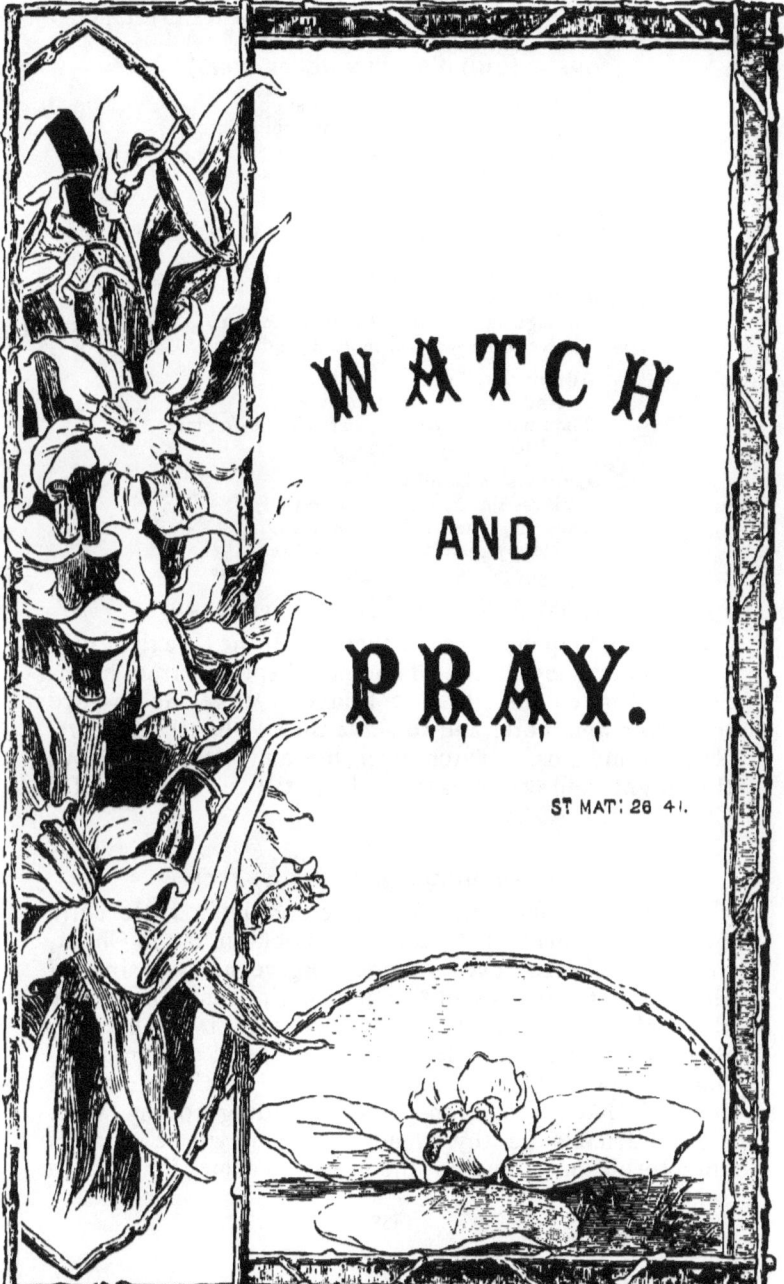

PRAYERS SUITABLE FOR CHILDREN.

ONE.—(CHILD'S EVENING PRAYER.)

NOW I lay me down to sleep,
   I pray the Lord my soul to keep;
If I should die before I wake,
I pray the Lord my soul to take.

TWO.—(CHILD'S EVENING PRAYER.)

JESUS, tender Shepherd, hear me,
   Bless thy little lamb to-night;
Through the darkness be thou near me,
   Keep me safe till morning light.

All this day thy hand has led me,
   And I thank thee for thy care;
Thou hast clothed me, warmed and fed me,
   Listen to my evening prayer.

Let my sins be all forgiven,
   Bless the friends I love so well;
Take me, when I die, to heaven,
   Happy there with thee to dwell.

THREE.—(CHILD'S EVENING PRAYER.)

O LORD, help me to thank thee for all the love thou hast this day shown me. Thou hast kept me from harm, and hast given me all that I have. Make me to love thee more and more, and to serve thee with all my heart. Forgive my sins. Watch over me and all whom I love this night, and keep us in safety till a new day, for Christ's sake. *Amen.*

FOUR.—(CHILD'S MORNING PRAYER.)

O LORD, I thank thee that thou dost let a little child like me kneel at thy throne. Look on me in Christ, and for his sake love me and forgive all my sins. I thank thee for the rest of the past night, that I have seen the light of this day. Lord, keep me all through this day. May thine arm lead me, and guard me from all harm. May I walk and act as a child of Christ; may I love all that is good, and live according to thy word. Let my friends be thy friends, and may we be thine in this world, and thine in the world to come, for Christ's sake. *Amen.*

PRAYERS FOR FAMILY DEVOTION.

ONE.—(EVENING PRAYER).

The following prayer was found in manuscript (German script) on a half-sheet of very old paper, in a German Bible, Luther's version, printed in 1545. The Bible has been in private or public libraries for probably between two and three hundred years, and the manuscript is presumably two centuries old, at least, if not older, though there is no way of determining the date exactly. The translation was made by the late Rev. Thomas J. Conant, D.D., the well-known Biblical scholar, and now appears for the first time in book form.

EVENING PRAYER TO OUR FATHER THROUGH JESUS CHRIST.

AH, my dear Father, I thank thee that thou so graciously hast guarded me this day. Ah, my Father, I beseech thee that thou wouldst forgive me all my sins which I have to-day committed against thee. Ah, dearest Father, I beseech thee, for the sake of Jesus Christ, my Redeemer and Saviour, hear my prayer! I am a poor sinner; but Christ has paid for me the penalty of my sins, out of his great love to me. Christ I set before thee as the surety for my sins. I beseech thee that thou wouldst guard me this night also, from the workings of the Devil and his train, so that they may not harm me. Let thy holy angels pitch their camp around me. Be thou my strong defence, O Lord; for evening is coming on, and the day has declined. Guard all my dear ones and friends; also my enemies. Ah, Lord, forgive my enemies, for they know not what they do. And should this night be the last of my life, ah, then I beseech thee that thou wouldst be gracious to me in my last dying hour. Ah, grant me a calm, blissful end, for the sake of Jesus Christ. *Amen.*

Our Father, etc.

TWO.—(MORNING OR EVENING.)

HEAVENLY FATHER, we thy children come to offer up our prayer and praise to thee. May they be offerings well pleasing. Thy mercies are new every morning and fresh every evening. Great is thy faithfulness.

For health and strength we thank thee, for the light of this day, for all its blessings; but above all for the gift of thy dear Son, to redeem us from sin and to open unto us the gates of everlasting life. For his present grace, his interceding love and his Spirit's power, we give thee thanks. For thy Church, its ministry and sacraments, thy holy Word, and for the examples of those who have departed in the true faith of thy holy Name, for the hope of a life to come, and the promise of thy coming again, we gratefully adore.

Make us ever mindful of thy love. May we never fall from thee, nor be led by sorrow or adversity to either question thy wisdom or deny thy goodness. May we be willing to receive at the Lord's hands evil as well as good. Pity our weakness and give us strength against the hour of trial sure to come. While on the earth, may we be trained for Heaven, and come off conquerors and more than conquerors; through him who hath loved us, thy Son Jesus Christ our Lord.

O merciful God, who hast written thy holy Word for our learning, that we, through patience and comfort of thy holy Scriptures, might have hope; give us a right understanding of ourselves, and of thy threats and promises; that we may neither cast away our confidence in thee, nor place it anywhere but in thee. Break not the bruised reed, nor quench the smoking flax. Shut not up thy tender mercies in displeasure; but make us to hear of joy and gladness through Jesus Christ our Lord. *Amen.*

Our Father, etc.

THREE.—(MORNING PRAYER.)

WE desire this morning, O our God, to approach thee through the only way whereby sinners may come to thee, thine own dearly-beloved and only-begotten Son. Thou hast given us quiet rest, and when we awoke thy hand sustained us. At the beginning of another day we seek together, as a family, thy blessing and grace. Keep us, O our Father, through this day, from all evil, and, above all, from the contamination of sin. As the children of a holy God, and the sincere disciples of the holy Jesus, may we spend this day in accordance with our solemn profession. If thou art pleased this day to give us the exercise of authority, enable us to act with tenderness and Christian discretion. If we are subject to reproach or oppression, give us, O Lord, the spirit of meekness and submission, that we may thus adorn the doctrine of our Lord. Enable us to rejoice in our neighbor's prosperity, instead of envying him, as we will do if left to our own natural tendencies. Make us not slothful in business, but fervent in spirit, serving the Lord. Preserve us from making the world our god. Let us not trust in uncertain riches, but in the living God, who is the soul's only sure, and abiding, and everlasting portion.

Accept of our united thanks in that thou has set us together as a family, making us, in this manner, mutual helps, and comforts, and defences to each other. May each of us discharge the duty which is assigned us by thee, as in thy sight. May we exercise a spirit of contentment and submission to thee, in respect to the station thou hast assigned us in life. May the Spirit himself dwell in us, and keep us from evil. And unto thee, the Father, the Son, and the Holy Spirit, be praise everlasting. *Amen.*

Our Father, etc.

FOUR.—(MORNING OR EVENING.)

O LORD, we desire to draw near into thy holy presence, in the name of him whom thou hearest always, thy blessed Son. We have sinned against light, and privilege, and warning, and mercy. We mourn our deep-rooted depravity, our constant proneness to alienation and departure from thee; the feebleness of our faith, the fitfulness of our love and the imperfection of our best services, the mingled motives in our holiest duties. We come anew, casting ourselves on the infinite fulness of our Saviour. Give us out of his inexhaustible treasury, even grace for grace. Let us walk as thy children, advancing in conformity to thy blessed mind and will. May we earnestly strive after greater spiritual attainments—laying aside every weight, and running with patience the race that is set before us.

Give us grace to bear about with us, in our daily duties and engagements, the solemn thought—we are soon to be with God. Let us not postpone the all-momentous question of our salvation. May we feel that now is the accepted time, and that it may be the only time! Let it be our constant aim and endeavor to know what the will of the Lord is; and knowing that will, may we have strength given us to obey it. May we murmur at nothing that brings us nearer thee.

O God, our Saviour, dwell in this household, make every member of it thine. May those who are absent feel that thou art near them. May those that are in distress be comforted by thee. Do thou increase the devotedness of thy children; give them more of the character of Christ and prepare them for the Christian's rest.

Prosper thy cause and kingdom everywhere. Let Satan's kingdom be destroyed—the kingdom of grace advanced—the kingdom of glory hastened. Save thy people—bless thine inheritance; feed them also, and lift them up forever! Give to each of us this day thy gracious benediction; and when the days of earth shall merge into the ages of eternity, may it be ours to spend them in the full fruition of thee, our God, through Jesus Christ. *Amen.*

Our Father, etc.

FIVE.—(MORNING OR EVENING.)

MOST holy and blessed God, before whom the angels veil their faces, fill us with awe and reverence as we draw nigh to thee. As unworthy as we are, thou hast invited us to come. In thy dear Son's name, and not for anything that we are, or for anything that we have done, do we make now our petitions unto thee. Give to each of us, dear Lord, a clear knowledge of our duties and responsibilities, and besides this, wisdom and strength, that these may be discharged by us with diligence and fidelity.

Whatsoever good thing our hand may find to do in this life, may we do it with our might, remembering that the night of death cometh when no man can work, and that after death there is the judgment. May no evil thoughts or angry tempers, may no doubts or fears disturb us, but may we ever put our trust in thee and find guidance, hope and consolation in the blessed gospel of thy Son.

May our hearts be so rooted and grounded in love for thee that no difficulties, however great they may be, may discourage us in the way of well-doing. Increase in us that which is lacking; raise up that which is fallen; restore to us that which has been lost; quicken within us that which may be ready to die; so that we may serve and obey thee in all things, through Jesus Christ our Lord.

We pray as well for thy blessing for all those who are dear to us, wherever they are, that they may be filled with the knowledge of thy will in wisdom and understanding, and in one heart and mind may ever seek thy glory and the salvation of souls; through Jesus Christ our Lord.

O Lord, we beseech thee, mercifully hear our prayers, and spare all those who confess their sins unto thee; that they, whose consciences by sin are accused, by thy merciful pardon may be absolved; through Christ our Lord. Amen.

Our Father, etc.

SIX.—(MORNING PRAYER.)

O LORD, we thank thee for the tender care with which thou hast watched over us during the hours of sleep, and for the comfort and health in which we arise this morning. Help us to carry into the busy hours of the day all the holy impressions and resolutions of thy day. Grant us grace to pursue our secular calling in a Christian spirit. May our most trivial occupations be ennobled by the principles of the gospel of Christ; may all our work be sanctified by the Word of God and prayer.

May we honor thee by the uprightness and integrity of our conduct, by the unselfishness and generosity of our spirit, and by our endeavor in all things to obey the law of Christ. Whilst not slothful in business, may we be fervent in spirit, serving the Lord. And Father, we pray that in our home life we may act worthily of thee. May we be ever conscious of the presence of our Lord, and seek to manifest his spirit. May we be gentle and forbearing toward each other, and faithful in rendering to all in the household their respective dues. May we minister to one another's welfare, and guard against selfishness in thought and word and deed.

Save us from the snares of ambition and the desire of human applause, and help us to walk humbly with our God. May those who are young, especially, learn to value everything according to its tendency to make them just and pure and good. May they become truly wise through the teaching of thine Holy Spirit.

Let us not be off our guard this day. Suffer us to run into no sin, but keep us in all our ways. May we be in the fear of the Lord all the day long, and may the remembrance of thy presence be our strength. Graciously forgive all our sins, and preserve us by thy mighty power through faith unto salvation, through Jesus Christ our Lord. *Amen.*

Our Father, etc.

SEVEN.—(MORNING PRAYER.)

O LORD our God, we desire, on this morning of a new day, to present ourselves before thee, and to bless thee for thy continued goodness. We are again reminded of our manifold obligations unto thee, and of the strong claims which thou hast upon our gratitude, our love and our obedience. We adore thee as the maker of all things, as the righteous governor of the universe, as the God of grace and of salvation. And we pray that we may each of us have a personal interest in the blessings of this salvation, and find it to be light and life to our souls. May each of us be enabled this day, and through the whole world of our life, to live as it becomes those whom God hath delivered from the power of darkness, and hath translated into the kingdom of his dear Son.

O Lord, let thy kingdom come, and let thy will be done in earth as it is in heaven. Hasten the glory of the latter day, even the day when the earth shall be full of the knowledge of the Lord, as the waters cover the sea. And as thou hast promised that Christ shall have the heathen for his inheritance, and the uttermost parts of the earth for his possessions, O let this promise be speedily accomplished, and let Christ be acknowledged in all lands, when all nations, drawing water with joy out of the wells of salvation, shall say, " Praise the Lord, call upon his name, declare his doings among the people." We ask all in the name and for the sake of Christ. And unto the Father, the Son, and the Holy Ghost, one God, we ascribe all praise and glory. *Amen.*

Our Father, etc.

EIGHT.—(MORNING PRAYER.)

O LORD, our heavenly Father, accept our morning sacrifice of praise and thanksgiving for the protection of the night, and for the early blessings of this day. To thee we owe all that we have and are. May the appreciation of thy goodness so grow upon us that we may love thee more and serve thee better.

As day shall be added to day, may we become more obedient to thy will and more earnest and self-forgetful in thy work. Let nothing separate us from the love of God that is in Christ Jesus, and finding our happiness in doing his will, may we secure his favor. May we lay aside every weight and the sin which doth so easily beset, to run with patience the race that is set before us, looking unto Jesus, the author and finisher of our faith, who for the joy that was set before him, endured the cross, despising the shame, and is set down at the right hand of the throne of God.

And as thou hast promised to give the Holy Spirit to them that ask, we humbly pray for this gift, that we may be kept from carelessness and hardness of heart, from fretfulness and impatience, from vanity and pride, from self-seeking and covetousness, from the unhappy desire of becoming great, from repining at thy dispensation; and from neglecting thy warning.

And as thou dost take from us these, will thou grant unto us such love and joy, and peace and long-suffering, such gentleness and goodness, faith, meekness and temperance, that we may daily crucify the flesh with its affections and lusts. And this we ask not for our own merits, but for the sake of him who hath loved us and died for us, thy Son, our Saviour Jesus Christ.

Be thou, O God, our protection, and watch over our paths with guiding love, that among the snares which lie hidden in our paths, we may so pass onward with hearts fixed on thee, that we may come to thee and be forever with thee. We ask it for Jesus Christ's sake. *Amen.*

Our Father, etc.

NINE.—(MORNING PRAYER.)

ALMIGHTY GOD, the Creator and Preserver of mankind, unto whom we come as our Father in Jesus Christ our Lord, we do most humbly and heartily thank thee for the mercies of the night, and for the blessing of this morning. We bless thee for the sleep which has refreshed us, and for the bread which thou hast given us. As thou didst watch over us in the darkness, watch over us through the day. Teach us by thy good word, and by thy Holy Spirit. Keep our feet in the way of salvation. Protect us from temptation, and strengthen us by thy grace. Take away from us all bitterness of temper, and preserve us from sin.

Grant each of us courage, faith, patience in trial, and loving submission to thy most holy will. Help us to be faithful in all our work, and to look to thee for our reward. Abide with us in joy and in sorrow, in prosperity and in adversity. Grant us quiet hearts amid the uncertainties of the day, and breathe upon us thy peace. Abide in our home, and make us all the children of thy household. The sick we commend unto thee, praying for their recovery, if it please thee; and beseeching thee that thou wilt give unto them and unto us all, the good and glad hope of everlasting life through our Lord Jesus Christ.

Hear thou, O God, the cry of the poor and the needy, and suffer us not to harden our hearts against them. Come near to all whose hearts are heavy and sore, and give them thy help in all their trials. Reveal thyself to all men, and hasten the days of universal righteousness and peace. Grant us thy forgiveness, for our sins are many; grant us thy strength, for we are very weak; increase our faith in thee, for our fears oppress us; and fill us with the joy of thy salvation; all of which we humbly ask in the name and through the merits of Jesus Christ our Lord, who hath taught us to pray, saying:

Our Father, etc.

TEN.—(MORNING PRAYER.)

O LORD, our heavenly Father, we thank thee for the light of another morning. This day thou hast spared us, and we would give this day to thee. In all our employments may we seek thy favor. May we be watchful for opportunities to serve thee, especially in those things which belong to thy kingdom and the salvation of souls. May we be true laborers in thy harvest, and each in his place make full proof of our ministry and the power of grace in our own souls.

Make us ever truly humble before thee. May we never be high-minded, nor trust in uncertain riches, but in thee the living God, who givest us richly all things to enjoy. May we remember that thou, the Father of mercies, art the sole author of all our privileges and blessings, and that to thee we must render a strict account of the use we make of them.

And to thy hands do we now commit ourselves, and all of our affairs, beseeching thee so to bless, direct and guide us, that we may pass this and each succeeding day of our lives, confident of thine approval and of thy acceptance at the last day; through the merits and mediation of our Lord and Saviour Jesus Christ.

Almighty God, whose kingdom is everlasting and power infinite, have mercy upon this whole land; and so rule the hearts of thy servants, the President of the United States, the Governor of this State, and all others in authority, that they, knowing whose ministers they are, may above all things seek thine honor and glory; and that we and all the people, duly considering whose authority they bear, may faithfully and obediently honor them: in thee, and for thee, according to thy blessed Word and ordinance; through Jesus Christ our Lord, who with thee and the Holy Ghost liveth and reigneth, ever one God, world without end. *Amen.*

Our Father, etc.

ELEVEN.—(MORNING OR EVENING.)

LORD, teach us to pray. We know not how to pray as we ought; but it is written, "The Spirit helpeth our infirmities." O send forth thy light and thy truth; let them lead and guide us. Lord, we confess our sinfulness, that our hearts are depraved, and our lives unholy; and especially do we humble ourselves for the sins of thy people. O may the record of their history, mercifully preserved in the Scriptures, be profitable to us. Help us to discover the beginnings of sin in them, and to avoid the same. May we be alarmed by the awful consequences to which their sins exposed themselves and others, and not therein follow their example.

While we behold thy readiness to forgive, may we be induced to come to thee with our confessions and prayers. While we see that thy good Spirit was not withheld, notwithstanding their rebellions, may we be encouraged to seek this precious gift. And O suffer us not to rest short of the sure and certain consciousness that he abideth in us. May we not grieve him by our sins, nor quench him by our neglect. May we enjoy the communion of the Spirit. May our souls be filled with his light, quickened by his power, and comforted by his grace. By his agency may we be qualified for our duty, and made faithful and successful in it.

Do thou control every thought, and direct every action. In the family, may we cultivate the graces that adorn it in all kindness, and condescension, and love. And in our intercourse with the world, forbid, Lord, that we should ever give occasion to the adversary to speak reproachfully. May the fruit of the Spirit abound in us and others, even love, joy, peace, long-suffering, gentleness, goodness, faith, meekness, temperance. We are thine, O Lord. We acknowledge thy claim upon us. In Jesus we devote ourselves to thee. And do thou accept of us for the Redeemer's sake. *Amen.*

Our Father, etc.

TWELVE.—(MORNING PRAYER.)

FATHER in heaven, hear us through Jesus Christ, thy well-beloved Son, our Lord; and accept our thanks for thy protection of us during the night and for thy favor this morning. We thank thee for refreshing sleep; for the new day; for the comforts of our home; for food and raiment; for all our kindred whom we love; for the help and sympathy of our friends; and for all which thou dost make us able to do in aiding the needy.

We pray thee to fit us to use our time, our possessions and all our powers and opportunities for the good of others, and for our own improvement, that we may serve thee well in our several places and employments. Guard us from danger. Make us prosperous and fruitful in the work of our hands and the care of our hearts.

We have hitherto experienced thy divine goodness; may it continue to bless us. Thy forbearance with us has been wonderful; oh, may it never fail us. Let thy loving kindness crown our days. For the sake of our Redeemer, forgive our sins, which we confess before thee; and may his blood cleanse us from all sin. May the Holy Spirit so renew and sanctify us that we may walk in the way of thy commandments with joy. Let the words of Christ dwell in us richly, and the perfection of his life and character become more and more our own through the supply of his grace. Oh that obedience, prayerfulness, compassion and kindness like his may ever appear in our spirit and conduct.

Show thy mercy, O God, to all penitent souls. Make transgressors obedient to thy law. Bless our rulers. Relieve all who are in distress; heal the sick; comfort the sorrowful; cheer the faint; save the lost. Give light and life to thy church. Spread the gospel far and wide. Hasten the coming of that kingdom which is righteousness and peace and joy in the Holy Ghost. And thine be the glory for ever. *Amen.*

Our Father, etc.

THIRTEEN.—(MORNING OR EVENING.)

ALMIGHTY GOD, our heavenly Father, we render thee most hearty thanks for the spiritual and heavenly nourishment of thy blessed word, wherewith our souls are constantly refreshed, our faith strengthened, our love kindled, our hope renewed. We humbly beseech thee to give us grace, not only to be hearers of thy word, but doers of the same; not only to love, but also to live thy gospel; not only to favor, but also to follow thy godly doctrine; not only to profess, but also to practise thy blessed commandments; that whatever of thy truth we outwardly hear and inwardly believe, we may show forth the same in our conversation and living, unto the honor of thy holy name, the comfort and help of our Christian brethren, the health and welfare of our souls. We ask it in the name of Jesus Christ our Lord. *Amen.*

Our Father, etc.

FOURTEEN.—(MORNING OR EVENING.)

ALMIGHTY GOD, who art the fountain of holiness and felicity, who by thy word and Spirit dost conduct thy servants in the ways of sanctity and of peace, instructing them by thy truth, inviting them by promises, and winning them by love, grant unto us so truly to repent of our sins, so carefully to avoid our errors, so diligently to watch over all our own actions, so industriously to do our duty, that we may never willingly transgress thy laws; but that it may be the work of our life to obey thee, the joy of our souls to please thee, the satisfaction of all our hopes, and the perfection of our desires, to live with thee in the holiness of thy kingdom of grace and glory; through Jesus Christ, our Lord. *Amen.*

Our Father, etc.

FIFTEEN.—(MORNING OR EVENING.)

MOST merciful God, who art of purer eyes than to behold iniquity, and hast promised forgiveness to all those who confess and forsake their sins; we come before thee in an humble sense of our own unworthiness, acknowledging our manifold transgressions of thy righteous laws. O gracious Father, who desirest not the death of a sinner, look upon us, we beseech thee, in mercy, and forgive us all our transgressions. Make us deeply sensible of the great evil of them; and work in us a hearty contrition; that we may obtain forgiveness at thy hands, who art ever ready to receive humble and penitent sinners; for the sake of thy Son our Saviour.

And lest, through our own frailty, or the temptations which encompass us, we be drawn again into sin, vouchsafe us, we beseech thee, the direction and assistance of thy Holy Spirit. Reform whatever is amiss in the temper and disposition of our souls; that no unclean thoughts, unlawful designs, or inordinate desires may rest there. May we seek those things which are above, where Christ sitteth on the right hand of God. And may our life be so hid with Christ in God now, that when he, who is our life, shall appear, we may also appear with him in glory.

Extend, we beseech thee, the arms of thy compassion beyond the bounds of our own habitations. Send down thy blessings, temporal and spiritual, upon our relations, friends, and neighbors. Reward all who have done us good, and pardon all those who have done or wish us evil, and give them repentance and better minds. Be merciful to all who are in any trouble; and do thou, the God of pity, administer to them according to their several necessities; for his sake who went about doing good, thy Son our Saviour Jesus Christ.

O most loving Jesus, pattern of charity, grant that the grace of charity and brotherly love may dwell in us, and that all envy, harshness, and ill-will may die in us; fill our hearts with such kindness that by constantly rejoicing in the happiness and good success of others, and by putting away all envious thoughts we may follow thee, who art thyself the true and perfect Love. *Amen.*

Our Father, etc.

SIXTEEN.—(MORNING PRAYER.)

MOST blessed heavenly Father, we thy dependent creatures desire this morning to draw near the footstool of thy throne. Vouchsafe us, we entreat thee, thy presence. We would enter on all our duties supplicating thy favor, feeling that all the happiness the world can give cannot compensate for the want of thy blessing.

We would look away from ourselves unto him who is our only Redeemer. We cast ourselves at his feet, feeling that if we are saved it must be by him alone. O may we feel it our greatest honor to live for Jesus. Let us seek, as thy stewards, to fill our place, whatever it may be; to "adorn the doctrine of God our Saviour" just in the station in which his providence has placed us—feeling the happiness of an active and devoted obedience. Take away from us whatever is unholy. Let us walk as the expectants of a glorious immortality. May we feel that we are pilgrims, soon to be done with the world, and at home with God. O be thou our constant guide in all our journeyings. Let us never hesitate when and where thou callest us. Make us to feel that all the circumstances of life—its joys and its sorrows—its comforts and crosses—are arranged by thee and ordained for us in adorable mercy and ineffable wisdom. Bless all near and dear to us. Defend our friends by thy mighty power. Surround them with thy favor and bring them at last to the enjoyment of thyself. Bless especially those now before thee. We commend each and all of us this day to thy keeping. Let us enter upon its duties with our souls stayed on thee, and seek to show the world that we have been with thee, and that thou art a present help in every time of need. We ask these blessings in the name and for the sake of the Lord Jesus. *Amen.*

Our Father, etc.

SEVENTEEN.—(MORNING PRAYER.)

OUR FATHER who art in heaven, for thy mercy in guarding us during the past night, and in granting us the light of a new day we thank thee. Thou didst not allow fire to consume our dwelling, nor disease to attack suddenly any of its inmates, nor death to snatch us unprepared from time to eternity. And now, thou art continuing to us not only life, and health, but those reasoning and moral faculties by which we may apprehend thee as the Creator of our souls and the providential ruler over all the events of our earthly existence. Help us by the instruction of thy word and Spirit thus to recognize thee more and more as the source of all our daily joys as well as the fountain of unceasing and everlasting spiritual blessings. We are unworthy of all these high favors.

Grant us grace, we do beseech thee, in the name of thine only begotten and well-beloved Son, for whose sake thou art always willing to hear our prayers, to realize more deeply our unworthiness in contrast with thine own loving kindness and tender compassion; and therefore to approach thee with an ever increasing sense of gratitude and love.

Unto whom can we come, O Lord, for guidance as well as thanksgiving, save unto thee who hast been our shield against the dangers, and our strength against the temptations of the past? May we accept the benefits of the past as pledges of what thou art willing to do for us to-day and in the future.

For Jesus' sake inspire us with a child-like trust. Teach us by thy gracious spirit to be docile, humble, contented, confident in thy truth and unfalteringly restful in thy promises.

Forgive us our sins; implant within our souls such right principles and pure motives that we shall be led to refrain day by day from trnasgression and its consequent miseries.

Prepare us to discharge the duties and to enjoy the privileges of this day. Direct us to find our highest happiness in thoughts of thee, and of what thou hast done for us by sending Christ as a prophet to instruct us in our ignorance, as a priest to atone on the cross for us in our sinfulness and as a king to reign over us, defending us from evil impulses that rise within, and from the assaults and deceitful solicitations that spring from Satan without.

Let our hopes and our yearnings reach out toward Christ as our ever perfect and ever blessed model. May the same mind that was in Jesus be in us. Let Christ be formed within us, the hope of glory. Remind us often, O Lord, of the words uttered by Jesus, and of the graces exemplified in his conduct and character. Help us to imitate him and to grow ever more like him in all heavenly qualities. Thus shall we be fitted to bear all afflictions, and to resist all temptations. And thine, O God, shall be all the glory through Jesus thy Son, our elder Brother and Redeemer. *Amen.*

Our Father, etc.

EIGHTEEN.—(MORNING PRAYER.)

OUR HEAVENLY FATHER, in thine infinite goodness we are permitted to come to thee again this morning. We give thee hearty thanks for the mercies of the past night. Thine angels have camped about our dwelling, though we have not seen them. We have dwelt in safety, because thou, Lord, hast kept us. Receive our thanksgiving for thy providence that has watched while we have slept. And now, let thy loving kindness be our portion this day. We come to thee that we may be fitted for our duties. We have no wisdom or strength of our own. We easily go astray. Do thou graciously shepherd us this day. Open for us the green pastures of thy grace. If any perils await us grant us thy deliverance. Shield us from sin. Give us victory over temptation. Make us faithful in our work. May we serve and endure as seeing him who is invisible.

Bless every member of this family. Bind us close in thy love. Make us helpful to one another and to all who are around us. In thy mercy remember all who may need thy special grace this day. Comfort the afflicted and sustain the burdened and rescue the fallen. May thy kingdom come and thy will be done in earth as it is in heaven; and thine shall be the praise through Jesus Christ, our Redeemer. *Amen.*

Our Father, etc.

NINETEEN.—(MORNING PRAYER.)

WE thank thee, our Father in heaven, for the light of this new day. The night is thy gift, and so is the day. We have had rest and food for our bodies, and now we humbly pray for spiritual renewal and strength. O how rich is the privilege of meeting thee at the family altar! Here give us, we beseech thee, O Lord, the kindling fire which comes from on high, so that when we enter into the employments of the day, we may be conscious that the Holy Spirit is with us and that he is able and willing to help us. Give us courage and wisdom to honor thee in all things, so that "whether we eat or drink, or whatsoever we do, we may do all to the glory of God."

Bestow upon us, we pray, an increasing sense of our need of thee and an increasing sense of our ability, if we have thy grace, to reveal thy spirit and honor thee in all the duties to which thou dost call us. We render thee thanks for all thy temporal gifts. So many are the mercy drops, that, blended together, we are carried forward on their strong current. May we not simply rejoice and be glad for them, but may we be thankful in heart and have grace to *live* our thankfulness day by day!

Above all, we thank thee for Jesus Christ our Saviour. Help us to trust in him. May we open the door that he may come in and abide with us! .... Help us, O Lord, our Redeemer, to meet the temptations and trials and sorrows of this day and of every day with calm and cheerful fortitude, and may we always "endure as seeing him who is invisible!" Send forth thy light, Sun of Righteousness, into all the earth! May the day soon dawn when the whole earth shall rejoice in thy salvation! Forgive our sins; bless our loved ones; renew thy Church, and bestow upon thy chosen a precious baptism of the Holy Spirit. We ask in Christ's name and for Christ's sake. *Amen.*

Our Father, etc.

TWENTY.—(MORNING PRAYER.)

MOST gracious Lord and Father, we come before thee this morning to thank thee for thy tender care throughout the night. Thou hast given us quiet sleep and refreshing slumber. Thou hast let no danger come nigh us, and hast brought us, with renewed strength and vigor, to see the light of another morning. We ask thy guidance for this day; keep our steps from stumbling and our feet from falling. Go with us to our business, and let thy presence abide with us and thy wisdom guide us in all our transactions.

Stay in our home, and let thy loving kindness be round about us, helping us perform our duties faithfully. Keep our thoughts pure, our tempers serene, our hearts holy. Keep us from disaster, and at last bring us, an undivided family, to our eternal and heavenly home, where we may worship and glorify thee forever. *Amen.*

Our Father, etc.

TWENTY-ONE.—(EVENING PRAYER.)

O LORD, our heavenly Father, look down in mercy upon this family, and bless us and keep us from harm. May we remember thee as we lay ourselves down to sleep, and think of thee in the night watches. When it is dark about us, thine eye seest us, for the light and the darkness are both alike to thee, and there is nothing hid from thy all-searching eyes. May we remember this, O Lord, and thus be prevented from sin.

And when the night of death has come, and our eyes closed forever to the light of the sun, may we be gathered to the rest and the rewards of the many mansions in the skies, and worship thee in the temple where there is no need of the light of the sun, and where our Lord and Saviour is the light thereof; for his Name's sake. *Amen.*

Our Father, etc.

TWENTY-TWO.—(MORNING PRAYER.)

ALMIGHTY GOD, we enter on the duties of this day imploring thy favor and blessing. We leave all our affairs in thy fatherly hand. Thou sendest both prosperity and adversity; thou makest poor and makest rich. Let thy will rule all things for us, and give us what thou seest best for our welfare. We seek not great things for ourselves in this world, but rather choose that good part which shall never be taken from us.

Give us, O Lord, this day not to please ourselves, but thee, the living God, who givest us richly all things to enjoy. May no discontent or pride or envy lurk in our hearts. May no disparagement or ill-will pass our lips. May no unseemly lightness, fear or idleness mark our conduct. But in all things may we live as becomes our profession, and as those purchased by the precious blood of Jesus Christ.

May it please thee to give us the constant assistance of thy Holy Spirit to guide us in our ways; and by his blessed influence may we be enabled to love thee above all things, and to love our neighbors as ourselves.

Finally, grant to every member of this family, and to all our friends wherever they may be, thy peace and heavenly consolations. Make us to be of one heart and mind, loving and serving thee on earth, and becoming day by day better prepared for that eternal kingdom which thou hast promised to thy faithful servants by and through thy Son, our Saviour Jesus Christ.

Almighty and everlasting God, who, of thy tender love towards mankind, hast sent thy Son, our Saviour Jesus Christ, to take upon him our flesh, and to suffer death upon the Cross, that all mankind should follow the example of his great humility; mercifully grant that we may both follow the example of his patience, and also be made partakers of his resurrection; through the same Jesus Christ our Lord. *Amen.*

Our Father, etc.

TWENTY-THREE.—(SUNDAY MORNING.)

OUR HEAVENLY FATHER, this is the day which thou hast made holy; we will rejoice and be glad in it. Draw thou near to us and help us to draw near to thee. May we walk all the day under the sunshine of thy gracious countenance. Whom have we in the heavens, O God, but thee; and there is none in all the earth that our souls would desire besides thee. . We draw near to thy footstool, under a deep sense of our unworthiness. We acknowledge the depravity and corruption of our nature; the sins and shortcomings of our practice. We bring our guilt to the great propitiation, even Jesus Christ.

Blessed Saviour! give to us a sense of pardon. May we see this day thy glory, as we have seen thee heretofore within thy holy temple. May every temporal mercy which gladdens our lot be sweetened and hallowed, and endeared by the thought that it comes to us through Christ. May blessings and trials, comforts and crosses, health and sickness, joy and sorrow, bring us only nearer to thee, and redound to the glory of thy great name.

Subdue whatever is inconsistent with thy mind and will. May our hearts become holy temples, and our lives living sacrifices. Fit us for thy glory. Let our eye be ever heavenward. Let religion become more "the one thing needful." May we grow more meek and child-like in submission to our heavenly Father's will. Breathing a perpetual Sabbath-spirit on earth, may we be fitted for that rest which shall never be broken, which awaits us in the kingdom of the redeemed.

We pray for all who are to minister to us this day, and may every good impression on the minds of those who hear the gospel to-day, be rendered permanent and saving. Bless us, even us, O God, who are now surrounding thy footstool. As thou hast knitted us together in the same earthly ties, do thou unite us in the better bonds of the everlasting covenant. Make us all partakers of the resurrection-life of thy people; that though death may sooner or later separate us here, we may meet at last where separation is unknown. Through Jesus Christ. *Amen.*

Our Father, etc.

TWENTY-FOUR.—(SUNDAY EVENING.)

MOST blessed Lord, we praise thee for all the manifestations of thy character in thy works and thy ways; but especially at the close of this day of rest, sacred to the remembrance of a once crucified, but now risen Saviour, we would extol thee. We bless thee for the full and free overtures of mercy which are addressed to us through the divine Redeemer, and for all the benefits that are treasured in him. Grant that we may never be moved aside from the hope that is in Christ; that through the blood of the covenant alone we may ever look for pardon, and all needed spiritual blessings; that by faith in him we may learn from this day to avoid those ways that are evil, and to obey thy law: thus may we become companions of all them that fear thee.

And may the holy Book, that records the things that belong to our peace, ever be prized by us as the charter of our privileges, the storehouse of our treasures. May we learn to make it the man of our counsel, the frequent companion of our solitude, our guide in seasons of difficulty, our refuge in danger, our comfort in affliction. Lord God of the Sabbath, vouchsafe to us thy presence and countenance on this evening of thy holy day. Let this prove truly a season of rest and refreshment to each one of us. Remember thy word of promise unto thy servants, that where two or three are met together in thy name, there thou wilt be in the midst of them.

Give testimony to the word of thy grace wheresoever and by whomsoever it may have been proclaimed this day, so that many who have hitherto been living far from thee may choose thee as their portion, and, with deep repentance, entreat thy favor. May the sick and sorrowful know that thou art with them, and in the issue learn thy loving kindness from their affliction. Thou knowest what is best for thy children far better than we know. May sickness as well as health, adversity as well as prosperity, be accepted by us as coming from thy loving hand. And when the night of death closes round us, may we be ready and waiting for thy summons to that better land above where we shall meet our loved ones and our blessed Saviour. All these things we ask, for Christ's sake. *Amen.*

Our Father, etc.

REV. THEODORE L. CUYLER, D.D.

TWENTY-FIVE.

SPECIAL PRAYER FOR SUNDAY MORNING.

INFINITE and loving Father, we lift our eyes unto the hills from whence cometh all our help. For our only help is in the name of the Lord who made the heavens and the earth. We thank thee for thy guardian care over us during the night. We thank thee that we have lain down and slept in peace and safety, for the eye that never slumbers kept watch over us. We rejoice in the gift of another Sabbath, and we pray, that we may all be " in the spirit on the Lord's day." Enable us to lay aside all the thoughts and the things of the world, and the toils and the cares of the week that is past. Forgive us all the sins we have committed; and grant thy blessing on all that we have attempted to do for thy glory during the six days that have gone with their account to heaven. This is thy day; may we remember to keep it holy as the Sabbath of the Lord our God. We rear our family-altar at the very threshold of the day, and invoke thy gracious presence with us through all its hours. We know not what the day may bring forth; we know not what temptations may assail us, or what perils may be before us, or what trials may be in store for us; but if thou, O loving Father, art close beside us every moment, no temptation will overcome us, and we shall be prepared to meet whatever thou in thy wisdom shall send upon us. We need thee every hour; for we are very weak and very wayward. O, pity our weakness and send us strength. Pity our ignorance, and send us light! Pity our guiltiness and pardon us for the sake of him whose atoning blood cleanseth from all sin. Search us, O God, and try us, and see what evil may be in us, and now create a clean heart in every one of us.

As thou hast given us another Sabbath we pray thee to bestow upon us a precious Sabbath blessing. Both in our homes and in thy sanctuary, may it be a golden day of prayer and of praise; and while we rest from worldly toils, may our souls be on fire with all holy activities in thy service. Let us be like the children of Israel at Elim when they gathered under the palm-trees and beside the overflowing wells of water. Send down upon us the heavenly manna of thy word, and may it satisfy all the hunger of our souls. May we feed upon this bread of life; may we come as the hart that thirsteth after the water-brooks, and draw with joy out of the wells of thy salvation.

If we go up to thy courts, wilt thou graciously go with us; and help us to worship thee in sincerity and truth. Let us enter thy gates with thanksgiving and thy courts with joyful praise. We long to meet our beloved Master there, and like the disciples on the mount may we "see none but *Jesus only*!" O, thou kind and tender Shepherd who knowest all thy sheep by name, gather thy flock to-day in the green pastures, and may each one listen to the loving Shepherd's voice. O, thou Divine Physician, there will be many before thee whose hearts are sick with sin, and wounded by many falls. Take pity on them. Lift them up and set the fallen on their feet again. Open blinded eyes and unstop deaf ears, and wake those who are dead in trespasses and sin! Bless to-day our own beloved pastor, and all thy ministering servants and thy missionaries in every clime. Baptize them with the Holy Ghost and with fire! May they be fearless for the truth, and may they all rejoice to hide self behind the cross of Christ and direct all eyes to *Him* who taketh away the sins of the world. Make this a day of glorious power when every stroke that is struck for God shall echo in heaven; and may there be great joy there over many sinners who have repented.

We invoke thy blessing upon all Sabbath schools. Instruct the teachers and make them wise to lead their scholars unto Christ. Let every teacher be an armor-bearer for the little ones who are to be equipped for the coming battles of life. May this be a happy Sabbath in every mission school and chapel and house of charity—where Jesus shall lay his hand on the heads of poor children to bless them—and in hospitals may he shed upon every sufferer's couch the sunlight of his countenance. Remember tenderly all those who are to-day detained from thy house by the privations of thy providence. As they cannot come to the house of the Lord, may the Lord of the house visit them, and put his everlasting arm underneath the sick and the sorrowing. Graciously bind up all broken hearts, and pour the oil of thy love into wounded spirits. Help them and help all of us to feel that this world is not our rest; and may it be a training-school in which we shall learn even hard lessons cheerfully, and always see God's loving hand through eyes that are washed with tears. Enable us to rejoice in the Lord always, and in everything give thanks!

Come, Lord Jesus, and be our elder brother, and abide here under our roof as thou didst with thy beloved friends at Bethany. Give thyself to every one of us, so that we all, parents and children, may be a part of thy glorified household when thou shalt make up thy jewels. Listen now, gracious Lord and Intercessor, as in thy name we humbly pray.

Our Father, etc.

COMMON FORMS FOR GRACE AT MEALS.

OUR heavenly Father, sanctify to our use, we beseech thee, these provisions of thy love, and us to thyself and thy service. *Amen.*

ACCEPT, O Lord, our grateful acknowledgments for the mercies we are now about to receive. Teach us thy statutes; and enable us, as we live by thy bounty, to acknowledge thee in all things, and spend our lives in thanksgiving and praise to thee. We ask for our Redeemer's sake. *Amen.*

IN thee, O Lord, we live, and move, and have our being. Keep us ever mindful of our dependence upon, and our obligations to thee. Do thou graciously forgive our sins, and sanctify us by thy Spirit. Grant us also, now, a Father's blessing with the bounty of thy providence; for Christ's sake. *Amen.*

O LORD, our heavenly Father, we thank thee for these renewed manifestations of thy love and bounty. Thou art ever graciously supplying our daily needs. Do thou also feed our souls with the bread of life; and strengthen us that we may do thy holy will, through Jesus Christ. *Amen.*

O LORD, bless unto us these bounties which thou hast graciously bestowed upon us, and sanctify ourselves to thy service, that we may live for thee alone, through Jesus Christ our Lord. *Amen.*

O LORD, the earth is full of thy riches, and of these thou art constantly bestowing abundance upon us. Let not thy bounteous fulness steal our hearts away from thee, but sanctify unto us these and all other blessings, and let us find acceptance in thy sight; for our Redeemer's sake. *Amen.*

WE accept, O Lord, these gifts as from thee who art the giver of every good and perfect gift that descendeth from above. Teach us, in receiving them, as we live upon thy bounty so to live to thy glory. For Christ's sake. *Amen.*

O LORD, our heavenly Father, thy mercies are new every morning and fresh every evening. Give us hearts of gratitude and praise for all thy blessings. Make us thy children, devoted to thy praise; and let us find acceptance in thy sight, for our Redeemer's sake. *Amen.*

BLESS, heavenly Father, this food to our use, and ourselves to thy service; through Jesus Christ our Lord. *Amen.*

ACCEPT, Lord, our thanks for thy mercies. Bless this provision of thy bounty. Feed our souls with the bread of life; and grant that we may sit with thee at thy table in thy kingdom; for thine own Name's sake. *Amen.*

WE give thee thanks, O God our Father, for all these material bounties. Let our souls not want for the bread of life, and teach us, in receiving both temporal and spiritual mercies, to be ever mindful of thee, the giver of all good; for our Redeemer's sake. *Amen.*

LORD, we bless thee for these provisions of thy grace. May our hearts go out in thanksgiving and praise for all thy mercies. May we hunger and thirst after righteousness, that our souls may be filled, and we be enabled to glorify thee in our lives here and hereafter; and thou shalt have all the praise, now and forever. *Amen.*

THE LORD'S PRAYER.

(ALL MAY UNITE IN THIS PRAYER, AS AN OCCASIONAL FITTING CLOSE AT FAMILY WORSHIP.)

OUR Father, who art in heaven, hallowed be thy name. Thy kingdom come. Thy will be done in earth, as it is in heaven. Give us this day our daily bread. And forgive us our trespasses, as we forgive them that trespass against us. And lead us not into temptation, but deliver us from evil: For thine is the kingdom, and the power, and the glory, for ever and ever. Amen.

www.ingramcontent.com/pod-product-compliance
Lightning Source LLC
Chambersburg PA
CBHW030601300426
44111CB00009B/1068